Praise for

Baby Hearts

"This is a vivid, illuminating, and wise portrayal of emotional development in the early years. These gifted authors highlight the importance of close relationships for the unfolding of personality, self-esteem, and understanding of others."
—Ross Thompson, Ph.D., University of California, Davis

"Healthy emotional development is at the core of all learning. Parents who read *Baby Hearts* will become masters at understanding their young children's feelings and how to foster their positive relationships, self-esteem, and emotional control. Engaging, practical, and scientifically based, *Baby Hearts* is a terrific book for all parents."
—Lise Eliot, Ph.D., author of *What's Going On in There? How the Brain and Mind Develop in the First Five Years of Life*

Baby Minds

"This creative approach to early parent-child interactions is richly illustrated throughout with real-life examples. *Baby Minds* will help you catalyze your child's intellectual and emotional growth."
—Bart Schmitt, M.D., Professor of Pediatrics,
The Children's Hospital of Denver

"Fantastic! *Baby Minds* is an important resource for all caregivers of young children. Applying only half of the ideas in this book would insure the child's preparedness for success in school."
—Kathryn Barnard, Ph.D.,
Department of Family and Child Nursing,
University of Washington

Also by Linda Acredolo, Ph.D., and Susan Goodwyn, Ph.D.

BABY SIGNS
*How to Talk with Your Baby Before
Your Baby Can Talk*

BABY MINDS
*Brain-Building Games
Your Baby Will Love*

baby hearts

hearts

A Guide to Giving Your Child
an Emotional Head Start

**Linda Acredolo, Ph.D.,
and Susan Goodwyn, Ph.D.**

Bantam Books
New York Toronto London Sydney Auckland

BABY HEARTS
A Guide to Giving Your Child an Emotional Head Start

A Bantam Book / July 2005

Published by
Bantam Dell
A Division of Random House, Inc.
New York, New York

Book design by Lynn Newmark

Bantam Books is a registered trademark of Random House, Inc., and the
colophon is a trademark of Random House, Inc.

Library of Congress Cataloging-in-Publication Data
Acredolo, Linda P.
Baby hearts : a guide to giving your child an
emotional head start / Linda Acredolo and Susan Goodwyn.
p.   cm.
Includes bibliographical references and index.
ISBN 0-553-38220-9
1. Infant psychology.   2. Infants—Development.   3. Toddlers—Psychology.
4. Toddlers—Development.   5. Child rearing.   I. Goodwyn, Susan.   II. Title.

BF719.A36 2005
649'.122—dc22   2005046401

Printed in the United States of America
Published simultaneously in Canada

www.bantamdell.com

10 9 8 7 6 5 4 3 2
RRH

This book is dedicated with respect, gratitude, and
affection to our academic mentors,

Professor Herbert Pick, Ph.D. (University of Minnesota),

and

the late Professor Richard Cromer, Ph.D. (University of London),

two splendid researchers who modeled for us the integrity,
perseverance, and humanity that doing good science demands

Contents

Acknowledgments   xi

Introduction: Welcome to *Baby Hearts*   xv

1. Nature's Contribution: The Biology of Emotions   1

Part I: The "Big Five" Goals for Healthy Emotional Development   *21*

2. Welcome to the World: Feeling Loved and Secure   23

3. I'm Feeling Sad: Expressing Emotions Effectively   55

4. Kid Kindness: Evoking Empathy and Caring About Others   83

5. I've Got a Friend: Developing Healthy Friendships   105

6. I Can Do Anything: Having Self-Esteem and Self-Confidence   129

Part II: The "Big Five" Challenges to Healthy Emotional Development   *151*

7. Monsters and Meanies: Addressing Fear and Anxiety   157

8. No Need to Hide: Dealing with Shyness and Withdrawal   185

9. Tempers and Tantrums: Handling Anger and Defiance   209

10. Sticks and Stones: Avoiding Hostility and Aggression   235

11. Everyone Makes Mistakes: Steering Clear of Shame   261

12. The Puzzle Pieces of the Heart: Putting It All Together   279

Appendix: Quick Reference Guide: Words of Wisdom and
    Tricks of the Trade Revisited   285

References   294

Photo Credits   299

Index   301

Acknowledgments

They've always been there, through the labor pains of three books and countless years of our efforts to juggle our personal and professional lives. They've always been there, two wonderful men who operate as our life support systems when things get tough (which is most of the time) and our most cherished sources of rest and recreation on those rare occasions when we've managed to relax. These two stalwart men are Linda's husband, Larry Stark, and Susan's husband, Peter Bradlee, and this time we're putting them right at the top of the list of those who deserve our thanks. Thanks, guys, for all the years you've been our biggest fans, our most loyal friends, and our shelter when we sorely needed comfort and love.

We also want to thank three individuals who have consistently stepped up to the plate over the last few years to help us deal with the day-to-day demanding work that otherwise would have prevented us from even starting, let alone finishing, this book. Without the daily donations of blood, sweat, and tears by Linda Easton-Waller, Lisa Holwagner, and Ron Berry, we would have even *more* miles every day to walk before we sleep. You are appreciated more than we can ever express.

Two other individuals who deserve our thanks for their continuing support are our brilliant, dedicated, and extraordinarily patient literary agents, Angela Miller and Betsy Amster of The Miller Agency. Their willingness to tackle complex and frustrating issues on our behalf has won them both our admiration and gratitude. Our affection they won a long time ago.

A sincere thank-you also goes to our wonderful editors at Bantam Books, Toni Burbank and Philip Rappaport. Their enthusiasm for *Baby Hearts* all along the way was just the inspiration we needed to keep our spirits up and our computers humming.

As usual, we couldn't have written this book without the help of countless families who have helped us over the years with our research. The generosity of parents never fails to amaze us. And a very special thanks goes to all the families who contributed the delightful photos that make the book come alive for readers.

And here's one final thank-you. This book, the third in our trilogy of books for parents, represents much more than just our own work. Without the splendid efforts of our colleagues in developmental psychology around the world, the story of the emotional life of babies would never have been discovered, let alone be ours to write. We have identified over 120 of these scientists by name in the pages of the book, but even at that, we've hardly scratched the surface. Of those we didn't have space to cite, some stand out as particularly deserving. These include a number of pioneers in the area of infant emotions whose efforts early on, in the 1940s through the 1970s, inspired not only the two of us, but legions of other young researchers to dig even deeper into the hearts and minds of little children and their parents. Listing them here is one small way to express our appreciation. These pioneers include Kathryn Barnard, T. Berry Brazelton, Urie Bronfenbrenner, Joe Campos, Peggy Emerson, Stanley Greenspan, Harry Harlow, Mavis Hetherington, Eleanor Maccoby, Lois Murphy, Paul Mussen, Harriet Rheingold, James Robertson, Rudolph Schaffer, Robert Sears, and René Spitz. Without their efforts, emotional development in early childhood would still be a mystery waiting to be solved—and *Baby Hearts* would have been an *exceedingly* short book. We hope we have continued their efforts in a way that would meet with their approval.

Introduction

Welcome to *Baby Hearts*

Making the decision to have a child—it's momentous. It is to decide forever to have your heart go walking around outside your body.

—Elizabeth Stone, author

We chose these words to begin *Baby Hearts* because they seemed to us to capture the depth of feeling we ourselves experienced when first given our newborn babies to hold. We each were blessed with two wonderful children, now grown, who changed our lives forever—and for the better. The fact that the moments when we first "met" each of them remain so vivid in our memories is testimony to how intense our feelings were at the time and how overwhelmed we were by the responsibility we'd just been given. We both remember being awed by the miracle of birth—and amazed that the hospital staff was actually allowing us to take these helpless babies home! They seemed to trust us to care for these children more than we trusted ourselves.

Such feelings are almost universally shared by parents of newborns. The desire to do right by their children is strong in those early days and, fortunately, remains strong in the vast majority of parents from then on. But how, exactly, does one "do right"? How does a parent know what to do when confronted by the myriad daily problems that inevitably arise in trying to guide a child through the ups and downs of life? There's no one answer to this question, of course. But what there is—and what we plan to share with you in this book—is advice drawn from research studies conducted in laboratories around the world, particularly advice relevant to the emotional lives of children.

Our previous books, *Baby Signs* and *Baby Minds*, were both focused on the intellectual side of development, how babies communicate and how they think. In *Baby Hearts* we are switching gears and tackling a very different aspect of life during those first critical years, one that has been described by researchers as among the most intriguing and important frontiers of child development research: how babies *feel*. However, before we begin explaining why researchers believe this to be the case, what their research has revealed, and how you can benefit from knowing more about it, we want to take a moment to share with you the story of how we came to write this book.

When a Baby's Actions Speak Louder Than His Words

Many of you are already familiar with our first book, *Baby Signs: How to Talk with Your Baby Before Your Baby Can Talk*. In that book we describe the benefits to children and parents alike of encouraging babies and toddlers to use simple signs to communicate before they can talk. We also summarize the two decades of research we conducted at the University of California at Davis to back up our claims. One major component of this research program was a long-term study funded by the National Institutes of Health (NIH) in which we compared signing and nonsigning babies as they moved through infancy into the preschool and elementary school years. A story told to us by the mother of one of the babies in the signing group taught us how much more knowledgeable babies are about their feelings than we had imagined and, ultimately, provided the inspiration for *Baby Hearts*.

By the time he was fifteen months old, Zack knew over thirty signs, and both he and his mother, Cathy, were thrilled with the world of communication that signing was opening up for them. In fact, in addition to the many signs he had learned directly from Cathy, Zack had also made up some signs of his own, including a sign to let his parents know when he was afraid. If a big dog or a scary person came too close for comfort, Zack would simply start patting his chest vigorously with the palm of his hand. Seeing this, his parents would quickly scoop him up into the safety of their arms and all would be well. That was impressive enough, but it was an event that took place in the middle of one night that really made Cathy take notice. And when we heard about it, we did the same. Here's what happened.

It began one night about 2:15 A.M. when Cathy heard Zack begin to wail. As she hurriedly entered his room, he stopped crying, looked toward a clown doll sitting on his dresser, and began repeatedly patting his chest with his open palm. "I knew right away what was wrong," Cathy told us. "He'd gotten the doll as a present earlier that day, and I thought it would be nice for him to have it close by when he woke up in the morning. Boy, was I wrong. He was telling me quite clearly that he was afraid of the doll. I guess a clown doll during the day isn't exactly the same as a clown doll at night!" And just as she suspected, as soon as Cathy took the doll away, Zack settled back down to sleep.

But what if Zack hadn't had that sign to use to let her know he was afraid? This is the point that gave us goose bumps when we heard it. "Just think," Cathy continued, "if all I'd seen when I walked in the room was Zack crying and pointing at the doll he'd enjoyed during the day, guess what I would have done? I would have thought he was crying because he wanted the doll and would have put it in the crib *with* him! Not exactly the way to build a trusting relationship."

Emotional Intelligence Starts Young

What we found so important about Cathy's story was that at only fifteen months, Zack had recognized and labeled his own emotion and, in doing so, had helped his mother respond to him in exactly the right—rather than in exactly the *wrong*—way. Does this mean that Zack is an emotional genius? Many scientists, along with many parents, would conclude just that. Although it's clear to everyone that even tiny babies are capable of expressing internal emotions through crying and smiling, until very recently most child development professionals have assumed that the kind of evaluation of his own emotions that Zack had done, followed by the purposeful communication of that emotion through a symbol (patting the chest), was well beyond the ability of a fifteen-month-old child.

However, taking a closer look at the records of other children in our signing studies, we found clear evidence that Zack was not alone in his emotional sophistication. Other babies, it turned out, had also used "emotion" signs well before they could say the words, for example, to communicate that they were happy, sad, or angry. They would sign "gentle" when their mother was being too rough changing their diaper or sign "hurt" when they had an ear infection. Obviously, "talking" about feelings is far from a rare event, at least for toddlers lucky enough to have access to simple signs. (For descriptions of these emotion signs as well as many other helpful signs, see the glossary at the end of *Baby Signs*.)

Our search for other evidence of emotional intelligence in infants and toddlers then began in earnest. We quickly discovered that our observations were consistent with discoveries being made in research laboratories around the world. Far from being a time when humans are oblivious to what happens to them, suffering only in the here-and-now from the obvious problems of hunger, thirst, and cold, the first years of life are critically important to a child's future emotional, social, and even intellectual development. What's more, give them a chance and infants and toddlers will tell you so—just as Zack did.

You've Come a Long Way, Baby!

It's taken babies an embarrassingly long time to convince the adults around them that they (babies) are smarter than they look, especially about emotions, and that what happens to them even in the first months of life leaves a lasting impression. As we said, it's always been clear that babies cry when they are unhappy and smile when they are pleased with themselves or the world. But until the middle of the twentieth century, most people, researchers included, assumed that these emotional expressions were simply automatic reactions to what was happening in the moment, reactions without any long-term consequences. A baby might be upset at a particular point in time, but that emotion was not thought to leave any kind of permanent trace in the baby's mind or heart. And it certainly wasn't anything that adults needed to be concerned about. Crying, after all, was "good for the lungs." Hmph!

Fortunately, such an uncaring attitude seems incredible to any parent who has taken a recent child development course in high school or college. However, its truth is sobering evidence of how far the science of developmental psychology has come in the last forty years. In his captivating book about the history of research on emotions and babies, *Becoming Attached,* Dr. Robert Karen describes specifically the attitude of researchers and politicians to the frequent death of orphaned babies cared for in well-run institutions of the early twentieth century. To the adults of the day, "These little creatures were not yet people and could not have real human feelings. They didn't become sad or lonely. If they deteriorated, there were other reasons: They may not have been hardy; they may have been broken by disease. But they certainly did not need others in any emotional or psychological way." (p. 14)

Additional evidence of the progress made in the last forty years is found in the profound changes that have taken place in adoption policies. Ask any adult today what the best age is for a child to be adopted and, nine times out of ten, the answer will be as soon after birth as possible. And that's absolutely correct. But, you say, isn't that just common sense? Unfortunately for centuries of children, the answer was no. Because nothing that happened during the first two years mattered anyway, the idea was to wait until age two or three so that adoptive parents could be sure what kind of child they were getting!

What Parents Want to Know

It's not only in terms of broad policy issues like adoption that developmental psychologists are making a difference. A great deal of what is being discovered on a daily basis is directly applicable to the lives of parents just like you. And yet the information clearly isn't reaching those most interested in receiving it.

Here's one way we know that there is a serious information gap. In a recent

How Times Have Changed . . . Thank Goodness

If you want to feel proud of what you already know about how to raise an emotionally healthy child, compare your beliefs to those of a prominent 1920s psychologist, Dr. John Watson:

> Treat them as though they were young adults. . . . Never hug and kiss them, never let them sit on your lap. If you must, kiss them once on the forehead when they say good night. Shake hands with them in the morning. Give them a pat on the head if they have made an extraordinary good job of a difficult task. (1928, pp. 21–22)

Your "gut level" negative reaction to his advice is in part a product of the wealth of very good research on emotional development emanating in recent years from laboratories around the world.

survey of 1,022 mothers and fathers of children under the age of three conducted by Zero to Three, a national organization dedicated to the healthy development of infants and toddlers, parents reported that, although they believe they can have the greatest impact on their child's emotional development (rather than their physical or intellectual development), this is also the domain they reported knowing the least about. Parents described great difficulty identifying their babies' emotions and desires. And even when they are able to figure out what their children are feeling, they reported great uncertainty about how best to respond. What they need most, they said, is specific information—guidelines, strategies, and activities—to help them improve their parenting

What Grown-Ups Know (and Don't Know) About Development

Civitas, a national nonprofit organization, reports the following statistics from a survey to determine how effective researchers have been in their efforts to educate parents of young children.

- ◆ 60 percent of adults did not realize that even babies under six months of age can sense an adult's mood and be affected by it.
- ◆ 62 percent incorrectly believed that six-month-old babies can be spoiled, and 44 percent believed that to be true even of three-month-olds.
- ◆ 42 percent did not realize that by two days of age, a baby can recognize his mother's voice.
- ◆ 34 percent did not know that children begin to develop their sense of self-esteem during the first two years of life.
- ◆ 62 percent were not sure or incorrectly thought that spanking children helps children develop self-control.
- ◆ 67 percent incorrectly thought that the bond between working parents and their children cannot be as strong as the bond between nonworking parents and their children.

Source: Civitas, 2002, "What Grown-Ups Understand About Child Development: A National Benchmark Survey," reported in *America's Family Support Magazine* 21 (Winter 2003): 17–20.

skills. Based on these responses, the authors of the Zero to Three study concluded: "The scientific community, communications media, and health and development professionals need to translate research and practice findings into clear, practical messages for parents."

Our Goal with Baby Hearts

Quite simply, our goal with *Baby Hearts* is to help close this information gap by providing you with exactly the kind of information parents all over the world are asking child development experts to give them: clear, practical messages that can take some of the guesswork out of bringing up baby. At the same time, we hope to create in you a sense of wonderment at how smart your baby is about emotions, how much she senses about your feelings long before she can understand your words, and how much love she has to give *and* how much she wants to give it.

Everything you're about to learn about babies has always been true, of course. It's just taken adults, researchers included, a long time to catch on. Fortunately, researchers have become very clever about devising ways to empower babies to "talk" to us. And what wonderful teachers they are! To whet your appetite, here are just a few of the lessons babies have taught us in recent years, lessons we will return to at greater length in later chapters.

- ◆ It's no accident that newborn babies get upset when they hear other babies crying. Empathy is such an important emotion that newborns come into the world primed for it. (And yet they don't get upset if they hear a tape-recording of *themselves* crying. They find that sound fascinating!)
- ◆ Even four-month-olds are aware when someone talking to them is happy with them or angry—just by the tone of his or her voice. Say something sweet, and they smile. Become angry, and they grow wide-eyed and worried. (Now, which would you like *your* infant to experience?)
- ◆ Three-month-olds are *extremely* sensitive to shifts in eye-to-eye contact with the important people in their lives. If Mom breaks eye contact, even fractionally, baby will notice. What's more, he is quite likely to become upset if his attempts to regain Mom's attention fail.

- From birth, babies notice whether their caregivers are quick to respond to them when they signal distress by crying—and reward them by crying *less*.
- By eight months, babies not only can "read" the emotional expressions on their parents' faces, but also are smart enough to use that information to guide their *own* reactions to what is going on around them.

Frankly, we have so much information to share that the challenge has been to organize *Baby Hearts* in a way that makes it easy to read as well as informative. As parents of former toddlers ourselves, we know how frantic life can be. Under such circumstances, to be truly helpful, a book must be both well organized and engaging. In the end, we decided to take our cue from the kinds of descriptors parents use when asked to define a "happy" child. The typical description is a child who feels safe and secure, has high self-esteem, is self-confident, is sensitive to the concerns of others, and is well liked by those around her. After an introduction to the biology of emotions in Chapter 1 we have organized Chapters 2 to 6 of *Baby Hearts* around these positive goals:

- Feeling secure (Chapter 2)
- Expressing emotions effectively (Chapter 3)
- Showing empathy for others (Chapter 4)
- Developing healthy friendships (Chapter 5)
- Feeling good about themselves (Chapter 6)

We start each chapter using the same "News Flash!" format that worked so well in our *Baby Minds* book to highlight especially interesting and important research findings relevant to the topic. And at the end of each chapter, you'll find a section called "Words of Wisdom and Tricks of the Trade" in which we offer lots of concrete advice and ideas for how to apply the research you've just read about to daily life with your own child.

In later chapters we turn from these positive goals to some of the main worries that parents voice when life with baby/toddler gets a bit rocky. Fortunately, recent research has much to offer here as well. The concerns include:

- Fear and anxiety (Chapter 7)
- Shyness and withdrawal (Chapter 8)

- Anger and defiance (Chapter 9)
- Hostility and aggression (Chapter 10)
- Feelings of shame and guilt (Chapter 11)

In Chapter 12 we summarize with a reminder that parenting is the most challenging task you'll ever face. Finally, in the Appendix we provide a quick review of the specific parenting tips included in the twelve preceding chapters. Organized by topic, the list makes it easy for readers to refresh their memories about what the tips are, where they are described in the book, and the approximate age when each tip begins to be relevant.

In short, our goal for *Baby Hearts* is to share with you information that will make your parenting experience more informed, more relaxed, and more fun. Think about what you've read, take advantage of the many tips we include along the way, and soon you will be providing the kind of nurturance your baby needs to grow into the happy, emotionally healthy child that is every parent's dream. Yes, your child will still make you feel like your heart is walking around outside your body, but at least you will feel much more confident that *both* are safe.

1

Nature's Contribution: The Biology of Emotions

N E W S   F L A S H !

There's More to "Mothering" Than Meets the Eye, Scientists Discover

New York, New York. What happens when Mommy Rat runs away from home, leaving her litter of pups to fend for themselves? They get hungry—*very* hungry. No surprise there. But according to Columbia University professor Myron Hofer, there's a lot more than that going wrong when Mom "turns tail" and runs. In fact, hunger is one of the least of the abandoned rat pups' problems. Like a harp that stays silent without someone plucking at its strings, rat pups left without the cuddling, licking, and delicious smells and rhythms that constitute mothering in their world lack the ability to maintain many critical biological functions, the control of which is necessary for life itself. Their body temperatures drop, their heart rates increase, their breathing becomes erratic, their sleep-wake cycles are disrupted, their growth and stress hormones go haywire. In short, the result is true biological chaos, a level of disorganization that can kill.

Researchers studying human mothering say there's an important lesson in all of this for us. Like the rat pup, the human infant may look like an independent little unit (especially in those identical little maternity ward cribs), but that's a serious, even deadly, misperception. The newborn human baby is dependent on our tender loving care for much more than food and diaper changes. Just like rat pups, human babies require proximity to a warm body—one that breathes with regularity, strokes and cuddles, smiles and smells—to keep their biological systems in line. Or one could say, like the silent harp, human babies need their parents' love to create the sweet, concordant rhythms that make for the beautiful music that is healthy life.

Biological Regulation: An Evolutionary Gamble

Myron Hofer's work with rat pups is both exciting and exceedingly important. Instead of seeing motherhood through a veil of sentimentality, he has proved that what parents routinely do (or *should* do) with their babies is absolutely critical for their survival. There were earlier clues, of course, particularly in the many tragic cases of failure-to-thrive syndrome in orphanages, where food was plentiful, beds were clean, but anything approaching mothering was considered too expensive, too time-consuming, and totally unnecessary. These babies literally withered and died. And now we know why.

Both the problem and the strength of the human baby is that she is a work in progress. If human babies were prewired upon entry into the world, there would be no capacity to change, to adapt to different environments, to *learn*. In other words, if human babies were *only* a product of "nature" rather than equally dependent on "nurture," human progress would have ground to a halt a long time ago. Instead, evolution took a chance, sending us newborn babies that are far from ready-wired, trusting that it could also nudge the big humans around these helpless creatures into providing them the attention needed to get their immature biological systems up and running in an organized, self-sufficient way.

Parents as the "Gelatin Molds" of Early Development

Human babies may arrive totally dependent on their parents to keep their biological rhythms working right, but they don't stay that way. Over the first nine months of life, the infant gradually becomes able to exert his own control over his breathing, heart rate, sleep-wake cycles, stress reactions, growth hormones, and the like. But it doesn't happen automatically. Again, this progress is not prewired. The ac-

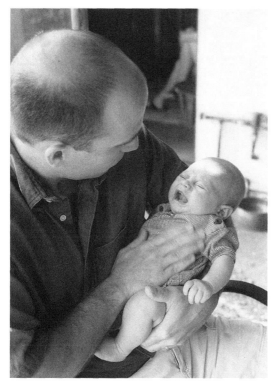

Newborn babies are totally dependent on their parents to keep their bodies and their emotions regulated. Pete's efforts here to soothe his tiny son Henry will help get Henry's stress hormones back under control and eventually will pay off in Henry being able to soothe himself.

tive support parents provide the baby during those early months helps shape his own control mechanisms. Feeling the parent's breath go in and out sets a pace for the baby's breathing. Hearing the parent's voice stimulates synchronized body movements. Being predictably roused from sleep and soothed back into it stabilizes sleep-wake cycles. The warmth of the parent's body and stroking of the baby's skin regulates his temperature. Touching the baby's face stimulates sucking. On and on it goes. But if that parental support is itself erratic or disorganized, then the baby's developing ability to regulate himself will be compromised accordingly.

When we explain the gradual development of biological regulation and the important role played by parents to our undergraduate students, we like to use the metaphor of the gelatin mold. The function of a gelatin mold is to contain the liquid gelatin until it slowly solidifies enough to hold its own shape once the mold is removed. Typically, the shape that results is a lovely, rippled mound with a flat spot on top for a dollop of whipped cream. But the shape the gelatin finally assumes won't be so pretty if one or all of the following things go wrong: (a) the mold itself is bizarrely shaped, (b) the mold is removed before solidification is complete, or (c) the mold itself is too flexible to provide a consistent shape.

In this metaphor, babies, of course, are represented by the gelatin, with parental interactions, daily routines, and physical closeness acting as the mold that holds the gelatin together until it can solidify. Without the mold, the gelatin simply runs all over the place, achieving no coherent shape as it hardens, just as a baby's biological rhythms disintegrate into chaos without the strength and warmth of a parent's arms to hold them in place. That one person's breathing, heartbeat, and nearness might exert such power over another person's behavior may at first seem far-fetched—but notice what happens the next time you find yourself close to someone who yawns!

Individual Differences in the Gelatin

Children differ in many ways, including how much support they need early on to regulate their biological systems. Continuing the metaphor, they differ in how solid their gelatin is to start with. Although some babies seem to develop reasonable sleep-wake cycles within weeks, for other babies the process can take months. Similarly, some babies will be soothed quickly when upset, while others require rocking for what may seem like hours. And some babies can sleep through the sound of the vacuum cleaner, while other babies flinch at the sound of a car door closing outdoors. Such differences can be genetic in origin and can run in families. In other cases, particular characteristics of the prenatal environment (the amount of maternal stress, for example) may be playing a role. Whatever their source, these individual differences in the newborn baby's gelatin contribute significantly to differences in infant temperament apparent from Day 1, the topic we turn to next.

Inborn Temperament: Variety Is the Spice of Life

What a boring world this would be if we were all alike, if we were all cut with the same cookie cutter. How would those of us who are shy be wooed into joining the action? How would those of us who jump in with both feet be persuaded to look before we leap? Fortunately, nature has guaranteed that we *aren't* all alike, even at the very beginning.

Sudden Infant Death Syndrome (SIDS)

On a very serious note, there is good evidence that some babies need more help than others to keep their breathing regular, particularly when they are asleep. These babies, it is hypothesized, are the ones at most risk from dying of sudden infant death syndrome, or SIDS. As evidence, researchers note the young age at which most SIDS cases occur (before four months) and an impressively lower incidence of SIDS in cultures where baby and mother routinely sleep together, proximity that presumably provides the child with a stable breathing pattern and frequent arousal episodes.

There is a downside, however, to cosleeping. New research strongly suggests that the fewer items in the sleep environment that might accidentally cover the baby's mouth and nose (pillows, crib bumpers, blankets, etc.), the lower the chance of SIDS. Many pediatricians worry that the parent's body or bedclothes pose such dangers. As a compromise, some parents are using baby beds that attach directly to the side of their own bed, allowing easy access and close monitoring without the added worry of obstructing the baby's breathing.

By far the most successful recommendation of all came in 1994 in the form of the "Back to Sleep" campaign launched by the American Academy of Pediatrics. The aim was to shift parents from routinely putting babies to sleep on their tummies to *always* putting them to sleep on their backs. As a result of these efforts, the incidence of SIDS in the United States is estimated to have declined by 40 percent.

The fact that babies differ from Day 1 is hardly a surprise to most parents— at least on an intellectual level. However, thanks to years and years of exposure to the well-behaved, cuddly babies popular among advertisers and greeting card designers, too many parents (particularly first-time parents) are indeed surprised at—and not fully prepared for—their baby's unique personality. It's as if they were expecting the perfect rose and received a happy-go-lucky sweet pea instead. It's cute, all right, but why doesn't it stand up tall and straight in the vase?

That's why it's so important for parents to know about the variations in what researchers call infant temperament. Once you know the wide variety from which the florist can pick, you'll be better prepared to enjoy the surprise when your doorbell finally rings and your particular flower is delivered. "Oh, goody! A sweet pea!"

CATALOGING INFANT TEMPERAMENTS

Carrying the metaphor a bit further, researchers tell us that there are four particularly popular flowers—or inborn temperaments—in the florist's greenhouse (none of which, by the way, is the perfect rose). Before identifying these four, let's first describe how this conclusion was reached. We have two pediatricians, Alexander Thomas and Stella Chess, to thank for the original, painstaking cataloging of infant temperament. Based on exhaustive interviews with parents of 136 children followed from age two to adulthood, they identified nine dimensions along which children reliably differ:

1. Activity level
2. Adaptability (Are transitions hard?)
3. Willingness to approach new things
4. Tolerance for frustration
5. Intensity of emotions (both positive and negative)
6. Distractabiity
7. Predominant mood (positive or negative)
8. Predictability of rhythms
9. Sensitivity to external events (stimuli)

Recognizing that some of these categories overlap, Chess and Thomas consolidated the groupings down to three: the "Easy" baby, the "Difficult" baby, and the "Slow-to-Warm" baby. As more and more researchers began viewing babies through these lenses, it gradually became apparent that Chess and Thomas's divisions were not giving "activity level" a prominent enough place. The result, as Alicia Lieberman reports in her excellent book *The Emotional Life of the Toddler*, was a gradual consensus that a fourth category needed to be added: the "Active" baby.

As we discuss each of these in turn, it's helpful to keep in mind that the four represent certain average profiles, or prototypes. In reality, of course, every baby's personality reflects a unique blending of the nine variables just listed. As we'll discuss later, it's also crucial to keep in mind that "biology is not destiny"—that although nature is the starting point for personality, nurture's forces (including *you*) have a huge role to play thereafter.

THE FOUR MOST COMMON FLOWERS

With all this as prelude, just what are the four most common flowers in the greenhouse and the inborn temperaments they represent? They include:

1. Baby Sunflower (aka the "Easy" baby)
2. Baby Holly (aka the "Difficult" baby)
3. Baby Orchid (aka the "Slow-to-Warm" baby)
4. Baby Dandelion (aka the "Active" baby)

We have chosen the plant analogy for several reasons. First, and most obviously, the specific plants and flowers really *do* seem to share characteristics with the babies they represent and, therefore, provide an easy way to remember the distinctions. The second reason is perhaps even more important. Although different

Just as different kinds of flowers have their own unique characteristics, babies have their own personalities from birth. Parents, like gardeners, need to understand how best to cultivate each one. The four most common temperaments are represented here by Baby Sunflower (the "Easy" baby), Baby Holly (the "Difficult" baby), Baby Orchid (the "Slow-to-Warm" baby), and Baby Dandelion (the "Active" baby).

from one another in many ways, each adds great beauty to the world—even the misunderstood dandelion, whose vivid yellow head creates golden meadows in the summer sun. Just as is true of every child on this earth, each of these plants adds greatly to the variety that is the spice of life. In addition, to grow tall and fine, all four plants require a specific blend of sun, soil, and water—just as each child, no matter what her inborn temperament, needs her parents' uniquely suited tender loving care.

> Parents are gardeners—planting the seeds of faith, truth, and love that develop into the fairest flowers of character, virtue, and happiness in the lives of their children.
>
> —J. Harold Gwynne, author

Here are the four flowers in more detail.

Baby Sunflower: The "Easy" Child. What distinguishes a sunflower? First and foremost, it's easy to grow. Look in almost any nursery school's child-tended flower garden and you'll find sunflowers for that very reason. Even four-year-olds can't kill them! Second, they face the sky as if eager for each new day's gift of sunlight. Third, they have an inborn tendency to grow straight and tall, inspired from birth to show off their warm and happy petals to any and all who pass by.

The "Easy" baby is like that too. She wakes up happy, her rhythms are fairly predictable, she adapts to change without undue protest, she's open to new experiences but not impulsively so, she's moderate in both her positive and negative expressions of emotions, and she's fun to be around. In short, she's got the sunny, easygoing disposition that all parents assume their baby will have. Fortunately, according to Chess and Thomas, 40 percent of parents are right.

Baby Holly: The "Difficult" Child. There's beauty in the holly bush's dark-green foliage and brilliant berries, but first one has to deal with the overall prickliness of the leaves. With tiny thorns at each of their six corners, these leaves are ready to scratch and poke at the least invasion of their territory, causing even the most skilled gardener to don sturdy gloves to prune and care for them.

Like the holly bush, the "Difficult" baby is by nature "prickly" and a challenge to nurture well. Constituting 10 percent of Chess and Thomas's sample, these children are easily upset, irregular in their habits, react irritably to changes in routine, are emotionally intense, and are difficult to console. And yet, under this prickly veneer, there truly *is* a loving and lovable child whose fine points (and we don't mean thorns) just need to be cultivated with care—and the proverbial kid gloves. One of our goals in *Baby Hearts* is specifically to help parents with their own versions of Baby Holly learn how to garden successfully.

Baby Orchid: The "Slow-to-Warm" Child. Think about a gardener with a passion for orchids and one typically imagines someone with great patience, someone willing to take the time and trouble to coax this beautiful flower out of the shade into the sun, all the time being careful not to let it get overwhelmed lest it quickly wilt and wither. And its beauty is delicate rather than robust, with petals that are easily bruised and colors that are subtle rather than brilliant.

"Slow-to-Warm" children (15 percent of Chess and Thomas's sample), like the orchid, require great patience on the part of their caregivers. As the name implies, these children need time to adjust to new things, to observe from the sidelines before joining the action. They aren't intense in their responses unless pushed too hard and too fast, at which point they bruise easily and withdraw fast. Their overall caution extends to their preferred forms of play—quieter activities like book-reading and puzzles rather than the rough-and-tumble play attractive to many of their peers.

Parents often worry that their Baby Orchid is *too* cautious and would benefit from being forced to confront fears and anxieties. Such a strategy usually backfires, however, leaving the child even more cautious and parents even more frustrated than before. The better strategy, says new research, is for parents to overcome their bias against their child's caution and simply accept that they must be patient, always on the lookout for ways to *gently* encourage their "Orchid" to show off his delicate beauty to the rest of the world. (See Chapters 7 and 8 for additional research on cautious children.)

Baby Dandelion: The "Active" Child. Yes, dandelions are beautiful! Their bright, happy heads reach exuberantly to the sun, and, later, their wispy, white seedpods blow wildly in the wind. That's all wonderful, of course. But when talk turns to dandelions, the characteristic most likely to be mentioned is the fact that

The "Colicky" Baby

"Poor Lisa and Jimmy. The baby has colic." So goes the sympathetic lament when we hear about a baby who never seems to stop crying. But what *is* colic? Is it a disease? Are the children crying because they are in pain? And is a colicky baby simply a Baby Holly (irritable baby) by another name?

The truth is that scientists do not yet understand what causes colic. They can, however, describe it fairly accurately. Colic begins when a baby is about two weeks old, peaks at two months, and generally is gone by four months. Such a simple description, however, doesn't begin to do justice to the misery experienced by baby and parent alike between the two end points.

The major symptom of colic is prolonged crying (and we mean *hours*!) generally starting in late afternoon and continuing through the evening. And nothing seems to work reliably to get the crying to stop. The baby looks like he's in pain—with clenched fists, back arched, distended abdomen, legs bent over the tummy, and grimacing. However, less than 5 percent of cases are likely to be related to diagnosable organic problems like cow's milk, lactose, or fructose intolerance.

The best guess at the moment is that colic is a "regulatory" problem, meaning that the baby's nervous system just can't stop once it gets set on a negative path. Colicky babies actually don't cry any more often than non-colicky babies. It's just that when a colicky baby starts crying, it's like a freight train out of control going down a hill. There's no braking mechanism strong enough to halt the momentum once it gets going.

It's also important to note that colic is not a temperamental quality. A colicky baby is *not* simply a Baby Holly. Here's the difference: Although crying episodes are longer than normal in both cases, irritable babies actually cry more often than either non-colicky or colicky babies (with their cries triggered by greater sensitivity to minor events) and don't outgrow these tendencies at four months as colicky babies do.

So what's our advice to poor Lisa and Jimmy? Simply to grin and bear it knowing it won't last forever—and, in the meantime, to find as many folks to help them deal with the baby as they can.

they are incredibly hard to control. First they're here, then they're there, and then in the blink of an eye they are *everywhere*!

So it is with "Active" children. Especially when they are too young to have developed any self-control, their exuberance makes them very challenging to parent. They are simply busy, busy, busy! They run rather than walk, climb obstacles rather than go around, and never look before they leap. Parents of these children face many challenges, particularly from other people. Strangers often are dis-

> When my kids become wild and unruly, I use a nice safe playpen. When they're finished, I climb out.
>
> —Erma Bombeck, humorist

turbed by the active child's energy and impulsiveness and come too quickly to the conclusion that it's the parent's fault. "If that were my child..." frequently begins the whispered criticism behind the parent's back. The truth is that parents of Baby Dandelions deserve a special award for hanging in there—and more than an occasional pat on the back rather than criticism behind it.

WHERE DO TEMPERAMENTS COME FROM?

We've described these four different temperaments as inborn. By this we mean that they are apparent very early in a child's life—at least by four months of age, when the newborn's rhythms start to settle down. Contributing to this description is growing evidence suggesting a genetic base. In other words, at least to some extent, temperament is inherited. How do we know? From looking at twins. Comparisons of identical twins—twins who have identical genes—with each other yield greater similarities in temperament than comparisons of fraternal twins— twins who share no more genes than normal siblings. In other words, if one of your identical twins is a Baby Dandelion, hold on to your horses; the other one is likely to be one too.

There is even speculation that the nervous systems of these various groups have different set points in the oldest part of the brain (the brain stem at the top of the spinal cord) where automatic, unthinking reactions to events are triggered. These ancient systems are designed to react efficiently to sudden danger—producing the famous fight-or-flight responses via higher heart rates, faster respiration, disrupted digestion, increased muscle tension, and heightened perceptual awareness. Such responses enabled our reptilian ancestors, such as the crocodile, to quickly slip into the water with lightning speed if alerted to danger.

What is meant by the term "set point"? According to Washington University psychiatrist Robert Cloninger and his colleagues, if our set point on this continuum is high, it takes a relatively greater danger to trigger a reaction, whereas if our set point is low, it might take only a whisper of a threat to cause us to pull back in fear. Most of us, thankfully, are somewhere in the middle. Some individuals, however, quite likely including Baby Dandelion and Baby Orchid, must learn to deal with set points more toward the extremes.

IS BIOLOGY DESTINY?

We just spoke about Baby Dandelion and Baby Orchid learning "to deal with" their more extreme set points. This is a critical statement that can be restated this way: Biology is *not* destiny! The advantage that humans have over our reptilian ancestors is that we can, in fact, learn to control our behaviors, if not our fundamental emotions. With careful and consistent support from caregivers, both Baby Dandelion (the "Active" child) and Baby Orchid (the "Slow-to-Warm" child) can learn to control their reactions to the wonders and worries of the world around them. Because such control depends a great deal on development of the highest and most sophisticated layer of the brain, the cerebral cortex, the development of the necessary self-control takes time. But, in keeping with the theme of nature and nurture as a partnership, without appropriate guidance from loving and patient adults, it's not likely to develop at all.

Nature Meets Nurture: Learning to Manage Emotions

All this talk of self-control brings us to a third topic we want to address before jumping into the individual issues that form the heart of *Baby Hearts*, something researchers these days refer to as emotional self-regulation. That's a very formal term for the simple idea that healthy emotional development involves gradually

How to Help Your Baby? "Know Thyself"

How can you, as a parent, prepare yourself to provide the kind of support your own particular "flower" child needs? One way is to assess what researchers call the good-ness of fit between the two of you. What this boils down to is an assessment of your *own* temperamental qualities to see if they mesh easily with those of your child. For example, if you are a high-energy person with the emotional intensity and love of novelty characteristic of the "Active" child, then you and Baby Dandelion are likely to have an easier time relating to each other than you and Baby Orchid. The reverse is true too. A quiet, contemplative parent is likely to find a highly active or difficult baby a major challenge. Unless a parent is aware of his or her biases, temperamental mis-matches can be challenging to the parent-child relationship. In such cases negative interactions and frustrations are likely to start the ball rolling in the wrong direction from very early on, making course corrections increasingly difficult as time goes by.

Here are a few questions to get you started thinking about your own temperament:

◆ Do you enjoy meeting new people (like Baby Sunflower and Baby Dandelion), or does the prospect make you nervous (like Baby Orchid)?

◆ Do you prefer to explore new places (like Baby Sunflower and Baby Dandelion), or do you return to the tried and true (like Baby Orchid and Baby Holly)?

◆ Do you worry when your day isn't planned in advance (like Baby Orchid and Baby Holly), or do you welcome the unexpected (like Baby Dandelion)?

◆ Do you find it easy to sit still (like Baby Orchid and Baby Sunflower), or do you prefer to be on the go (like Baby Dandelion)?

That's the idea. And don't forget to consider the possibility of temperamental mismatches between your baby and other important caregivers too.

learning to manage (control) one's own emotions. It's just not a good idea, no matter what your age, to be so overcome with fear that you hide yourself away, or even so overcome with joy that you forget to look both ways before you cross the street. Like the discussions of biological regulation and temperament, the subject of emotional self-regulation is so fundamental to emotional development in general that at least a brief description is appropriate in this introductory chapter.

Also like the discussion of biological regulation and infant temperament, it provides a great example of how nature and nurture interact to nudge children along their developmental journey.

STEP 1: FROM BIOLOGICAL REGULATION TO EMOTIONAL REGULATION

Let's start with "nature," a reasonable choice given that's where every baby starts. As we described, newborn babies are even more helpless than they look. Although they seem to be compact little units with a life unto themselves, in reality they depend on being "plugged into" good caregiving ("nurture") in order to keep their biological systems functioning properly. What's more, this outside support (remember the gelatin mold?) gradually enables them to take over the job themselves as their brains and bodies mature—a push toward greater sophistication fueled by "nature" but shaped by "nurture."

At the very beginning, the helplessness of the child is so all-pervasive—involving everything from learning when to suck, to controlling body temperature, to being able to keep breathing regularly—that the issue is really total *biological* regulation. However, as the early months proceed and these vital biological systems gradually settle in, babies' job of learning to regulate themselves starts to narrow down to the devilishly sticky problem of specifically keeping emotions under some kind of control.

Why is emotional regulation important for babies? If emotions were only a psychological phenomenon, the task would be significant enough. But emotions, especially for young children still limping along without the help of sophisticated brain centers (see the next section), are very much *physical* issues too. For example, if left unchecked, the emotion of distress that leads to crying will eventually unwind a baby's whole body—causing symptoms as minor as hiccups, to catastrophes as serious as disruptions in breathing. And, even more critically, prolonged and frequent experiencing of highly stressful situations—and here we mean more than the frequent crying of the colicky baby—can *permanently* alter the chemistry of the brain through the release of large amounts of stress hormones like cortisol, resulting in problematic emotional patterns that become more and more difficult to change. Emotionally adverse environments can affect the brain even to the point of producing very substandard physical development (psychosocial dwarfism) and health (failure-to-thrive syndrome). (For more detail on the topic of the impact of severe stress on the developing brain, see Liu et al., 1997, and Perry et al., 1995.)

In other words, helping babies keep their emotions—especially the negative ones—within reasonable bounds is one of the most important responsibilities of a parent. Soothing a crying baby may seem like a good idea just from a noise perspective, but it's even more important for the baby!

STEP 2: FROM EMOTIONAL REGULATION TO EMOTIONAL SELF-REGULATION

As babies grow more complex and begin moving around the world on their own, relying on their parents to monitor and modulate their emotions becomes less and less practical. Fortunately, "nature" has thought of this and has managed to build in to human babies the desire to gradually take over the task of managing their own emotions. It's this passing of the buck back to the child that scientists refer to as emotional *self*-regulation.

What does emotional self-regulation actually look like? We will be talking a good deal about the various forms it takes as we introduce specific topics in later chapters, but here are a few examples.

- ◆ When feeling bombarded by stimulation, babies learn to turn their heads away and may even start playing with their fingers to calm themselves down.
- ◆ When feeling anxious or upset, babies learn to comfort themselves by sucking on their thumb.
- ◆ When toddlers are in unfamiliar settings or with unfamiliar people, they learn the value of holding on tight to a favorite toy.
- ◆ When toddlers become anxious about new events or people, they learn to check out their parents' faces for cues about what's happening.
- ◆ When toddlers are required to wait, they learn to distract themselves by doing other things.
- ◆ Finally, once children can *talk* about emotions, they learn that doing so helps diffuse the intensity of their feelings.

Clearly, there's a lot for babies to learn. And who will your own baby need to learn all this from? There's no doubt that her teachers will include grandparents,

An important shift takes place in the middle of the first year, when babies begin to be able to soothe themselves instead of always relying on their parents for emotional regulation. Luke demonstrates how creative babies can be when they really need some help.

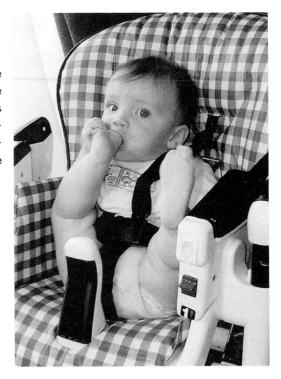

siblings, babysitters, and peers—but Mom and Dad are definitely the most influential teachers of them all. Don't worry, though; we plan to provide lots of lesson plans throughout the rest of the book.

The Brains Behind It All

No introduction to the biology of emotions would be complete without at least some discussion of the role played behind the scenes by the greatest of all evolutionary inventions: the human brain. "Behind the scenes" is an apt description, because we are rarely (if ever) aware of how much is going on up there when we experience even a fleeting emotion such as mild surprise, let alone a complex emotion such as love.

The love we feel for our children is magical, not mechanical. It seems to well up from deep inside of us, melting our hearts, making us smile, sometimes even bringing tears to our eyes. And when our children return this love, the magic is doubled. Love does indeed make our hearts sing.

But how does all this happen? What exactly is going on when we cuddle with our children, body to body and heart to heart? It may surprise you to learn that a large part of what is going on is actually brain to brain. What's more, it's not just two brains in sync with each other; it's more like three brains each, for a total of six.

THE TRIPLE-DECKER BRAIN

Thomas Lewis, Fari Amini, and Richard Lannon, three psychiatry professors at the University of California, San Francisco, School of Medicine, provide a wonderful description of the relation between our multiple brains and our experiences of love in their fascinating book *A General Theory of Love*. In it they explain how human emotions are really the result of incredibly rapid and complex cross-talk among three separate "mini-brains," each one a separate product of evolution. Presented in the order in which they appeared over the eons, these three include the reptilian brain (the brain stem), the limbic or "emotional" brain (deep within our skulls), and the cerebral cortex or "thinking" brain (the wrinkled sheet of tightly packed nerve cells that covers it all).

In the Beginning: The Reptilian Brain. Let's start at the most basic and historically earliest level, the reptilian brain. The name, not surprisingly, comes from the fact that this primitive structure located at the top of the spinal cord has been a vital factor in the survival of every species since the age of reptiles. What does this part of the brain, more typically called the brain stem, have to do with the feelings we call emotions? Pretty much nothing—at least not by itself. After all, one can hardly credit reptiles, which routinely have hundreds of hatchlings that they care nothing about, with any depth of feeling.

And yet without the reptilian brain, our own emotions wouldn't be nearly as helpful—or hurtful. The reason is because the systems included in the brain stem—particularly those that make up the autonomic nervous system—are responsible for helping us react with lightning speed to danger. Such reactions often are referred to as fight-or-flight responses. For example, when a little boy's hand suddenly enters the visual field of a blue-bellied lizard sunning on a rock, the images from the lizard's eye travel immediately to its primitive reptilian brain and set in motion changes in very basic bodily functions (heart

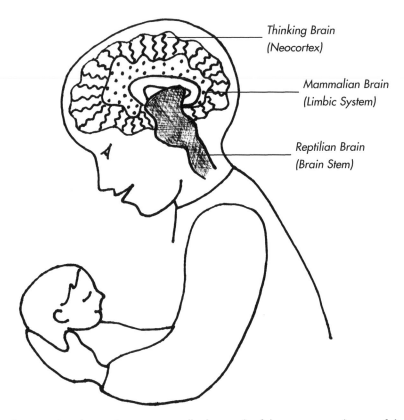

Thinking Brain
(Neocortex)

Mammalian Brain
(Limbic System)

Reptilian Brain
(Brain Stem)

Our emotional experiences are really the result of three separate layers of the brain all working together. The "triple-decker brain" shown above as a mother cuddles her infant includes the primitive reptilian brain (the brain stem), the emotional mammalian brain (the limbic system), and the human thinking brain (the neocortex).

rate, breathing, muscle tone, etc.) that enable the lizard to move to safer quarters in the blink of an eye. The same thing happens when that little boy jumps out at us from behind a door, shouting "Boo!" Like the lizard, we react immediately, in our case jumping three feet in the air while clutching at our pounding hearts.

But unlike the lizard, our reaction doesn't stop there. Because of the development later in evolution of the other two levels of the triple-decker brain, we also react with specific feelings (most likely fear, followed by relief, followed by irritation) and specific thoughts (for example, "That kid will be the death of me!").

With Fur Came Feelings: The Limbic Brain. The appearance of mammals on the evolutionary scene was the advancement that ushered in emotions—or what we more colloquially term "feelings." Just because they have them doesn't mean that all mammals are consciously *aware* of these feelings—a gift granted humans by the further development of layer three, the cerebral cortex. It does mean, however, that much of mammalian behavior is motivated by internal states that linger over time and get them in and out of much more complex interactions with their peers (not just predators). Much to the delight of kittens, puppies, and human babies, for example, mammal parents don't eat their young! Instead, mammal mothers are programmed to engage in quite elaborate behaviors designed to help insure their youngsters' survival. They feel *drawn* to their young through some version of parental "love." Also unlike reptiles, mammals create bonds with other adults of their species to form mating pairs, families, or even troops. All of these behaviors are made possible by the complex activities of the limbic brain.

> If evolution really works, how come mothers only have two hands?
>
> —Ed Dussault, humorist

How does the limbic brain accomplish all this? Essentially by *coordinating* the activities of any part of the body even vaguely involved in emotions. This includes the various biological functions controlled by the reptilian brain (like heart rate, breathing, etc.), as well as any emotion-relevant thoughts or perceptions flowing down the pipeline from the top layer, the thinking brain (the cerebral cortex). It also includes all hormones involved in emotions—such as stress and sex hormones—via one of its own structures, the hypothalamus.

The limbic brain, and especially its main component, the amygdala, is like a master switchboard operator, receiving phone calls from lines coming into the board from various parts of the body and then figuring out what lines these calls should be connected to on their way out. For example, when three-year-old Johnny suddenly runs into the street, it's Mom's amygdala that senses the danger and then triggers the adrenaline rush that fuels her sudden intake of breath, her accelerated heartbeat, and her mad dash to save him from harm. Without the amygdala, in other words, little Johnny might not be here—and chances are good that neither would we.

And Then There Were Three: The Thinking Brain. The human cerebral cortex is the latest evolutionary comer. This gray and profoundly wrinkled sheet, scrunched up right under our skulls, is what enables humans to think, plan, remember, and talk—activities that, nine times out of ten, involve some kind of emotion. Looking at the newborn baby in our arms, we not only feel love welling up in our throats, but also think about how much we love her, sing her praises to others, and plan for her future. And where does the particular lilt to our voice come from when we whisper "I love you!" in her ear? Straight up from the limbic brain to the speech centers in the cerebral cortex. In other words, we speak because we have a cortex, but we speak of love because we *also* have a limbic brain. Teamwork extraordinaire.

NURTURE PUTS ITS STAMP ON NATURE

All this talk about brain structures, with the inevitable emphasis on biology, might make it seem as if the environment is pretty marginal to a child's developing experience of emotions. On the contrary, the environment is very important. For one thing, there is the obvious role played by witnessing specific events—like the boy jumping out from behind the door or our four-year-old blowing us a kiss. There's no denying that a large percentage of our emotions occur in reaction to something happening "out there."

However, the environment you provide your baby has much more influence over brain activity than just the triggering of momentary reactions. For good or bad, the emotions your baby experiences in reaction to individual events make an actual *physical* impression on the brain. Each one leaves a kind of footprint in the form of chemical changes, and the more often a particular emotion is felt in a particular context, the deeper that footprint becomes—much the same way a trail through the woods becomes worn deeper with each succeeding hiker. If the accumulating experiences tend mainly to evoke smiles and contented coos on your baby's part, then the accompanying changes in the brain move its development in a positive direction.

If negative experiences predominate, however, then the changes to brain chemistry can leave a negative trail deep enough that it's hard for succeeding footprints to turn any other way. The result is an increased tendency to experience the world as negative even when it's not. That's why feeling secure in the arms of a parent's love is so critical to a baby's emotional future. And that's the subject to which *Baby Hearts* turns next.

PART I

the "big five" goals for healthy emotional development

2

Welcome to the World: Feeling Loved and Secure

N E W S   F L A S H!

A Secure Attachment: Memories Are Made
of This, Say Researchers

University Park, Pennsylvania. Although hardly an Academy Award winner by ordinary standards, the puppet show that three-year-old Bennett has just settled down to watch is actually a huge winner in the eyes of the child development research community. Written and directed by University of Pennsylvania scientists Jay Belsky, Becky Spritz, and Keith Crnic, the individual scenes played out on the tiny stage are revealing something extremely important about how children as young as Bennett experience the world and what role a child's earliest relationships play in determining their views.

Just how is all this being accomplished? First, the individual scenes were selected to include happy events (like a puppet receiving a birthday present) and sad events (like a puppet spilling his juice). In addition, sometimes the puppets said nice things to their pint-size viewers, while other times they teased them in not so nice ways. Then, after the entire multiact play was over, the researchers interviewed the children to discover which events they remembered and which ones they didn't.

The results were intriguing. Some children, it seems, are significantly more likely to remember the details of happy events, while others are more likely to remember the details of sad ones. That in itself is interesting. But the most important finding of the study was what predicted which tendency a child would show. The key predictor came from an earlier visit to the lab when the children were only twelve months old. During that visit each child had experienced a sequence of seven, three-minute episodes designed to evaluate the quality of the relationship they enjoyed with their mothers. Based on how they reacted during these short sessions, Belsky and his colleagues were able to categorize these relationships as either "secure" or "insecure." And it was this difference that predicted whether the children would remember pleasant or unpleasant events two years later during the puppet show. Those children who enjoyed a warm and secure relationship with their mothers early on were significantly more likely to remember the nice things that happened, while those whose relationships were marked by anxiety and mistrust were significantly more likely to remember the unpleasant events.

Jay Belsky explains: "The lesson is clear. How babies feel about their parents during the first year of life plays a powerful role in how they experience events that happen after that. If they start off feeling safe and secure, then their focus has a good chance of continuing to be on what's wonderful about life. But if they aren't so lucky, and especially if their relationship continues to be problematic, then the negative views they develop in that first year are likely to color their experiences for years to come."

Bottom line? Thanks to modern researchers like Belsky, Spritz, and Crnic, we now know that what happens early in life is more important than most of our grandparents ever suspected.

What's All the Excitement About?

All parents want their children to grow up feeling safe, secure, and loved. Unfortunately, however, not all children end up this way. One of the main reasons is that dealing with a baby is a good deal harder than movies, advertisements, and greeting cards suggest. Most newborns cry at least two hours per day. What's more, they sleep only sporadically, have lots of poopy diapers, get runny noses and ear infections, and spit up and drool. Once they are mobile and capable of thinking their own thoughts, life gets even more complicated. No longer dependent on adults, they are soon into everything and resentful of attempts to thwart their plans. When you stop to think about it, the wonder is that so many parents *do* manage to provide the unselfish gifts of time, energy, and love so critical to starting babies off on the right foot emotionally.

And how they start off *is* critical. That's what all the excitement is about. Thanks to research that has followed children from infancy to adulthood (especially work by Everett Waters, Alan Sroufe, and Jim Elicker started in the 1970s at the University of Minnesota), we now know for sure that children's experiences during the first three years of life have an enormous effect on every aspect of their emotional lives thereafter. Forming a strong bond with his or her baby must, therefore, be every parent's first and foremost goal. This emotional bond, or secure attachment, as it's referred to by child development professionals, is considered crucial to emotional well-being because it establishes children's "working model" for future relationships: how they will expect to be treated by peers, teachers, neighbors, and, eventually, romantic partners. More specifically, we now know that children who develop a secure attachment bond with their parents...

- ◆ Show more empathy toward others.
- ◆ Establish friendships more easily.
- ◆ Are more cooperative, generous, and less aggressive.
- ◆ Do better in school.
- ◆ Are less likely to experience anxiety and depression.
- ◆ Enjoy more rewarding intimate relationships throughout their lives.

In fact, research shows that the quality of a child's attachment during the early years is a powerful predictor of how securely attached his or her *own* children will be in the far-distant future.

We don't mean to imply that relationships after the first three years are inconsequential. That's far from true. A relationship with parents that starts off secure can turn sour because of divorce, separation, or other unforeseen circumstances, with the result that the child shifts from positive to negative expectations about life. In contrast, a relationship that starts off less than perfect often (but *not* always) can be counteracted with consistent, gentle caring, thereby edging a child toward a more positive outlook on life. All things being equal, however, it's hard to disagree with the principle that a child is much better off starting life feeling secure and loved.

Given all we now know about the power of early relationships to shape a child's life, it's safe to say that there is no more critical chapter in all of *Baby Hearts* than the one you are about to read. And even in subsequent chapters you'll see more references to the importance of the attachment bond than to any other single concept. There's just no getting around it: Making sure your baby feels loved and secure is the cornerstone of emotional development. How to do that is what this chapter is all about.

A secure and wholesomely loved child goes forth to meet new experiences in a spirit of adventure and comes out triumphant.

—Rodger A. Pool, educator

The Birth of a New Idea

As we mentioned in the introduction, the notion that the first years of life make an impression on young children is a fairly recent idea. Sigmund Freud had talked about the importance of breastfeeding and the dangers of faulty toilet training at the turn of the twentieth century, but most of his "data" were collected from therapy sessions with adult patients. The idea that scientists should actually observe interactions between babies and their parents didn't gain momentum until decades later with the pioneering work of two researchers: John Bowlby and Mary Ainsworth.

THE PIONEERS OF ATTACHMENT THEORY

John Bowlby, a clinical psychologist in London during the late 1940s, began noticing similarities between two groups of children: children orphaned by World War II and children referred to him because of criminal activity. Both groups, Bowlby observed, had trouble connecting with other people and were often described as emotionally aloof or detached. But equally important was his discovery that the criminal children, like the orphans, had experienced physical or emotional "separation" from their parents during their earliest years. Bowlby concluded that the emotional problems the children were experiencing were the result of being denied the consistent affection of adults whose presence and support they could count on. He theorized that the desire for such relationships is innate, that human babies are

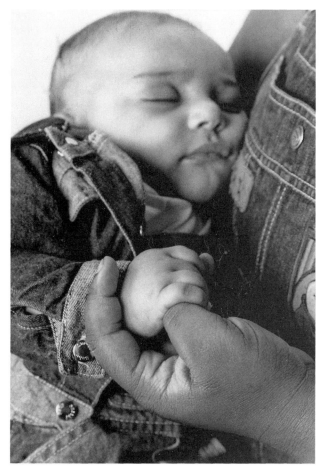

Helping babies feel loved and secure is the most important gift that
parents can give. Called the attachment bond by researchers, the emotional relationship between parent
and child sets the stage for the development of a lifetime of emotions.

born *eager* to bond with the important people in their lives. These "attachment figures," as he called them, provide infants and toddlers with a secure home base from
which they can safely venture out to explore the world.

Bowlby's theory would have remained just that—a theory—had it not been for
the creativity of his American research partner, Dr. Mary Ainsworth. It was
Ainsworth who finally figured out a way to look at a particular parent-child relationship and determine whether it was providing the security the child needed.
Based on Bowlby's notion that babies view their favorite caregivers as secure home
bases, Ainsworth decided to see what would happen when babies were placed
under a bit of stress—nothing unusual, just very short periods of separation from
Mom (or Dad) or the presence of a stranger. Bowlby's theory predicted that babies

with good attachment relationships would quickly and confidently seek comfort from their caregivers, while babies with poorer attachment relationships would be less certain of help from their caregivers and would respond very differently. And that's just what Ainsworth and legions of researchers who have followed her lead have found using the most frequently cited research procedure in developmental psychology today, a procedure aptly named the "Strange Situation."

ASSESSING SECURITY: THE STRANGE SITUATION

Taking little Bennett from the news flash as our example, here's how the Strange Situation works. Bennett, age twelve months, and his mother arrive at Jay Belsky's lab at the University of Pennsylvania and are shown into a playroom containing a few chairs and a wide variety of toys. After a minute or so to get settled, Bennett and Mom experience seven, three-minute episodes, one right after the other:

1. Mom and Bennett are alone in the room.
2. A stranger joins them.
3. Mom exits, leaving Bennett alone with the stranger.
4. Mom returns and the stranger leaves.
5. Mom exits *again*, this time leaving Bennett all alone.
6. The stranger returns and tries to comfort Bennett.
7. Mom returns for good and the stranger leaves the two alone to reconnect.

All of the episodes are videotaped and then watched and *re*watched by the researchers. Their goal is to determine how willingly and effectively Bennett uses his mom as a source of companionship and comfort.

WHAT WE'VE LEARNED ABOUT ATTACHMENT BONDS

The Strange Situation has provided researchers with a valuable tool for distinguishing optimal, secure attachment relationships from less than optimal, insecure relationships. In addition, by looking in more depth at the lives of children who fall into each category, researchers have been able to find predictors—specific patterns of interaction, family circumstances, and infant characteristics that predispose a parent and child to develop a particular kind of bond.

But before we talk in more detail about these predictors, here is a sketch of what a secure attachment looks like, along with descriptions of three subcategories of insecure relationships. Keep in mind that although Mom is used in the sketches, the descriptions can apply equally to a child's relationship with Dad or any other important caregiver.

Secure Babies. Fortunately, most babies (about 65 percent in middle-class American samples—the group most available for study) fall into this category. These lucky babies enjoy their moms and trust them enough to explore the world as long as they remain close by. In the Strange Situation they are content to play with the toys, occasionally sharing them with Mom; they become distressed when Mom leaves and then are genuinely relieved to see her return, finding comfort and solace in her welcoming arms.

Insecure Babies. The remaining 35 percent of babies fall into one of three groups of insecure attachments. Although the groups differ in important ways, all these babies share one thing: They all lack trust in the willingness or ability of their caregiver to help them when they need it. These descriptions of how they behave in the Strange Situation illustrate this point.

 ◆ **Insecure resistant (or ambivalent) babies.** An unusually high level of anxiety keeps these 15 percent of babies clinging to Mom. What makes them different from children who are merely very timid is the fact that they act this way *even when no one else is around*. It's as if they don't trust their mothers to protect them unless they are holding on tight. Not surprisingly, they are *extremely* upset when their mothers leave. Given their distress, you might expect these babies to be really glad to see Mom return. However, in sharp contrast to the enthusiastic reception the mothers of securely attached babies get, insecure resistant babies appear visibly ambivalent. They may approach their moms or agree to be held but simultaneously push away and refuse to make eye contact. It's as if they hold a grudge. They seem to be communicating "You did it to me again! I trusted you, you let me down, and I'm not ready to forgive you yet." Researchers believe these babies have grown frustrated by their mothers' hit-and-miss records of appropriate caregiving over the first year.
 ◆ **Insecure avoidant babies.** Unlike the babies in the secure and insecure resistant groups, the 20 percent of babies in this attachment category act as if they

couldn't care one way or another whether their mothers are around. They play by themselves and don't express relief or joy when Mom returns after an absence. Are these babies simply so secure that behaving independently comes easily? No. Physiological measures (like heart rate) indicate that even though avoidant babies look content, they are actually anxious and upset. In other words, they are in need of comforting and protection but, sadly, don't see any point in trying to get it from their caregiver. Why? Parents of avoidant babies tend to withdraw emotionally from their children, sometimes due to depression, sometimes due to anger or resentment, and still other times because that's the way they themselves were raised. Whatever the reason, these parents fail to provide the unconditional affection and warmth that convince a child that other people can be trusted to help when he is in need. The only option, therefore, is for the child to try to take care of himself.

◆ **Insecure disorganized babies.** Infants in this group are an altogether special

Babies love playing with their daddies, in part because fathers are more likely than mothers to engage in rough-and-tumble activities. Here Baby Jack enjoys a ride on Dad Jim's shoulders.

Make Room for Daddy!

Up until the mid-1970s, research papers about the early emotional lives of children could justifiably cause a reader to conclude that, except for their contribution of chromosomes, fathers were pretty irrelevant to the lives of their babies. Fortunately, all that has changed. Sparked by the independent efforts of Ross Parke and Michael Lamb, two developmental researchers who are also devoted dads, a large body of data now documents the important roles fathers play in the lives of children—by both their presence and their absence. Here's just a sampling of what we now know.

◆ Just as is the case with moms, the quality of the interactions between babies and their dads determines whether the attachment bond between them will be secure or insecure.

◆ Attachment relationships between babies and fathers are independent of their relationships with their mothers. A baby can be securely attached to one parent and insecurely attached to the other.

◆ Babies in cultures all over the world tend to prefer Dad over Mom as a playmate because of the natural tendency of fathers to enjoy more high-energy, unpredictable activities. (How many times have you seen a *mother* holding her baby high overhead, balanced on one palm, and swooping the baby through the air while making airplane noises?)

◆ Because mothers in two-parent households are the ones most likely to hold and soothe babies, children tend to prefer Mom over Dad when they are hurt, sick, or unhappy—although Dad is a welcome substitute when Mom is not available.

The older children get, the more important dads become to their emotional and intellectual lives. Sons observe them closely and imitate their attitudes and behaviors. To some extent daughters do so too, but in addition, daughters use their fathers' reactions to them as a measure of how they can be expected to be treated by males in general.

case, often victims of serious emotional or physical abuse or both. The term "disorganized" comes from the fact that these babies behave erratically and unpredictably in the Strange Situation. For example, they may start crawling to Mom and suddenly turn away. They may start to hand her something and then throw it down. They stumble and fall, move distractedly from toy to toy, and don't seek comfort. The most common emotion they express is *fear*. These babies seem afraid of everything, *including* their parents—all too often with good reason.

Steps Along the Way

As was true for Baby Bennett, most children are twelve months old when their attachment relationships are assessed in the Strange Situation. Researchers figure that it takes at least a year for human babies to develop the brain power necessary to figure out who is and who is not being nice to them. There are, however, some predictable milestones along the way.

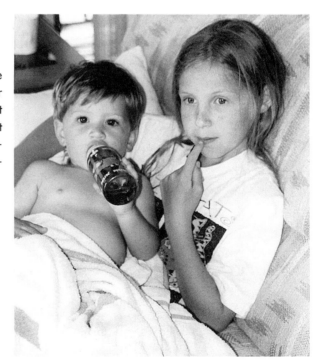

Although babies at first pick one person (usually Mom) to be their one-and-only favorite, by their first birthday they have expanded the list to include other very familiar people—such as the older cousin pictured here.

◆ **Birth to 6 weeks.** "Whatever feels good is great!" Although newborn babies are instinctively drawn to looking at people, it's the feel-good experiences those people provide (cozy contact, interesting sights and sounds, relief from hunger pangs) that seem to make an impression rather than the people themselves.

◆ **6 weeks to 7 months.** "Being with people is *especially* great." Suddenly babies begin to show a clear preference for people over other objects. What makes this change so obvious is the advent of what researchers call the social smile, so named because it's triggered specifically by interacting with people. Pick baby up and chances are good you'll be rewarded with a smile. A little later and it could even be a giggle.

◆ **7 to 9+ months.** "Anything but my favorite person is *not* great." As a baby's memory for faces and experiences improves, she begins to show a very strong preference for one particular person. That's why this period also marks the beginning of two not-so-popular developments: stranger anxiety and separation anxiety. (See tips for dealing with these very normal fears on page 175 in Chapter 7.)

◆ **11+ months.** "Being with any of my favorite people is great!" Although one person may be favored over all others for a short while, the baby's list of strong attachments quickly grows to include others who are important in daily life.

N E W S   F L A S H !

Four-Month-Old Music Critics Say "The Best Songs of Love Are Just for Me"

Hamilton, Ontario. Four-month-old Clara is sucking as hard as she can on that funny pacifier the nice lady put in her mouth. And the funny thing is that as long as she keeps sucking, she keeps hearing Mommy singing a song—and singing it so nicely too.

If your baby's pacifier doesn't automatically cause you to break into song, you may be wondering what's going on. It turns out that Clara and a group of other four-month-olds are all part of a study being conducted by psychologist Laurel Trainor at

McMaster University in Ontario, Canada, to find out just how fussy babies are about the music they hear. And the answer turns out to be very fussy indeed! Trainor, knowing from other research how much babies enjoy lullabies sung by their parents, decided to look a bit further into exactly what qualities of the experience were important to the infants. To find out, she hooked an audio recorder to a special pacifier so that the only way sound could be heard was if the baby sucked really hard. Trainor could then compare how "popular" a song was by how vigorously the babies sucked to hear it.

So what songs did she compare? That's the amazing part. She compared two versions of the same song both sung by the babies' mothers. The difference was that one song had been recorded when the mothers were actually singing to their babies, while the other version was recorded when the babies weren't there. The results were amazing. The infants clearly recognized the difference between the two versions and strongly preferred the recording of their mother actually singing to them.

Clearly, it's not just the music these four-month-old babies care about, or they wouldn't have worked harder to hear one tape over the other. But what is it? What does one version of Mom's voice have that's missing from the other? A group of adults who listened to the two types of recordings rated the direct singing as having a more "loving tone"—a tone that lets babies know their moms think they are pretty special. Singing to a baby, it seems, does much more than just entertain.

Predicting Attachment Success

Don't worry. Laurel Trainor's study does not mean that if you can't carry a tune, your baby won't love you. What it does mean, though, is that even very young babies can detect subtle differences between messages that are carried in loving tones and messages that aren't. And it's the ratio between the two that matters to attachment. Even before babies can understand the words themselves, they know from your tone of voice whether you're happy with them or not, and the more often you are angry, impatient, irritated, or just plain "blah" with them, the greater risk there is for an insecure attachment.

Tone of voice, then, is one factor that enters into the equation for predicting a secure attachment. Thanks to research over the last fifteen years, we also now know about many others. Here's a compact list.

WHAT'S IN YOUR HANDS

It Matters How "Sensitive" You Are. Most attachment researchers today agree that something they call parental sensitivity plays an extremely important role in determining whether a child will develop a secure or insecure attachment. What "sensitivity" means in this context is pretty specific. It's the ability to "read" your baby well (figure out what she needs) and then meet those needs in a timely fashion. In other words, a highly sensitive caregiver who hears her baby begin to cry will be familiar enough with the baby's temperament, daily schedule, and immediate situation to have a pretty good idea what the problem is and then will be willing and able to quickly provide whatever comfort the baby needs.

Of course, the phrase "timely fashion" is open to interpretation. Alicia Lieberman, a well-respected professor of psychiatry and author of *The Emotional Life of the Toddler,* provides some guidelines drawn from research data with very young babies reported in the *Journal of Pediatrics.* If a parent responds to a newborn baby within ninety seconds, then the baby is likely to calm down within five seconds. In contrast, if the parent waits three minutes, then the baby will take fifty seconds to calm down. In other words, every doubling of response time leads to a *tenfold* increase in the length of crying. As you can see from these figures, responding in a timely fashion is the easiest way to stop a baby's crying. In fact, research across the first year consistently shows that babies whose parents respond rapidly to their bids for attention cry significantly *less* often than babies whose

One Size Never Fits All

The response-time statistics Alicia Lieberman cites are, of course, based on the proverbial "average" baby (if one even exists!). A baby's temperament is clearly a factor in how easy or hard she is to soothe. One of the hallmarks of Baby Sunflower's temperament, after all, is the very fact she is easy to calm down, while Baby Holly is termed "Difficult" in part because she is both more easily upset and harder to soothe. The bottom line, however, is that parents who are appropriately sensitive understand their babies well enough to enter their temperaments into the equation and respond in ways that fit their babies' individual needs.

parents don't. In other words, the idea that responding rapidly to crying "spoils" babies, causing them to cry more often rather than less, is a total myth—one that causes pediatricians and psychologists alike to cringe every time they hear it.

The fact that a quick and appropriate response, especially to a newborn baby's distress, is so important makes sense once you remember how immature a baby's nervous system is for months after birth. Babies are simply not able to regulate their bodies on their own. Unless a parent responds quickly, very likely the act of crying will unwind a young baby's physiology to the point that it becomes harder and harder for him to stop. It's like a freight train that has no brakes. Once a train starts down the mountain and picks up speed, stopping it becomes more and more difficult. And older infants and toddlers face a similar problem because the longer they cry without any response, the more anxious they get that no help is coming, thereby increasing the number of things they have to cry about from one to two.

Of course, the reality is that parents can't always respond to their babies as quickly as they'd like, and an occasional lapse in sensitivity won't turn the attachment process sour. The overwhelming impression the baby must have, however, is that someone will be there when he needs help. And here's a bit of reality that parents often forget: Unfortunately, babies aren't in a position to cut us any slack because our *intentions* are good. They neither understand nor care about *why* we aren't responding in a timely fashion—for example, that the boss was on the phone or that big sister had just fallen down and needed attention. All babies know is that they didn't get what they needed when they needed it, and if this happens more than occasionally, their sense of security will grow just a bit weaker every time.

It's also important to remember that "sensitivity" encompasses more than just responding to a baby when she begins to cry. It also includes leaving the baby alone when she's sending signals that she needs to *stop* interacting for a while or wants to interact in a different way. By about the third month, babies are able to withdraw a bit when they feel overwhelmed by stimulation—they may look away, start gazing at their fingers, squirm, or begin to whimper. Some parents, particularly those who are trying too hard to live up to the image of the involved parent, take these signals as a personal challenge. They intend to win back the baby's attention or die trying. They may start tickling the baby, raise their voices even higher, move into the baby's line of sight, or even forcibly turn the baby's head back to face them. Such "intrusiveness," as researchers call it, also qualifies as insensitive. The point to remember is that sensitivity involves reading the baby's signals, even if what the baby is signaling doesn't fit your own idea of what should be going on.

It Matters How "Insightful" You Are. Being "sensitive," however, isn't the whole story. According to a 2002 study by Nina Koren-Karie and her colleagues at the University of Haifa in Israel, it's also important to be "insightful." These terms may sound the same, but according to the results of the study, insightfulness is actually an independent predictor of how securely attached a child is to a parent. While sensitivity describes the actions a parent takes in interacting with a child, insightfulness is more a mind-set or attitude.

Koren-Karie and her colleagues assessed insightfulness by videotaping mothers interacting with their twelve-month-old children and then reviewing the videotapes *with* the mothers. During these conversations, they looked for answers to these questions.

- ◆ Did the mother try to see experiences through her child's eyes? (Did she even understand the question?)
- ◆ Did she try to understand the motives underlying the child's behavior, acknowledging that it's sometimes hard to know?
- ◆ Was she open to new insights about the child and her style of caregiving, or was she rigid in her interpretations?
- ◆ Was she appreciative of her child's strengths and competencies even when discussing less than perfect behavior?
- ◆ Did she *enjoy* talking about her child in these ways, or did she find the conversations pointless or boring?

Using the Strange Situation to assess the attachment relationships between these mothers and their twelve-month-olds, Koren-Karie and her colleagues were able to demonstrate that those mothers whose babies enjoyed secure attachments were significantly more likely to enjoy these conversations, be open-minded, try to see things from their child's perspective, and express empathy for their children. Such mothers, the researchers concluded for want of a better word, were demonstrating "insightfulness."

A similar argument for the importance of "insightfulness" comes from work by developmental psychologist Daphne Bugental with abusive parents, showing what

Does Being "Sensitive" Mean Never Saying No?

When a four-month-old baby cries, the advice to meet her needs in a timely fashion makes intuitive sense. However, what about the two-year-old who cries because you're leaving for work or because you won't let her climb on the coffee table? Clearly, the older a child gets, the less appropriate it is to set as the primary goal stopping all crying as quickly as possible. Where do you draw the line?

It helps to remember that, unlike the four-month-old—or even the twelve-month-old—a two-year-old is able to grasp the reasons behind your decisions if they are expressed simply and consistently. If your decision is a sensible one and you deliver it with empathy, conviction, affection, and a clear explanation, then you are, in fact, being sensitive. The child may not like the decision, but she can learn to live with it, especially if she also has learned from Day 1 to trust in your love. Dr. Lieberman expresses it this way: "Toddlers learn meaning from their parents, and they can learn to tolerate distress much better if they have a sense that it is for a worthy cause."

can happen when parents are really *not* insightful. It turns out that a good predictor of which parents are most likely to abuse their children is whether they perceive even their very youngest children as having more control over situations than they do. They are, in other words, attributing totally inaccurate levels of "power" to their infants and toddlers, which in turn leads them to feel powerless and to strike back defensively. Their mantra seems to be "The best defense is a good offense."

It Matters How "Synchronized" You Are. In order to draw adult humans into caring interactions as quickly as possible, human babies have evolved in a way that makes them search for and revel in face-to-face interactions with caregivers where there's a synchronized give-and-take. Baby smiles and Mom smiles back. Baby frowns and Mom looks sad. Baby coos and Mom coos too.

An important characteristic of such interactions when they are working well is that the parent's response is contingent on what the baby does. In other words, the parent's response is timed to follow the baby's behavior and to be appropriate and predictable. Baby does A and parent follows with B. Baby does C and parent follows with D.

The hearts of small children are delicate organs. A cruel beginning in this world can twist them into curious shapes. The heart of a hurt child can shrink so that forever afterward it is hard and pitted as the seed of a peach. Or, again, the heart of such a child may fester and swell until it is misery to carry within the body, easily chafed and hurt by the most ordinary things.

—Carson Smith McCullers,
American novelist

Why is contingent responding so important? For one thing, it gives the baby the pleasure of calling the shots for a change, a pleasurable form of control in an otherwise uncontrollable world. However, according to Daniel Siegel, author of *The Developing Mind,* it serves another, even more important purpose. When a parent reflects back what a baby is feeling during these intimate face-to-face interactions, the baby enjoys what Dr. Siegel calls a sense of "feeling felt." He uses this term to describe the internal feeling that any of us experiences when we perceive that another person has truly connected with us emotionally, has shared a momentary bond of understanding or, to use another of Dr. Siegel's terms, "emotional resonance." We all thrive under these conditions, but babies do so especially for the simple reason that a baby's caregivers provide the only shelter the baby has in an unknown and unpredictable world.

This detailed emphasis on face-to-face interaction may sound like it requires exquisite planning on the part of parents, but in most cases, fortunately, responding contingently comes very naturally. And that's good because it turns out that human babies *require* such interactions for healthy emotional development. We know that's the case from watching what happens when this synchronized "dance" is disrupted. Dr. Edward Tronick, from the Harvard Medical School's Children's Hospital, has demonstrated how unsettling babies find such disruptions using a clever technique called the "Still Face" procedure. After filming a parent and infant interacting face to face in whatever way is normal for them, the parent is asked to suddenly assume a totally frozen face—neither smiling nor scowling—and remain totally passive and unresponsive to any bids for attention from the baby. The

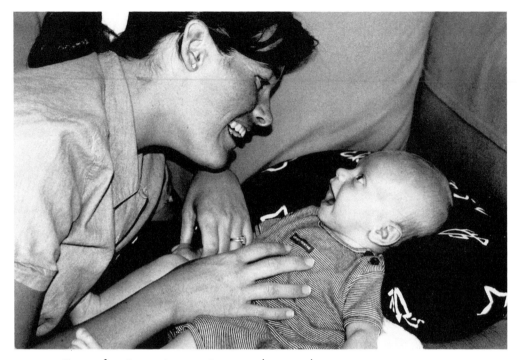

Face-to-face interactions are important because they encourage parents to get in sync with their baby. Such emotional matching on the part of parents contributes to the very young baby's sense of being understood and cared for.

result? Babies as young as four months turn out to be exquisitely sensitive to disruptions and quickly become despondent when such disruptions continue for more than a moment or two. Interestingly, babies understand when Mom turns away to talk to someone else; it's when there seems to be no good reason for the disruption that they become disheartened. Under those conditions, they seem to perceive their mother's behavior as rejection, and with that perception comes the fear that they have lost their hold on a safe and predictable world.

Elephants Aren't the Only Ones with Long Memories

Does what happens to babies at five months make a lasting impression? You bet it does! And if you don't believe us, consider the results of a recent study by psychologists Marc Bornstein and Clay Mash from the National Institute of Child Health and Human Development and Martha Arterberry from Gettysburg College.

In a test of the importance of face-to-face interaction between babies and adults, a group of five-month-old babies experienced the Still Face procedure first used by Ed Tronick and his associates (see page 39). Instead of the child's mother, however, the interaction was with an unfamiliar adult female. As is typical, the woman interacted normally for one minute and then stared for the next two minutes at the infant without reacting at all. As is also typical, the babies didn't like the change one bit.

However, of even more importance were the data gathered fifteen months later when the infants were twenty months old. At this point the original infants as well as a new group of infants were shown three videotapes, each showing a woman interacting as if with a baby. Two of the women were totally new to the original babies, while the third was the same woman from the earlier testing. Results? Yup, you guessed it. Although the new babies found all three videos of interest, the original babies were significantly less willing to look at the video of the woman with whom they had had a negative experience over a year earlier!

It appears even very young infants can carry a grudge!

It Matters How Happy or Unhappy You Are. Parents can be depressed for many reasons: marital discord, mental or physical illness, financial uncertainty— even too much to do and too little time to do it. Unfortunately, we now know that when depression persists, particularly in the case of the mother, the consequences to a baby's emotional health are serious. For one thing, depressed mothers are simply not lighthearted enough to engage their babies in the kind of synchronized interactions we just described. As Ed Tronick was quick to point out once he discovered the power of the Still Face procedure, if a momentary "still face" in the laboratory can cause a baby to become despondent, just think what happens when such rejection occurs on a daily basis. Human babies crave interaction, and when it's missing for long periods of time, they become depressed too.

In addition, depressed mothers are generally less likely to provide sensitive and timely caregiving. When you can't face the world and want nothing more than to pull the blankets up over your head, it's all too easy to let a baby cry too long, to ignore early signs of distress, and to rebuff bids for attention and affection. Sadly, these moms simply don't have the energy, patience, or joy in living that is required to deal effectively with the demands of the helpless human infant or the mobile and demanding toddler. As a result, the children of depressed mothers feel rebuffed and anxious, feelings that translate into insecure attachments.

WHAT'S IN YOUR BABY'S HANDS

With so much of what determines a secure attachment dependent on how *you* behave, you may be wondering if there's anything left for your child to contribute. The answer is a definite "yes!" What your baby contributes is her individual temperament and its powerful influence on how hard or easy she is to parent.

By temperament, of course, we're referring once again to the four flowers we described in Chapter 1: Baby Sunflower, Baby Orchid, Baby Holly, and Baby Dandelion. Here's how each inborn personality tends to affect the development of attachment:

◆ **Baby Sunflower.** This is the "Easy" baby whose generally sunny disposition makes him slow to get upset and quick to be consoled. His readiness to smile, interest in people, and openness to experiences tend to bring out the best in his caregivers. With these endearing traits, it's not surprising that, more often than not, Baby Sunflower ends up being securely attached.

◆ **Baby Orchid.** This is the "Slow-to-Warm" baby for whom almost any new event evokes caution, if not total withdrawal. Because she is wary of the world at large, Baby Orchid tends to really value the people she knows well, showering them with levels of attention and loyalty that are appealing to some parents but off-putting to others. Parents who are themselves quite adventuresome may find it particularly difficult to understand Baby Orchid's need for reassurance and support. As a consequence, they may end up being inconsistent in responding to her emotional needs, inconsistency that can result in an insecure resistant attachment.

◆ **Baby Holly.** This is the "Difficult" baby whose equilibrium is easily upset and difficult to reestablish. It's hard to know what will set Baby Holly off. In fact, the only thing predictable about Baby Holly is that she's unpredictable. Unfortunately, irritable babies are notoriously difficult to parent and frequently end up in insecure attachment relationships of one type or another. A study by developmental psychologist Dymphna Van den Boom in the Netherlands, however, provides some reassuring news. Just six hours of one-on-one coaching about how best to deal with their specific Baby Holly helped raise the percentage of secure attachments from 28 percent to 68 percent among low-income families with babies diagnosed as "irritable" (or "difficult") at birth. (In other words, organized interventions do help!)

◆ **Baby Dandelion.** This is the "Active" baby whose energy level keeps parents constantly on the go themselves. As we discuss in more detail in Chapter 9, some

Baby Hearts in Action: It Sometimes *Does* Take a Village

Whenever Susan talks to her students about attachment, she always includes the story of two children, one her grandchild, Brandon, and the other a neighbor child born the same week.

Little Brandon was not the cooing, cuddly cherub that first-time parents envision. Brandon's problem was that for the first four and a half months of his life he suffered from colic, that still-mysterious malady that keeps babies so uncomfortable that they scream inconsolably for hours at a stretch (see box on page 10). Fortunately, Brandon had a whole cadre of adults to cope with his need for constant rocking, walking, and soothing. In fact, it took the patience and stamina of five adults (two parents, two grandmothers, and one grandfather) to help little Brandon get through these first draining months without any of the emotional scars that frequently come when a mother is too exhausted, discouraged, and resentful to cope. Their reward? At four and a half months, a happy, gurgling, giggling baby, and at twelve years, an emotionally secure preteen.

The other baby, however, wasn't as lucky. Born to a single teenage mom living with her parents in the house next door, this baby also suffered from colic. But unlike Brandon's situation, this baby's grandparents traveled extensively and were seldom home. That left only two arms to hold him—a sharp contrast to the ten arms available to Brandon. "Night after night," Susan recalls, "we would hear that baby crying, and it would break my heart knowing that poor mom was all by herself." Because the neighbor family moved a few months later, Susan never knew how things turned out. All they could do was hope that somehow the young mother had found the enormous reserves of emotional and physical strength she needed in order to get her baby off to a good start.

"Don't worry, Mom. Everything's under control!" This little boy must have read the research showing that having other people around to help mothers with infant care makes it more likely that mother and baby will be able to develop a secure attachment.

parents end up angry and frustrated by their inability to control Baby Dandelion's behavior. These negative feelings can lead parents to lash out at their children in ways that result in insecure avoidant or even insecure disorganized attachments.

WHAT THE OUTSIDE WORLD CONTRIBUTES: EMOTIONAL AND PHYSICAL SUPPORT

Research by developmental psychologist Dr. Susan Crockenberg of the University of Vermont provides powerful evidence that the more physical and emotional support a mother has in her attempts to deal with a young baby, the more likely the outcome will be a secure attachment. The source might be a spouse, one or more grandparents, friends, or even social service professionals. It's easy to see why. Having someone else available to help take care of the baby enables a mother to get more rest, develop a better perspective on life with baby, and have access to a sounding board for worries and uncertainties.

Another helpful role that outsiders play is in supporting the family unit through tough times. For example, developmental psychologists Rand and Kathy Conger, now at the University of California at Davis, have documented how financial problems all too often result in parental depression and conflict, leading in turn to significant decreases in nurturing behaviors toward children. Balancing this out, however, is good news from the University of North Carolina, where developmental researcher Margaret Burchinal and her colleagues have discovered that families who are part of some kind of "community," whether it is a church group or neighborhood circle, find their parenting far less disrupted by economic hardship. In other words, friends coming to the aid of friends end up indirectly aiding children.

Words of Wisdom and Tricks of the Trade

The basic message of this chapter of *Baby Hearts* is that babies require unfailing love and support to enjoy an emotionally healthy future. Unfortunately, these goodies may be difficult to provide on those days when you are at your wits' end from exhaustion or when you are required to be away from your child for hours or days at a time. Now that we've dealt with the generalities of what promotes a secure attachment, here are some specific tips to help you get through the tough times and increase the probability that your child will grow up feeling loved and secure.

COMMUNICATING LOVE

The vast majority of parents say they love their children. And we believe them. However, not all parents know how to communicate their love to the very individuals most in need of being convinced—their children during the first three years of their lives. And, because babies come into the world understanding no language at all, if there was ever an audience for whom "actions speak louder than words," this is it. So, here are some actions to help get the message across.

- **Play with your baby face to face.** Remember that young babies love direct eye contact. Take lots of time each day to give your baby a healthy dose of the synchronized, face-to-face interaction that researcher Ed Tronick discovered is so important. And make sure you're genuinely engaged. Believe it or not, even very young babies can detect the smallest sign of inattention. Finally, be sure to be a highly animated partner. Use big-scale facial expressions and let your enthusiasm be apparent in your tone of voice. Your baby will love these times together—and, eventually, love you too.

- **Sing to your baby.** Rather than relying on prerecorded lullabies and infant songs, take a tip from Laurel Trainor's study described in the first news flash and sing to your baby yourself. Your neighbors might not appreciate it, but your baby definitely will. By doing so you are sending a message of love and affection. In addition, you are helping your baby become familiar with your voice and associate it with positive messages.

- **Whisper sometimes.** Whispering creates the impression of an intimate connection between two people. Use it to make your child feel special. And whispering is also an effective way to calm children down before nap- or bedtime—or whenever your little angel is in danger of going off the deep end.

- **Cuddle with a good book.** The close physical contact that comes when parent and child cuddle up to read a book works like a balm to soothe a baby's soul.

- **Play together.** Resist the urge to treat playtime as a time to get chores done. In the long run, it's much more useful as an opportunity to make sure that your baby's memories of you are happy ones. The type of play, of course, will change with age, but here's a suggestion from Linda's own childhood that can help make any type of play more fun: Just throw a sheet over a card table to create a special, secret "playroom" big enough for just the two of you. What a great place for a picnic on a rainy day!

- **Take advantage of the power of touch.** A stream of amazing research results from the Touch Institute at the University of Florida has added a powerful new parenting tool that is literally at every parent's fingertips. The use of physical massage has been found to help premies develop faster, sick babies get well quicker, stressed babies calm down, and even some colicky babies stop crying. All of these changes increase the chances that the parent-child relationship will flourish. (See the next box.)

The Power of Touch

Thanks to years of research by developmental psychologist Tiffa[ny] [and col]leagues at the University of Florida, we now have lots of proof th[at touch,] and massage in particular, is a powerful tool, literally at every [age.] Not only is it a lovely way to be together, but it also strengthens [a] baby's immune system, stimulates growth hormones, and releases opiates that suffuse a child with good feelings. Fortunately, there are many books and classes available on the subject, but in the meantime, here's some advice for how to go about it.

- Make sure the room is warm enough for your baby to be comfortable stripped to her diaper or naked.
- Sit on the floor with your back leaning against a chair or couch and your legs stretched out in front of you (supported by a pillow if necessary).
- Drape a thick, soft towel over your legs. Place your baby on her back on your legs with her head toward your knees.
- Apply some kind of nonpetroleum-based oil or lotion to your hands and rub them together until they feel warm.
- Starting with both hands on your baby's chest, slowly and gently rub outward toward her arms and then downward toward her toes. Repeat in rhythmic manner as often as you want, while maintaining eye contact, smiling, and singing or talking softly.
- Pay separate attention to arms, hands, legs, and feet. A gentle "milking" motion with one hand while the other hand provides support is often pleasing.
- Turn the baby onto her tummy and start again.

By the way, a clever variation with older children is to make massage part of a game by gently rolling a soft rubber ball across their bodies from bottom to top and then top to bottom.

BUILDING TRUST

Love and trust aren't the same thing. It's not unusual to love someone you can't count on and to count on someone you don't love. But love and trust need to be

...ing hand in hand for babies to develop a secure attachment relationship. ...ere are some tips for building trust.

◆ **Be sensitive.** Remember, research clearly shows that responding quickly to your baby's cries and bids for attention is a critical ingredient in establishing a trusting relationship. Don't worry that picking up your baby whenever she cries will "spoil" her and teach her to cry more to get your attention. Crying is a baby's way of communicating that she is hungry, wet, tired, or hurting. But babies also cry because they need to be close to you—what child development professionals call contact comfort. Remember, babies whose needs are met in a timely fashion during their first few months actually cry less frequently as they grow older than do those whose parents adopt a less responsive approach. If you are concerned about teaching your baby independence, rest assured that responding to her cries also leads to more self-confidence and self-sufficiency.

◆ **Learn from your baby what works.** Watch for subtle clues to what is most effective with your *particular* baby. Write your ideas down and test them out. If Grandma is more effective in calming your baby down, analyze why that might be. Is she humming? Is she walking at a different rate? Is she holding him more or less firmly than you do? Also, don't follow advice blindly just because it's "supposed" to work. For example, while it's true that some babies respond well to being swaddled tightly, all this does is enrage others. And whatever you do, try as hard as you can to communicate genuine love and concern while you do it.

◆ **Encourage your baby to sign.** Remember little Zack from the very first news flash? It was his ability to communicate with a sign for "afraid" that enabled his mother to understand that he wanted her to take away the scary doll. Had he *not* known how to sign, she would have misinterpreted his crying and put the doll right in the crib with him. This is just one example of the way the use of signs can help parents "read" their babies well and, therefore, respond appropriately.

◆ **Make very few promises and keep the ones you do.** "I promise I'll be there in just a minute." "Just one more phone call and then we can read." "We'll go to the park when I'm done." Sound familiar? Promises like these are fine—as long as you keep them. Children may not be good at math, but they do notice when broken promises start adding up. Remember, trust is a valuable commodity that is hard to recapture once it's gone.

◆ **Work hard at being a secure home base.** Your child should view you as a safe

refuge no matter what he does or what he is worried about. This doesn't m
close your eyes to unacceptable behavior, but it does mean that your c......
should never cause your child to question your love or your availability. It also
means trying hard not to be "too busy" when you get a request for a cuddle.

◆ **Establish routines.** The word "trust" also implies "predictability," and "predictability" yields "security." That's why so many child-rearing books recommend
building as much predictability as possible into your child's daily life. Here are
some tips for doing so.

  ◆ **Establish bedtime routines.** Establishing a set of steps that lead to lights
  out helps children make the transition from play to sleep in a gradual way.
  Including some enjoyable activities in the routine (cuddling with a book)
  gives her something to look forward to.

  ◆ **Use songs as signals.** Incorporate songs into your daily routines. That way,
  simply hearing the first bars of "Are You Sleeping" or "Rubber Ducky, You're
  the One" can become signals for what's to happen next (Answers? Bedtime
  and bathtime.)

  ◆ **Create family traditions.** Establish Friday nights as movie and popcorn
  nights or Saturday nights as family game nights. Doing so creates a feeling
  of belonging for everyone in the family. And don't forget that your family
  videos make some of the most entertaining movies of all, even for toddlers.

IF YOU NEED TO LEAVE YOUR CHILD

No parent can be with her child all the time. No matter how much we love our
little ones, we often find it necessary to be absent, either for hours at a time
while at work or days at a time while traveling on business. And then there's the
all-important "respite" time when Mom and Dad need to enjoy some well-
earned hours by themselves while a babysitter takes over. Here are some point-
ers for dealing with these inevitable absences in ways that can help your baby
maintain his sense of security.

◆ **Remember, you are still number one.** First of all, don't worry that any of your
child's caregivers will take your place in his heart. Research consistently shows
that bonds with parents remain a child's most important relationships, even in the
face of substantial amounts of time spent in alternative care.

Baby Hearts in Action: "Give Me Your Best Shot, Mom!"

The advice to explain to your child *why* you need to be away from her is basically sound. Not only does it provide a sense of when you'll be back, but knowing that her discomfort is for a worthy cause can help a child cope, according to Dr. Lieberman. However, don't count on the information automatically changing "Don't go, Mommy!" into "Go with my blessings, Mom." Susan's daughter, Lisa, was taught this lesson by her two-and-a-half-year-old son, Brandon, one day when it was time for Lisa to depart for her new job. Attempting first to appeal to Brandon's materialistic side, Lisa explained, "Mommy needs to work so that Daddy and I can buy you nice things," to which Brandon replied with a plaintive "I don't *want* any nice things, Mommy!" Taken aback, Lisa next tried to appeal to his sense of kindness and empathy: "Mommy needs to work so she can help people have healthy teeth." Brandon's reply? Scarcely missing a beat and holding even tighter to her leg, he wailed, "I don't *want* people to have healthy teeth. I want them to have *bad* teeth!" Stifling her urge to laugh, Lisa gave up trying to placate him, hugged him one more time, and left.

◆ **Communicate confidence, not anxiety.** Whether you must go back to work for financial reasons or choose to pursue your career, it's important to know that your baby can "read" your emotions in your tone of voice and facial expressions. Feeling guilty about your employment situation doesn't help you or your baby. It only communicates your anxiety, thereby making your baby anxious too. Instead, focus on feeling at ease with yourself and relaxed about the time you *do* spend together.

◆ **Provide reasons.** Remember Dr. Lieberman's advice (see page 38) that even very young children will cope better with distress if they know it's for a good cause. Start early talking about the reasons you need to be away. Even though your baby may not understand all your words at first, you will be establishing an important habit and her comprehension will gradually increase.

◆ **Say when you'll be back.** Always tell your baby (even if you think she is too young to understand) when you are leaving and when you will be back. Try to link your return to something she'll recognize, like "after circle time." This is a good habit to get in to even before she understands the words. By saying these things over and over, you provide your baby with "food for thought" that increases the likelihood that she will try hard to understand even earlier than she might otherwise, and then be comforted when she does. And never *ever* sneak away while she's not looking.

◆ **Join the worlds together.** Look for ways to join your baby's two worlds together. Whenever you can, spend extra time in her child care classroom, perhaps joining the fun at circle time once in a while. Videotape your child in her classroom and watch the tape together at home. Not only do such efforts increase the time you spend with your child; they also give "extra bang for the buck" by helping your child experience these two parts of her life as less separate. The more you can help your child integrate the two experiences, the more likely it is your child will remember and actually *feel* your presence even when you're not there.

◆ **Provide reminders from home.** When you leave your baby or toddler in care outside the home, preserve his sense of security by providing familiar things, such as a favorite stuffed toy, special blanket, books, or a familiar snack. Toddlers can even get a feeling of security from photos of you and other family members taped to their cubby or available in a small album they can carry with them. Such photos also provide babies and toddlers a way to let their caregivers know what they are feeling. A sad face combined with a finger pointing toward a photo of Mommy is a request for reassurance every caregiver will understand.

◆ **Use your voice as a source of comfort.** New research from the Penn State Children's Hospital is showing that sick children cry less when they hear soft music *plus* their mothers' voices than when they hear soft music on its own. With this in mind, make audio recordings of some of your singing sessions to be played in your absence, or tape yourself reading a favorite story. Maybe the babysitter can even turn the pages while your voice provides the text. And don't forget that videotapes of you and your baby can be powerful reminders of your loving presence.

KEEPING YOURSELF UNDER CONTROL

Even the most even-tempered mom with the most even-tempered baby sometimes gets pushed close to her emotional edge. Believe us, it happens to everybody. Here are some tips for dealing with those times you're feeling close to the edge.

◆ **Post a reminder.** Hang a picture or embroidery in a prominent place in your baby's room that includes a motto such as: "What I Do Today Makes a Difference for Tomorrow" or "This Too Shall Pass."

◆ **Understand your baby.** It can help you forgive your baby if you understand *why* he's acting the way he is. Recognizing that you are parenting a Baby Holly or a Baby Dandelion, for example, can provide clues to handling situations wisely. It's absolutely true that the more you know about how children develop, the better off you'll be.

◆ **Stay healthy.** Tempers rise when we are exhausted, and we are more likely to feel exhausted when we don't sleep enough, eat right, exercise, or enjoy time for ourselves. For exercise, try putting your baby in a stroller and taking a brisk walk once a day. For fatigue, take turns with your spouse sleeping late on weekend mornings, and put rest as a higher priority than chores when your baby is asleep.

> When you reach the end of your rope, tie a knot in it and hang on.
>
> —Mary Engelbreit, artist

◆ **Develop a support network.** Find neighbors, friends, or relatives you can call on when times get tough. Perhaps you can swap babysitting with someone.

◆ **If all else fails, seek professional help.** When you've tried everything and still feel overwhelmed, a good place to go for advice is to your trusted pediatrician. If necessary, he or she can refer you to a professional individual or organization equipped to help you deal with your problem.

LAST BUT NOT LEAST, KNOW THYSELF

More and more research is showing that our own childhood experiences and the values, assumptions, and emotions they leave as footprints across our lives exert a powerful influence over how we parent our own children. Daniel Siegel, M.D., and Mary Hartzell, M.Ed., make this point powerfully and persuasively in their book *Parenting from the Inside Out*. It makes sense when you think about it. The reason attachment bonds are so important is because they predispose children to go through life either trusting or not trusting others and either thinking well or thinking ill of themselves. Well, there's no automatic "reset" button to wipe all this away when we have children of our own to raise. An individual's parenting style tends to reflect how he or she views life, and this viewpoint is inevitably shaped by positive and negative experiences of the far distant past.

Unfortunately, few prospective parents realize how pervasive these influences are; rather they simply assume that their approach to parenting makes "perfect sense." That's why Siegel and Hartzell's book is so important. They firmly believe—and we absolutely agree—that time spent closely examining one's child-rearing beliefs and expectations, with professional help if necessary, is time well spent.

It's also very important to make sure you have the emotional energy to raise your baby in a way that establishes a secure attachment. This means taking concrete steps to deal with depression, marital discord, and/or any physical illnesses that might cause you to be distracted from that most important of all tasks: being truly "present" with your baby. It also means looking for help from every available source. One thing for sure, your decision to read *Baby Hearts* is a step in the right direction.

3

I'm Feeling Sad:
Expressing Emotions Effectively

N E W S   F L A S H !

Babies Use Hands to "Say" What's on Their Minds

Davis, California. The Center for Child and Family Studies (CCFS) at the University of California, Davis, may look like an ordinary child care facility, but looks can be deceiving. Yes, it has an infant/toddler classroom with the usual contents—miniature chairs and tables, fish tank, changing table, and lots of toys and books. But scratch the surface and you'll find some major differences. Here's why. Because of its proximity to child development research labs on the UC Davis campus, the center's staff is able to take advantage of cutting-edge research years before the ideas reach other centers.

The work of Drs. Linda Acredolo and Susan Goodwyn in the Psychology Department is a case in point. Back in 1982 the two researchers discovered that babies will eagerly learn to use simple gestures to communicate with the adults around them well before they are able to say words. What's more, by 1990 their research, funded by the National Institutes of Health, was showing many benefits to using such signs—including faster verbal development, decreased frustration, and higher self-esteem among others.

The importance of these results for child care professionals was not lost on the CCFS Infant/Toddler director, Kathleen Grey, and soon the two professors were helping Grey and other staff members at the center make signing an integral part of daily life in the infant/toddler classroom. The usual advantages were quickly evident. Despite having no words, the children could tell caregivers they were hungry, thirsty, needed their diaper changed, or wanted to read a book or see the fish. But what was even more exciting was the way the children, despite their very young ages, were able to use signs to talk about what they and their classmates were feeling. Here are some examples.

◆ Sixteen-month-old Marcus is lying on the changing table, one of the few places where the children are calm enough to listen to what's going on around them. Suddenly Marcus looks worried and makes the signs for "noise" and "sad." His caregiver, stopping a moment to listen, replies, "Why, you're right, Marcus. Ben is crying. He must be sad." A lovely example of concern about the emotional state of his friend.

◆ Like little Marcus above, fifteen-month-old Ellie suddenly stops in her tracks and makes the signs for "noise" and "sad." "Yes, Billy is crying. He's feeling sad," her caregiver responds. However, at this point Ellie goes one step further and suggests a solution. Much to her caregiver's amusement, Ellie adds two more signs: "bottle" plus "nap."

◆ Sixteen-month-old Maria is playing outside with the other children when she suddenly begins to cry. Her caregiver quickly comes over and comments, "Oh, Maria, you're crying. I guess you're feeling sad," whereupon Maria shakes her head emphatically and signs "angry!" "I stand corrected" is the caregiver's flabbergasted reply. And some folks think children this young don't know their own minds!

To even the most novice observer, it's clear that the use of signing in the classroom is providing these babies with a jump start on learning to communicate about emotions. The children's use of signs also is increasing the likelihood that the caregivers will talk about emotions with them and meet their needs in a timely fashion—two critical ingredients in maintaining a child's sense of trust and security.

Emotional Knowledge: What's at Stake?

Share even one day with a very young baby and you'll be hard-pressed to believe that babies have any trouble expressing their emotions. And in one sense it's very true that they don't. From the day they are born, babies wear their hearts on their sleeves, automatically crying when they are upset and smiling when they are happy. But these innate reactions to events are only a small part of what emotional communication is all about. To be effective members of the social world around them, children need to do more than just react. They also need to be able to *recognize* what they are feeling, keep their emotions from spiraling out of control, and communicate their feelings in socially acceptable ways.

Even these goals, however, don't tell the whole story. In order to get along well with other people, young children also need to be able to "read" the emotional messages being communicated by other people and learn to predict what those emotions might be in the future. "What does that look on Mommy's face mean?" "If I throw my food, will it make Daddy mad?" "Why do Mommy and Daddy look scared?" Once they are able to interpret these messages, they then need to learn how to react appropriately, how to handle the emotional messages others are sending. They may learn, for example, to stay clear when Daddy is mad, give Mommy a hug when she is sad, or get excited when their playmates are happy.

And what if children don't develop these different facets of what psychologist Daniel Goleman calls emotional intelligence? The research data are clear. Such children are more likely than their peers:

◆ To have problems getting along with other children
◆ To do more poorly in school
◆ To be less empathic
◆ To make home life more difficult for everyone
◆ To suffer from depression
◆ To be prone to anger, defiance, and aggression
◆ To deal less appropriately with the emotions of their *own* children down the line

Explaining how you can help your child avoid these pitfalls is what this chapter of *Baby Hearts* is all about.

What Babies Are Feeling

One fundamental question researchers have tried to answer is what emotions children of different ages actually are capable of feeling, that is, the point at which individual emotions appear. For example, can a two-month-old baby feel "jealous" or a two-year-old toddler feel "prejudiced?" Unless parents are aware of the steps

There's More to Emotions Than Meets the Eye

When students in our classes first hear us mention the development of emotional understanding, they assume we will simply list the ages at which children come to understand different facial expressions—smiling means "happy," crying means "sad," and so on. They quickly learn, however, that there's a lot more to it than that. Here are eight important facts about emotions that adults take for granted but that children must learn—and, with supportive parenting, tend to learn much more quickly.

1. Human emotions are vast in number and subtle in their differences. Consider these different feeling states: cranky, cowardly, curious, confident, coy, cagey, confused. And these are just ones that start with "c."
2. Emotions, even strong ones, tend to fade over time.
3. People often experience two or more emotions at once, sometimes even conflicting ones (for example, a "bittersweet" experience).
4. People can pretend to feel one way when they really are feeling another.
5. People may not actually be aware of their own feelings.
6. Certain emotions are not appropriate in certain situations (being gleeful at a deathbed or openly sad at a wedding).
7. Emotions can be powerfully influenced by being in a crowd.
8. Talking about emotions requires knowing your culture's peculiar metaphors for feelings, such as these English terms for "happy": tickled pink, pleased as punch, thrilled to death, happy as a clam, contented as a cat, on cloud nine.

With all this to learn, it's enough to make a child "as nervous as a cat on a hot tin roof."

within the emotional timeline, they can end up making unfortunate mistakes. Here's what happens all too often to inexperienced parents. In their frustration over frequent crying, fussing, or general troublemaking, parents sometimes attribute attitudes and motivations to their babies that are totally beyond the child's developmental level. "She's just trying to manipulate us" is one form this takes, or "He's just doing that to make us mad." The truth is that babies aren't capable of such Machiavellian feelings.

Uncovering the details of what forms of emotions babies *are* capable of feeling during the early years was in and of itself an impressive research accomplishment. The first major discovery was that there are two groups of early emotions, one group now commonly referred to as primary emotions and a second group referred to as secondary emotions. The first category, the primary emotions, includes all the emotions that are preprogrammed to appear at birth or soon thereafter and that are understood in similar ways no matter where a baby is born, be it in Borneo, Bolivia, or Boston. The second category, the secondary emotions, includes emotions that appear much later (eighteen to twenty-four months) and that are highly influenced by the cultural milieu within which the child develops. Let's take them one at a time.

OUT OF THE STARTING GATE: THE PRIMARY EMOTIONS

We are, pardon the term, "primarily" indebted to a very clever researcher at the University of Delaware for much of what we know about the timeline for the primary emotions—those that babies feel early in their lives. In the early 1980s, psychologist Carroll Izard devised a set of events for babies to experience while video cameras recorded their reactions. The events included things like the appearance of a normal human face, the appearance of a mask of a human face with its facial features all mixed up, an encounter with an ice cube, and the introduction of sweet- or bitter-tasting liquids. (He even filmed babies as they received routine vaccinations in order to study reactions to pain—not a popular assignment among his undergraduate research assistants.) Izard then had adults who hadn't seen the events judge what emotions the children's facial expressions revealed they were feeling. The consensus among the judges was remarkable.

From Day 1. Based on Izard's efforts, we now know that four emotions are present at birth:

1. Distress (to discomfort from any source)
2. Contentment (when all's well with the world)
3. Interest (to novel, nonjarring events)
4. Disgust (to unpleasant tastes)

Between Two and a Half and Seven Months. As infants become a bit more capable of analyzing what's going on around them and making comparisons, the second set of primary emotions begins to emerge. These include...

5. Joy (a reaction more intense than simple contentment)
6. Sadness (requiring a perception of a loss or disappointment)
7. Anger/Frustration (a feeling of being thwarted in some way)
8. Fear (requiring an analysis of an object or event as threatening)
9. Surprise (resulting from having one's expectations violated)

What happens past seven months is a gradual broadening and refining of the situations that trigger these primary emotions. For example, swaddling a four-month-old too tightly is likely to bring on anger; by eighteen months, however, the same child might erupt into anger over swaddling, but this time the result of frustration when his *own* attempts at swaddling—for example, of the family cat—are thwarted.

The sad face is marked by a down-turned mouth and eyebrows slightly raised near the nose. Although babies experience distress from birth, the experience of feeling sad takes longer to develop because it requires a sense of having lost something that was valued.

Luke's wide eyes, raised eyebrows, and open mouth are classic signs of surprise, one of the primary (basic) emotions that infants begin to experience around two months of age.

THE NEXT BIG STEP: THE SECONDARY EMOTIONS

You'll know your baby is making emotional progress when the emotions in the second category begin to appear sometime between eighteen and twenty-four months. These emotions are considerably more "sophisticated" than the earlier ones in that they require children to view themselves in relation to other people. Because other people are involved in some way, these emotions are sometimes called the social emotions or the self-conscious emotions. Here's the list along with examples of the thinking that goes on beneath the surface. Notice the role that other people play in each one.

10. Pride: "Look, Mommy! It was hard, but I did it!"
11. Eagerness to Please: "Daddy will be glad I did this!"
12. Embarrassment: "Oh, dear. I wet my pants. Everyone can see."

When I was a child, love to me was what the sea is to a fish—something you swim in while you are going about the important affairs of life.

—P. L. Travers, author of *Mary Poppins*

13. Guilt: "I shouldn't have done that. Mommy will be mad."
14. Shame: "I shouldn't have done that. I'm a bad girl!"

But why, you may be wondering, does it take eighteen to twenty-four months for children to pay attention in these ways to other people? After all, people have been a big part of their lives from the very beginning. There are two reasons.

Development of a sense of self. The first reason has more to do with a fundamental change in how children view *themselves* than in how they view others. We're talking here about the development of a sense of self. This process has always fascinated researchers, most notably Daniel Stern, whose book *The Interpersonal World of the Infant* provides an insightful analysis, and Bob Emde and his colleagues at the University of Colorado, whose data have contributed greatly to our growing understanding of this important milestone in development. Here are the basics of what these researchers suggest.

Although the roots of the development of the sense of self go back to birth and face-to-face interactions with Mom, the process really gets going around the first birthday when children, with the help of their parents, start noticing their own emotions. They do so, these researchers suggest, particularly in the case of frequently repeated, emotion-rich routines—such as tickling games, bedtime cuddling, mealtime routines, bathtub play, and the like. As children register in their fledgling memories more and more of these high-profile events, they start to string them together, gradually yielding a feeling of "continuity" of experience across time that eventually translates into a sense of self.

This process takes most of the second year, so it's not until sometime between eighteen and twenty-four months that children have a firm sense of themselves as entities separate from others, as independent agents in interactions with the people around them. This is an extremely important milestone, one that affects a great many facets of their lives in addition to making possible the secondary emotions. With the advent of a sense of self, children also can begin to organize a self-concept, record and retrieve memories of past events, and make plans for the future. (We'll have much more to say about this milestone in Chapter 6 in our discussions of self-esteem and self-confidence.)

Development of a sense of others. The second reason these more complex emotions take so long to develop is because they require children to understand, at least at a rudimentary level, that other people have thoughts and emotions of their own—that they can observe and judge a child and that those judgments affect how they react to the child's behavior. As Oxford researcher Paul Harris points out, we frequently see evidence of this new skill in the simple games of pretend that two- and three-year-olds enjoy—for example, games where children pretend to be feeling and thinking what a mommy or daddy thinks or feels.

This dawning awareness of the judgments made by others gains strength throughout the third year, so that by age three, most children have at least a vague sense of standards and rules by which they can evaluate *themselves.* In other words, because children now have available to them at least a few ideas of what's good to do and not good to do, it's no longer always necessary for another person to be physically present for a child to experience pride, shame, or guilt. Children now know on their own whether they've done something that warrants pride, shame, or guilt—at least when it comes to fairly simple things. However, it can take well into the elementary school years for children to internalize complex standards and rules and for them to understand abstract generalities like honesty and gratitude.

What Babies Know About Their Feelings

You now know a lot more about what your baby is feeling at a given age than your baby does. Not only are very young babies limited in what emotions they can experience, they are also severely limited in their ability to actually recognize those that they are experiencing. In fact, it's really not until language comes along between twelve and twenty-four months that children begin to sort out one emotion from another. Just as having available the words "olive," "chartreuse," "lime,"

Birth of the Green-Eyed Monster

Along with the birth of Child #2 comes the worry that Big Brother or Sister will resent all the attention paid to the new baby. But what about the baby? Won't there come a point when the tables are turned and the baby begins to resent having to share Mommy with the older child? In other words, when does the traditional green-eyed monster called jealousy appear on the scene?

One answer comes from a clever study by developmental researchers Sybil Hart, Tiffany Field, Claudia Del Valle, and March Letourneau that tested twelve-month-old babies under two conditions. In one, moms were asked to ignore their children while looking through a picture book. In the other, still ignoring their babies, moms were given a life-size baby doll to cuddle. If simply being ignored is what annoys babies this age, then both situations should be equally upsetting. But that's not what happened. Instead, these year-old children were *significantly* more distressed about the doll than the book, suggesting that they specifically resented seeing another "baby" get the cozy comfort of Mommy's lap. Looks like sibling rivalry is a two-way street from pretty early on.

and "forest" helps us make better sense of the color green, having labels like "mad," "sad," "angry," and "afraid" helps toddlers recognize how what they are feeling one minute differs from what they are feeling the next. Here are some milestones to watch for as recognition begins to dawn.

◆ The most frequently understood feeling words at eighteen months are "sleepy," "tired," "hungry," "good," "happy," "sad," and "need."

◆ Even though eighteen-month-olds can understand these feeling words, they aren't yet capable of producing very many themselves. For example, one study found that only 50 percent of eighteen-month-olds used the word "good" and only 7 percent used the word "sad." Children who are encouraged to use signs, however, begin labeling emotions months earlier.

◆ Most two-year-olds understand the labels for emotions commonly conveyed in facial expressions, including "happiness," "surprise," "anger," "fear," "sadness," and "disgust."

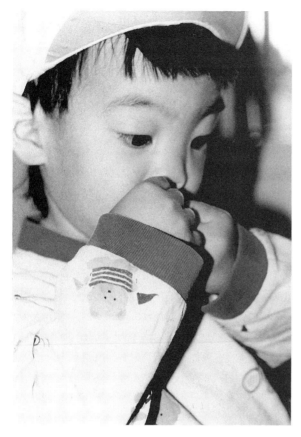

Children who are encouraged to use signs can begin "talking" about emotions at remarkably early ages. Here a little boy uses his personalized version of a sign for sad (fists down a little from his eyes).

◆ However, even for two-year-olds, the ability to comprehend feeling words outstrips the ability to use them in conversation. One exception is the extremely popular pair of expressions "I want!" and "No want!" These are definitely within the typical two-year-old's vocabulary.

◆ In contrast to the difficulty children have producing feeling words, children who are encouraged to use signs begin labeling internal feeling states (with signs) at much younger ages, often as early as fourteen to fifteen months. Popular sign examples are "sleepy," "hungry," "thirsty," "scared," "sad," and "I need." Little Maria described in the opening news flash certainly illustrates this point.

◆ Between two and a half and three years, improvements in both emotional awareness and memory enable children to begin remembering their past feelings and predicting future feelings. If you don't believe it, ask any three-year-old what she remembers about her last vaccination and how she feels about future ones.

What Babies Know About Others' Feelings

IN THE BEGINNING . . .

Human infants come into the world preequipped to get along with other people. They love looking at human faces, listening to human voices, being cuddled by human arms, and smelling the smells of the most important people in their lives. They don't, however, start off with the ability to understand the *emotional* signals others are sending through their voices, facial expressions, or posture. But they are certainly quick learners. By the time they are four months old (some researchers think sooner), babies are able to detect differences between adults who are interacting with them in positive ways from those who are interacting with them in negative ways—and are able to react appropriately.

How do we know? Researchers have used a variety of techniques to reveal how insightful even very young babies are about emotions. Here's one we think is especially clever. In a recent study, developmental researchers Diane Montague and Arlene Walker-Andrews from Rutgers University took advantage of the old, classic peekaboo game to see how savvy four-month-olds are about emotions displayed by other people. The researchers simply played peekaboo three times in a row in the normal way, each time ending with a gleeful "Peekaboo!" when the adult revealed her face. But then, on the fourth trial, two-thirds of the infants heard "Peekaboo" said in a very different way. One group heard it said with a sad tone of voice and sad facial expression, and a second group heard it said with an angry tone of voice and angry facial expression. The rest still heard it said in the original, gleeful way. The results were clear. Both of the first two groups stared longer at the adult on the fourth trial than they had during the typical trials, indicating they had noticed the change. In addition, those who heard the sad version turned their heads away and avoided any more than glances at the adult on subsequent trials—a reaction typical of much older infants and children to messages that convey sadness. In contrast, the four-month-olds became serious and especially vigilant in reaction to the angry adult, again a response typical of much older children and adults. In other words, these four-month-olds were already reacting to the emotional messages of other people in the same ways adults tend to do.

In fact, infants this young don't even need to *see* the other person to make a judgment about her emotions. Researcher Anne Fernald from Stanford University had four- to five-month-old American infants simply listen to (not look at) strangers speaking German and Italian. Some of the messages were traditional expressions of approval ("What a nice baby you are! You're so sweet"), while others were angry messages typical of adults who are trying to stop children from doing something ("No! Stop it! You mustn't touch that!"). How did these children who had never heard German or Italian before behave? They smiled at the pleasant messages and became very serious and vigilant in reaction to the negative ones, thereby indicating awareness of the emotional meaning carried in tone of voice alone, independent of information carried in facial expressions or the words themselves.

These findings don't surprise scientists interested in the development of attachment relationships. As we discussed in Chapter 2, infants thrive on synchronized, face-to-face interactions with the important adults in their lives and are remarkably sensitive to any negative emotions conveyed in these interactions. Sadly, this leaves infants of chronically depressed or emotionally hostile mothers very vulnerable to emotional problems themselves.

MOM AND DAD AS EMOTIONAL TEACHERS

Have you ever noticed what happens when a stranger approaches a toddler playing at a distance from his mother? If the child is any older than about ten months, chances are good that he will glance at his mom's face to see how *she* is reacting to the intruder. If she indicates she's pleased at the arrival, the child is likely to be at least somewhat reassured. If Mom indicates she's anxious, upset, or angry about the intruder, however, then the child is likely to become wary and upset himself. In other words, starting around ten months and continuing from there on, children depend on emotional messages from people they trust to teach them how *they* should feel about unexpected objects, people, and events. Researchers call this tendency to check with Mom and Dad social referencing, and there's overwhelming evidence that it's a powerful influence on the developing child's attitudes, fears, and expectations.

Mom and Dad aren't the only teachers, however. By twelve months, babies have learned to use the emotions of complete strangers in the same way. If a stranger stares in horror at a toy, most toddlers are likely to steer clear of it. If the

Any child can tell you that the sole purpose of a middle name is so he can tell when he's really in trouble.

—Dennis Fakes, humorist

stranger looks happy about the same toy, most toddlers will pick it up enthusiastically. Eventually, of course, peers become as important (and in the teenage years, even *more* important) than adults as guides to what's neat, not so neat, and downright revolting. If you don't believe us, try getting one sibling to eat brussels sprouts after his brother or sister has expressed unadulterated disgust at the idea. (We will have lots more to say about social referencing in future chapters.)

INTERPRETING EMOTIONS AS A SOCIAL SKILL

Speaking of peers, the more important they become in a child's daily life, the more critical it is that he develop a talent for *interpreting, understanding,* and *predicting* other people's emotions. Being able, for example, to tell when a playmate's feelings have been hurt, when she's sending signals that help is needed, or when her good humor about being teased has gone around the corner to irritation will go a long way toward making a child popular with his peers. And, unfortunately, *not* being able to read these cues is likely to lead to rejection. For example, studies of children who are routinely rejected by their peers show that a contributing factor is often the children's tendency to see hostility where there is none and to overlook bids for sympathy and cooperation. Clearly, anything parents can do to help their children meet the challenge of understanding the emotional world around them is well worth the effort.

The Hardest Lesson of All: Learning to Control Their Emotions

One additional important finding from the studies of rejected children is that the inability to control their own emotions puts children at an enormous disadvantage. Starting as early as the toddler years, children who are impulsive, defiant, or generally too emotionally intense are at greater risk of being rejected by both other children and adults. In other words, it's really important that children take big steps early in life toward the skill of emotional self-regulation that we first talked about in Chapter 1.

WHAT IS EMOTIONAL SELF-REGULATION?

As we explained in Chapter 1, babies come into the world with very little ability to keep themselves on an even keel. They are like rowboats in rough seas, tossed this way and that by physiological waves over which they have little control. Or to use the same analogy we introduced earlier, they are like liquid gelatin before it hardens and can stand up on its own. They need the support of the gelatin mold, represented by their parents, to help them regulate their emotions, particularly distress. Parents do this by responding quickly with physical comfort (warmth, rocking, swaddling), soothing sounds (lullabies, rhythmic words), and distractions (nursing, pacifiers, interesting toys).

> In automobile terms, the child supplies the power but the parents have to do the steering.
>
> —Dr. Benjamin Spock,
> parenting expert

STEPS ALONG THE WAY

But even though advances toward these emotional regulation goals begin as early as two to three months, there's still an awfully long way to go. The steps along the road toward emotional self-regulation have been described particularly well by researcher Ross Thompson from the University of California at Davis. He first identifies five ways adults manage their emotions and then reviews the fledgling efforts children of different ages make toward achieving these same goals. Underlying all these developmental advances, of course, are changes in the child's triple-decker brain described in Chapter 1, and especially the gradual development of an effective cerebral cortex—the topmost layer that enables humans to *think* about what they are feeling.

Baby Hearts in Action:
Gentle Is as Gentle Does

Eighteen-month-old Emily was an enthusiastic hugger. Unfortunately, she was also bigger and stronger than any other toddler in her class at the UC Davis Center for Child and Family Studies. All too often what would start out as a well-meaning hug would turn into a viselike grip, resulting in predictable and strident protests from her victims. Fortunately, the center had incorporated signing into its curriculum, thereby providing a solution. Every time caregivers spied Emily speeding toward another child, they would remind her, "Now remember, be *gentle*," using both the word and a sign for gentle—a soft stroking of the back of one hand with the other. And it helped. But the teachers had no idea how much it had helped until one day they saw Emily crawling as fast as she could toward her favorite target. About halfway there, as she put her left hand out in front of her on the floor, she suddenly stopped, stared at her hand for a moment, and then sat back up on her behind and made the sign for "gentle." She then proceeded on to the other girl who, this time, received a tender embrace instead of an overpowering bear hug. What the teachers had witnessed was a wonderful example of emotional *self*-regulation at a remarkably young age.

Fortunately, children don't stay totally dependent on their parents forever. With parental love and support, good modeling of appropriate emotional behavior, and actual *tips* for controlling themselves, children can eventually learn how to . . .

- Calm themselves when they are upset
- Unwind themselves when they are too wound up
- Resist the temptation to break rules
- Learn which emotions are appropriate and which are not appropriate in specific situations
- Trade immediate fun for the sake of long-term goals

To understand in more detail the steps along the way to skillful control of emotions, imagine you have been asked to speak to your city council about the need for safer playground equipment in your neighborhood park. The evening has arrived and you are so nervous that you're afraid you won't be able to utter a single coherent word. You know you need to calm yourself down. Here are five strategies you use, along with their childhood versions.

1. You divert your attention to safer things. As you drive to city hall, you think about your upcoming vacation instead of dwelling on your fears about the interview. In addition, when you get to the auditorium, you avoid looking at the video cameras used to record the meetings for the local cable channel.

THE KID VERSIONS. Diverting attention to safer things is the easiest and ear-

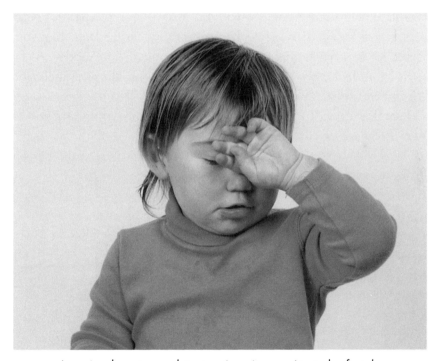

Learning how to regulate emotions is a major task of early childhood. One of the earliest strategies toddlers learn to use when they are upset is simply to turn away and/or cover their eyes. "Out of sight is out of mind" clearly rings true for them.

liest of the self-regulation strategies. By two to three months, babies are able to turn their gaze away from disturbing things and suck vigorously on a pacifier to calm themselves down. By age two or three years, they also have learned to cover their eyes or ears and physically to leave situations that are too upsetting. By age four or five, once imagination is an integral part of their mental lives, children under stress spontaneously let their minds wander to other things—either real or fantasy. And even later, by age eight to ten, they can purposefully divert their thinking to pleasant thoughts just as you did.

2. You seek help from others. Before you leave home, you rehearse your speech in front of your spouse and receive both advice and reassurance. Best of all, he agrees to go with you.

THE KID VERSIONS. The help-seeking strategy comes naturally to children from age seven months on as they come to trust more and more in the love and protection of their parents. That's essentially what the originators of attachment theory, John Bowlby and Mary Ainsworth, had in mind when they coined the term "secure home base" to describe how children view their parents. When your child hides behind your leg and peaks out at Grandma, she's really just trying to deal with her fear from a safe place. As children get older, the list of trustworthy sources of comfort grows beyond just you to include other adults and good friends.

3. You reinterpret the situation. Instead of dwelling on the intimidating faces of the council members, the dozens of people in the audience, or the thousands of viewers out in TVland, you pretend that you're simply expressing your views to a friend over coffee.

THE KID VERSIONS. Using the reinterpretation strategy requires mental gymnastics that are beyond the ability of most children until they are three or four. At that point, however, you might see a child change the outcome of a sad story ("Bambi's Mommy is just sleeping!") or laugh after falling down to convince himself he isn't really hurt. Parents use this strategy from the very beginning to try to influence their children's emotions. They exaggerate their happiness when a stranger approaches to try to make their child less afraid, or they say such things as "Hop up. You're fine" when their child falls down. As Dr. Thompson points out, however, parents need to be careful not to do this so frequently that their children either come to distrust them or become confused about what they really are feeling inside.

4. You express your emotions in an acceptable way. Instead of trying to hide how nervous you are, you begin your comments by admitting how nervous you are, using language to dissipate some of your anxiety. You also take three deep breaths just before the red light comes on and filming begins.

THE KID VERSIONS. The frequently heard parental admonition "Honey, use your words" represents an important coping tool children finally develop about age two to three. When language is finally available and they need no longer simply rely on crying, children find comfort in telling Mommy or Daddy why they are angry, afraid, or sad and getting hugs, kisses, and reassurance in return. As a result, once they can talk, toddlers are less likely to lash out in frustration at peers, lie down on the ground and have tantrums, or hold their breath until they're blue. They can also understand specific suggestions adults make, such as "Count to ten" or "Take a few deep breaths." Given the relief that language brings, encouraging children to use signs to express their emotions is a great way to accelerate progress toward this source of emotional self-regulation.

5. You choose to avoid highly arousing situations in the future. You promise yourself that, next time, you'll find someone else to make such presentations. You also decide not to watch any videotape of your appearance on the cable channel. No point in getting more upset.

THE KID VERSIONS. As soon as babies are mobile, they begin to take advantage of this avoidance strategy. Although they aren't in complete control of their lives, they can choose to play or not play with certain children, decide exactly how far they dare venture from Mom, and refuse to do certain things or go certain places. That's why it's so important, when an act of defiance does occur, to try to understand the motivation behind it. It may simply be the only way your child can think of to avoid an upsetting situation. An ounce of empathy and a pledge to stay close may be all she needs. Parents also help by learning to avoid situations they know will tax their child's ability to cope, such as becoming too tired, too hungry, too hot, or too overwhelmed by strangers.

Over time, children develop many of these coping strategies spontaneously. Until they do, however, you and your baby may be in for a rocky ride. The good news is that research has also revealed positive steps you can take to help your child begin learning to understand and control emotions during the first three years. The following news flash is a wonderful case in point.

N E W S   F L A S H !

Simple Words About Feelings Speak Volumes to a Child

Cambridge, England. It may be time for her nap, but eighteen-month-old Jessica isn't quite ready yet. Instead, she's still wandering around the house with a worried look on her face. At this point a young woman standing in the corner of the room comes to attention, poised with clipboard and pencil in hand to begin taking notes. Her pencil flies as the following exchange between Jessica and her mother takes place.

> MOM: What's wrong, Sweet Pea?
>
> JESSICA: Bee-bee!
>
> MOM: Oh, you're looking for your baby doll. Is that it?
>
> JESSICA: [Nods her head and continues looking]
>
> MOM: You want her to take a nap too? It makes you feel comfy-cozy to have her sleep with you, doesn't it?
>
> JESSICA: [Nods again]
>
> MOM: Well, we'd better find her then!

The exchange is just one of many that the young woman, a research assistant from Cambridge University, has recorded in an effort to help scientists Judy Dunn, Inge Bretherton, and Penny Munn learn more about how parents can best support the development of their young children's understanding of emotions. In fact, this study with eighteen-month-olds is only one of many conducted at Cambridge, each of which has pointed in the same direction.

"Our results are very clear," says Dunn. "The more frequently parents comment on, clarify, and explain the reasons for their toddler's emotions, the more sophisticated that child's understanding of emotions will be at age three." Not only were children like Jessica better able to identify and discuss their own emotions, they could also identify and discuss the emotions of others. In fact, thinking about emotions was so important to them that they even enjoyed incorporating feelings into their pretending games ("You be happy. I be sad") more than children whose parents didn't have such conversations. In short, when parents take time to talk to their children about emotions ("Are you feeling angry?"), they help them develop a richer emotional vocabulary and, in turn, the beginnings of a richer emotional life.

Words of Wisdom and Tricks of the Trade

What a wonderful contribution Dunn, Bretherton, and Munn have made to our understanding of emotional development! Could anything be easier? Simply by paying attention to your child's feelings and *talking* about them, you can go a long way toward helping him begin to sort out the intricacies of emotional life—what's going on inside of him and inside of other people as well. And the good news doesn't stop there. Researchers from other laboratories around the world have uncovered other tips for parents.

PREPARING THE FOUNDATION

Let's start first with general principles. If your goal is for your child to get a jump start on understanding emotions, research shows that you need to start thinking at birth about how to make emotions a "positive" thing in your child's life. Specific advice from researchers includes:

◆ **Build a secure attachment bond.** As we explained in Chapter 2, there's no better way to launch your child into her emotional future than to do everything you can to make sure she feels secure in your love and trusting of your protection. Developmental psychologist Howard Steele and his colleagues at University College, London, however, have gone beyond these generalities to provide definitive proof that attachment counts when it comes to helping children understand emotions. The children in their study were assessed at both twelve months and six years. The early visit was devoted to measuring the security of their attachment to their mothers using the Strange Situation, while the later visit involved a test designed to see how well they understood an inherently difficult aspect of emotional reality—the fact that people can experience *mixed* emotions. The researchers found clear evidence that those children who enjoyed secure attachment relationships at age twelve months were more sophisticated in their knowledge at age six.

◆ **Engage in synchronized interactions.** Remember the lovely, face-to-face emotional exchanges we described in Chapter 2, the ones that babies need in order to thrive emotionally from the very earliest months? Well, thanks to a study by developmental psychologist Ruth Feldman and her colleagues in Israel, we now know that the sharing of positive emotions during these interactions at three and nine months predicts the ability of twenty-four-month-olds to "regulate" their emotions (in this case, picking up toys when asked and refraining from touching candies when told not to). What's more, this was particularly true for the Baby Hollys in the group (the "Difficult" babies). The message is clear: It pays to get up close and personal with your baby from Day 1.

◆ **Encourage your baby to use signs.** Even though a child's first signs are more likely to be names for concrete things, such as "milk," "kitty," and "ball," these signs pave the way for the more abstract emotion signs that will come later, including those that will help your toddler tell you what he and others around him are feeling. What's more, the very act of modeling these signs for him ("Oh, you're sad!" accompanied by the "sad" sign or "I can see you're really mad" accompanied by the "mad/angry" sign) meets researcher Judy Dunn's suggestion that you take advantage of opportunities that come your way to talk about emotions. Here are some good signs to start with:

  ◆ **Sad.** Trace the path of a tear down your cheek.
  ◆ **Mad.** Clench fists and scowl.
  ◆ **Happy.** Place palm on chest and sweep upward.
  ◆ **Sleepy.** Rest head on hands.
  ◆ **Love.** Cross hands over the heart.
  ◆ **Afraid.** Pat chest rapidly.

REACTING ON THE SPOT

◆ **Help your child identify feelings.** Follow the example of Jessica's mother in the news flash and verbally label what you think your child is feeling. Of course, it's important to interpret his facial expressions and general behavior as accurately as possible. One way to avoid making a mistake is to start with a question, such as "Are you feeling sad?" Get in the habit of responding this way from the very first months as you interact face to face. By doing so you are familiarizing your baby with the verbal labels for feelings, an important step in developing emotional competence.

◆ **Acknowledge the use of signs.** If your baby uses a sign to let you know what she is feeling, be sure to let her know you understand and are willing to help if the feeling is negative, and are willing to share in her enjoyment if the feeling is positive. Think how much less frustrated you both will be when she can make it clear exactly what's on her mind. Validating feelings and meeting needs are important at any age.

◆ **Take advantage of conflicts.** Research shows that conflicts between siblings or playmates provide excellent opportunities for discussing emotions with children. For one thing, under such conditions children are pretty sure to volunteer a response when you ask them what they are feeling. What's more, for better or worse, you can count on having lots of chances to generate discussion in such contexts. (Researchers Deborah Laible and Ross Thompson recently documented an average of nineteen conflicts per hour in their study of two-and-a-half-year-olds!)

GENERATING DISCUSSION

◆ **Start a "happy/sad" bedtime routine.** Linda started this ritual with her children when they were barely toddlers. Take a moment at the end of the day to share events that made each of you "happy" and "sad." By including your own emotions in the conversations, you provide a model for how to talk about such things and also reinforce the point that parents have feelings too. Of course, when your child is very young, you will have to take his part as well, using your knowledge of events to suggest things he was happy or sad about. By doing so, not only are you helping him understand his emotions better, but you also are helping him develop effective ways to communicate his feelings and strengthen his memory for emotional events.

◆ **Branch out from "happy/sad."** As your child gets older and more able to participate, add other emotions to the "happy/sad" bedtime routine. What made each of you angry during the day? What was especially funny? Be sure to listen closely and uncritically to what your child says. There's no quicker way to quell a child's enthusiasm for talking about feelings than to find fault with what she says about them. ("No, you weren't *really* scared when the lights went out. You knew I'd protect you.")

◆ **Review photo albums or family videos.** Photos and videos spark memories of salient events, and nine times out of ten, these events involve emotions. Describe the emotions the people in the videos and photos seem to be feeling. ("Gramma looks so happy holding you in her arms.") Besides, whether it's a birthday party, a trip to the snow, or just fun in the backyard, chances are good that you and your child will both enjoy the chance to reminisce. Anything learned about emotions is just a wonderful plus.

◆ **Use storybooks.** "Why do you think Goldilocks ran away?" "How do you think the Three Little Pigs felt when the wolf was huffing and puffing?" Research shows that questions like these posed during book reading help children think more deeply about emotional issues.

Storybooks provide excellent opportunities for parents to discuss emotions with toddlers. Asking why Bambi is so sad or Goldilocks is so scared can get very young children thinking about emotional causes and consequences.

◆ **Speculate on the emotional dramas you witness from afar.** Whether you and your child are in the park, in a restaurant, or in line at the grocery store, chances are good that the people around you are expressing emotions. Point to strangers (at a distance) and ask your child to guess what they are feeling and why. Contribute your own guess, choosing another likely explanation, making clear you're not discounting your child's. As your child gets older, you can take turns, eventually even increasing the entertainment value by making up funny stories about why strangers are feeling the way they do. ("I bet he's feeling sad because he had to leave his pet gorilla in the car. What do you think?")

◆ **Start a "gratitude journal."** Teaching children to understand the complex emotion of gratitude takes more than simply badgering them to say "thank you." That's why we were delighted at this tip from a mother in Bakersfield, California: "When my son was only two years old, I began a 'gratitude journal' for him. Each night we would talk about the things we were thankful for that day and I would write them down in his journal. Once he learned to read and write, he made the entries himself while I made entries in a 'gratitude journal' of my own. Not only did my son learn what it means to be grateful, he also had a wonderful keepsake from his childhood."

◆ **Practice reflective listening.** It's very important in all of these discussions to listen carefully to what your child says and respond without lecturing or judging. One particularly helpful strategy is reflective listening, in which you summarize what you're hearing your child express, always offering the opportunity for her to correct you. ("I see. You're really mad at Jason because of what he did to your painting. Is that it?") Rephrasing the child's message in this way helps her label what's going on in her head, an important part of the development of emotional intelligence.

PROVIDING PRACTICE WITH EMOTIONS

◆ **Play the "show-me" game.** Make a game out of matching words to facial expressions by taking turns naming an emotion for the other person to demonstrate. ("Show me your ANGRY face.")

◆ **Use emotions in pretend play.** As you play "tea party," "grocery store," or any other pretend scenario with your child, remember to involve emotions. These are especially good opportunities to help your child express negative emotions such as anger, fear, sadness, and aggression. Using puppets helps too by enabling your child to distance himself from the feelings he's expressing. (Eavesdropping on the pretend scenarios is also a good way to get a sense of what your child's inner world is like at any given moment.)

◆ **Play the "silly song" game.** Take turns singing familiar songs, such as "Mary Had a Little Lamb" or the "ABC Song," with different emotional intonations and facial expressions. Your child will have fun suggesting what you should do next. ("Now sing it like you're angry!")

◆ **Make a "what are they feeling?" deck of cards.** The idea here is to create a small deck of playing cards where the four emotions—Happy, Sad, Angry, and Afraid—represent the suits. Each suit, in turn, is represented by appropriate pictures of people expressing that emotion cut from magazines, photo albums, or old picture books. Select about twenty cards from an old deck of playing cards and paste these pictures on the cards so that you have, for example, five cards with Happy faces, five with Sad faces, and so on. Use the cards to play easy card games like "Go Fish." ("I'm looking for a Happy face. Do you have one?" "No. Go Fish.")

TEACHING SELF-CONTROL

Self-control is a critical component of emotional self-regulation. Because it plays a special role in helping children deal with feelings of frustration and anger, we provide lots of tips on how to spur its development in Chapter 9.

Reaping the Benefits

Helping children get a jump start on emotional intelligence is one of the best gifts any parent can give them. In fact, with the ability to understand what she and others are feeling—and *why*—your child will have the tools necessary to develop the critical skills we highlight in the next three chapters: empathy, friendship, and self-esteem.

4

Kid Kindness:
Evoking Empathy and Caring
About Others

N E W S   F L A S H !

Surprising Newborn Nursery Credo:
"One for All and All for One!"

Padua, Italy. Picture the following scene. One-day-old Sophia is sleeping soundly in her bassinet in the maternity ward along with nine other newborns. The lights are dim and the supervising nurse, moving efficiently but quietly from baby to baby, is pleased to see that all are quiet and breathing regularly—that is, until she accidentally stumbles into the side of Sophia's bassinet. Startled by the sudden movement, Sophia's eyes pop open and she begins to wail. Question: What should the nurse do? Pick up Sophia and soothe her back to sleep? Certainly. But there's something else the nurse should do: Call for reinforcements because pandemonium is about to break loose.

Researchers—and nurses—have long known that when one newborn begins to cry, more will follow. What hasn't been so obvious is why. One reasonable explanation is simply that the increased noise level and unpleasantness of a baby's cry irritates other babies enough to cause them distress, something that might result if any loud, unpleasant noise were heard. It turns out that what's really happening is much more interesting—indeed, fascinating—than that. According to recent research by Marco Dondi,

Francesca Simion, and Giovanna Caltran, three scientists from the University of Padua in Italy, the tendency for babies to start crying when they hear other babies cry is an innate reaction to that specific event: distress among their human peers. How do the scientists know that's the case? Simply by adding a little twist to the situation. In addition to exposing newborns to tape-recordings of other newborns crying, they also exposed them to tape-recordings of themselves crying. Although both tapes were equally loud and unpleasant, the babies became distressed only when the cry was not their own. In other words, they were specifically geared to match the distress of other babies. If the cry was not from another baby, it simply wasn't worth getting upset about.

Martin Hoffman, researcher at New York University, would not be surprised by these results. He has long suspected that the "emotional contagion" seen in human newborns is one way nature has chosen to jump-start the development of empathy. Why should nature be so concerned with empathy? Because, say Hoffman and other modern scientists, empathy is the glue that binds humans together in ways that promote our survival as a species.

Why Empathy Is So Important

Empathy is the ability to share another person's emotional state. It's that warm, teary-eyed feeling that comes from watching touching commercials at holidays or the sadness and despair that overwhelm us when we see wrenching news footage of parents whose children have been abducted. In other words, it's feeling *what* someone else feels, not just feeling *for* them. And, as pointed out in the news flash, its existence is probably one reason the human species has survived as long as it has.

Unlike our reptilian ancestors, humans are social creatures who depend on each other in many different and important ways: to avoid predators ("Look out! There's a saber-toothed tiger!"), to gather resources ("You look over there for roots; I'll look over here for berries."), to share responsibility for helpless youngsters ("Would you mind holding Pebbles while I stoke the fire?"), and to learn new things ("Wow! That's a neat way to skin a bear."). With so much at stake, it makes sense that individuals with a knack for getting along with others would survive to pass on any genes that helped them do so. Chief among these, scientists suspect, were genes that endowed us with a natural proclivity to read and match each other's emotions—in other words, to be empathic.

Unfortunately, nature gambled a bit on us at the same time. Despite providing a jump start for empathy at the beginning of life, it did not guarantee that this important tool would continue to develop as we grow past infancy and become able to think for ourselves. Instead, nature left room for nurture—the environment—to determine the ultimate presence or absence of empathy. And that's where you come in. As we discuss in detail later in the chapter, there's a great deal that you can do to help your child develop into an empathic, caring individual.

What's more, it's extremely important that you do so *for your child's sake*. Here's what's at stake. Study after study shows that children high in empathy—and the sympathy that flows from it—fair better in life. They are more popular with their peers, they get along better with teachers and other adults, they have more successful relationships when they grow up, and, in general, they tend to live lives that garner them respect and affection.

> Teaching a child not to step on a caterpillar is as valuable to the child as it is to the caterpillar.
>
> —Bradley Miller, humorist

In contrast, young children whose empathic beginnings are stunted or derailed find themselves unable to understand or care how their behavior impacts others. As a consequence, they are more prone to hitting, biting, and other aggressive behaviors—none of which endears them to other children. Not surprisingly, they are far more likely to be rejected by their peers and to become involved in serious antisocial behavior as they grow older. This is clearly a future no parent would willingly wish on his or her child. Our goal with this chapter of *Baby Hearts* is to help you help your child become what nature intended: a kind and compassionate individual for whom empathy is as natural as breathing in and out.

STEPS ALONG THE WAY

Newborns have a long way to go from reflexively matching the crying of other babies to purposefully helping others out of genuine care and concern. Many of the changes reflect a child's growing cognitive awareness of being a unique person separate from others and, somewhat later, from the ability to understand events from another person's perspective. These are the "cognitive" components that underlie the development of empathy. The ultimate shape that empathy takes, however, depends equally on the "emotional" component—how the child *feels* about what's happening to someone else. How this component changes with age is in the hands of parents and caregivers. Here are some steps that empathy researcher Carolyn Zahn-Waxler and her colleagues at the National Institute of Mental Health have identified.

◆ **Birth to 8 months.** The automatic distress reaction of newborns to other people's distress continues through the first eight months, although with less and less crying. Instead, a baby's developing ability to regulate her own emotions (see Chapter 3) makes it more likely that she will try to calm herself by looking away and/or sucking her thumb. She does not yet understand the outside event that is triggering her own discomfort.

◆ **9 to 12 months.** Babies still automatically become upset at another's distress, but now they have additional strategies available to deal with it. Whenever possible, babies this age look at the faces of trusted caregivers to see how *they* are reacting (see Chapter 3's discussion of social referencing) and can calm themselves if they see that their caregiver isn't upset.

◆ **12 to 18 months.** Although still motivated by their own distress reaction, by now toddlers understand enough about cause and effect to identify the other person's situation as the problem and to want it resolved. In addition, they are beginning to remember what behaviors others use in such situations and, therefore, occasionally may try to comfort distressed children or adults by patting or hugging them. The goal, however, is as much to help the toddler feel better as it is to help the victim, and it's not unusual for a toddler to react aggressively in an effort to make the distressed person stop acting that way.

◆ **18 to 30 months.** During this period, toddlers develop a sense of self, a conscious awareness of themselves as people separate from others. They also begin being able to use simple words and phrases. These two cognitive advances combine with a developing awareness of emotional states in themselves and others to motivate toddlers to more frequently comfort other people, express sympathy, and explore reasons for the person's distress. For example, witnessing a parent in distress, a toddler may say, "Why cry?" But overall, toddlers still are primarily focused on their own feelings and aren't likely spontaneously to sacrifice something they value for the good of others.

◆ **30 to 48 months.** More and more, older toddlers and preschoolers take their cue from their own experiences, from what they see the important people in their life do in reaction to the *child's own* distress. Children who are hugged and kissed when they are upset are likely to hug and kiss others in distress. Unfortunately, children who are ignored, belittled, or punished when upset themselves are just as likely to repeat those behaviors. During this period we begin to see children whose natural progression toward true empathy is being derailed or even destroyed.

◆ **4 to 6 years.** By now children are smart enough to begin paying close attention to how the important adults in their lives react to their behavior toward other people. Like all good hedonists, high on their agenda is the strong desire to get goodies and avoid punishment. Therefore, if they have consistently been acknowledged for being kind, they are likely to continue being kind. Unfortunately, for some children, *any* attention is rewarding. As a result, if their good behavior has consistently been ignored and only their bad behavior has brought them attention, then the bad behavior is likely to continue.

◆ **7+ years.** Two major advances play a role in shaping empathy from now on.

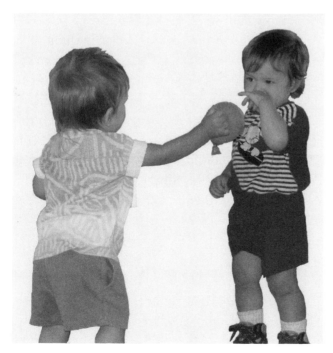

Seeing his little pal Kerrick upset about something, thirty-month-old Corey tries to cheer him up with a balloon. The fact that he tries to help his friend probably means that his parents have treated his own distress with empathy.

First, children become quite good at understanding how other people perceive events, even if those perceptions are different from their own. Researchers call this skill role taking or perspective taking. This skill enables children to understand better when and why people are distressed and to figure out ways to help. It also enables them to detect whether the important adults in their lives approve of their behavior or not. If (and that's an important "if") they love and respect those adults, then their desire for that approval—not just the goodies the approval can bring, but the approval itself—provides a critical motivation for behaving empathically.

A second important factor involves children's evolving images of themselves. No longer do they describe themselves simply in concrete terms—as tall, short, or good at video games. Finally their self-concepts start to include personality traits—like being a kind and helpful person or a dominant, don't-tread-on-me sort of person. These self-perceptions become harder and harder to change as children automatically seek to behave in a manner consistent with their image of themselves. By this point, the presence or absence of empathy is pretty much a done deal.

THE DEVELOPMENT OF MORAL VALUES

The steps in the development of empathy that we've just outlined are closely connected with the more general development of what parents typically think of as moral values. In addition to the values of kindness and compassion that come to mind with any discussion of empathy, the category usually includes references to honesty, cooperation, fairness, and responsibility. Although each term describes a different behavior, all of the behaviors have certain things in common: Their development depends on young children having these values modeled by parents whom they both respect and adore, who talk about the reasons for living by these values, who recognize and reward their children for adhering to them, and who discipline with a consistent yet compassionate hand. These guidelines are described in more detail at the end of the chapter.

FROM EMPATHY TO SYMPATHY TO ACTION . . . OR *NOT*

As we've seen, the roots of empathy lie in the personal distress newborns experience when they hear other babies crying. But newborns aren't alone. Witnessing the distress of others will engender feelings of distress within us no matter how

Giving Voice to Toddler Empathy

As we mentioned at the very beginning of *Baby Hearts,* just because children can't talk doesn't mean they aren't thinking about things—including emotions. Here is a true story illustrating how using simple signs enabled one child to express empathy (*and* sympathetic action) toward another.

Kara and Levi, both seventeen months old, were great buddies at their child care center and knew each other as well as any two seventeen-month-olds can. One morning soon after she had arrived, Kara noticed that Levi was crying and holding on tightly to his mother's hand. He clearly didn't want her to go. Kara, watching all this intently and beginning to frown herself, suddenly turned to her own mom, pointed to Levi, and ran a finger from her eye down her cheek—her sign for *sad.* "Yes, Kara, Levi is feeling sad this morning," replied Kara's mother, amazed that Kara could describe what Levi was feeling. But she was *really* amazed at what happened next. Quickly walking over to Levi, Kara looked at him with real concern in her eyes and began smacking her lips repeatedly. Although her mom immediately recognized the smacking as Kara's sign for *fish,* she didn't know why Kara was doing it. The mystery was solved by Kara's teacher. Whenever children had difficulty separating from their parents, the caregivers would take them over to feed the fish as a way to make them feel better. Kara had not only correctly identified and empathized with Levi's problem, but she had even come up with a very appropriate way to help. In the words of Kara's teacher, "Whoever says babies can't express empathy hasn't been around signing babies!"

Source: Adapted from Linda Acredolo and Susan Goodwyn, *Baby Signs: How to Talk with Your Baby Before Your Baby Can Talk,* 2nd ed. (New York: McGraw-Hill, 2002).

old we are. That's actually the definition of empathy—feeling what the other person is feeling.

Just feeling bad, however, doesn't do much to alleviate the other person's suffering. What needs to be added is an inclination to action, to figuring out what one can *do* to make the situation better. Researchers Nancy Eisenberg, Richard

Fabes, and their colleagues at Arizona State University have discovered important individual differences among young children in their ability to take this next step, that is, to put their personal distress on the back burner and move on to what they call "sympathetic action" in which children marshal their resources to help. The researchers have divided children into two groups, sympathizers and avoiders. Sympathizers develop the mind-set pretty early that they want and/or need to help, while avoiders are routinely so overwhelmed by their own internal upset that their highest priority becomes turning away from the situation in an effort to reduce their own distress.

In infants and toddlers, this "turning away" is quite literal—running in the other direction, often toward a caregiver who can comfort the avoider herself. Older children and adults, with their more sophisticated thinking skills, are much more creative in how they manage to reduce their discomfort upon witnessing someone's suffering. Here are some of the most common defense mechanisms

Baby Hearts in Action:
Confession of an "Avoider"

Susan knows all about the type of child researchers call an avoider. Why? Because she was one. Like the children Eisenberg, Fabes, and their colleagues studied, Susan would become so upset at witnessing someone in trouble that she would immediately flee the scene. When a fire engine roared down the street and all the other kids raced after it to see what was on fire, where was Susan? Running the other way. When a fight broke out on the playground and all the other kids were gathering around, where was Susan? Anywhere *but* near the action. Should a child burst out crying, would Susan be among the other kids running to see what was wrong? No way. She was the one running home as fast as her little legs would carry her. Fortunately, with greater maturity and broader experience, Susan overcame her childhood avoider tendencies. Just ask Linda, who has benefited time and time again from her best friend's strength and active support. (Tips for helping children become sympathizers instead of avoiders can be found in the remainder of the chapter.)

humans use and examples from slightly older children. Notice that, for the most part, they ring hollow—they sound more like the excuses they really are.

◆ **Blaming the victim.** Avoiders come up with some way that the person who is suffering brought the situation on his- or herself and, therefore, deserves the consequences. Not only does using such a strategy provide avoiders an excuse for inaction, but it also provides the comfort of thinking they know how to avoid the same fate. ("If that new girl hadn't worn such an icky dress, kids wouldn't be picking on her. It's her own fault!")

◆ **Diffusing responsibility.** Avoiders convince themselves that there are many other people in a better position to help, that it's not their job. This type of rationalizing is usually accompanied by an attempt to flee the situation as rapidly as possible. ("There are lots of kids in the park. I'm sure someone else will help that little girl who fell off the slide.")

Baby Hearts in Action: "Dry Those Tears; Mimi's Here!"

Susan's grandson Brandon was barely three when he started preschool. To ease the transition, Susan (known to all her grandchildren as Mimi) stayed with him for the first two weeks, gradually spending less and less time directly by his side. It was close to the end of this period that she witnessed the following heartwarming illustration of empathy in action.

One day, despite the general hubbub that always marks the start of the day, Brandon became aware that one of the little girls in the class was crying. Assessing the situation quickly, Susan answered Brandon's quizzical look by explaining "Yes, Brandon, she's sad. She's missing her mommy." As Susan watched from the sidelines, she was touched to see Brandon walk up to the girl and put his arm around her. But it was what Brandon said to the girl that really made Susan's heart sing. Indicating that he knew the perfect solution to the little girl's problem, he said with great confidence, "Don't cry. Mimi will take care of you. Mimi takes care of *everybody!*"

◆ **Shifting the blame.** Avoiders often blame others for their own unwillingness to help. This strategy enables people to avoid responsibility for lots of things: mistakes, accidents, being late. ("I'd help that little boy find his mother, but I promised Mommy I'd never talk to strangers.")

◆ **Doing a "cost-benefit" analysis.** Avoiders may decide that the cost to themselves is much too high to justify helping. ("I'd stop and help, but then I'd miss part of the birthday party I've been looking forward to.")

There is an additional reason why both children and adults sometimes find themselves shuddering at, and then turning away from, the suffering of others: They simply do not know how to help. Although a lack of know-how can be used as an excuse like any of the other defense mechanisms, in many cases it is an accurate reflection of the truth. Hearing about floods in Asia or civil wars in Africa can cause empathic feelings to swell, but the frustration of not knowing what we personally can do to help the victims can lead to reflexively turning our thoughts away to lower our empathic turmoil. Such a reaction is understandable and probably inevitable when events of this magnitude are involved. There's an important lesson here, however, for parents. As we will discuss in more detail later, helping children learn how to aid those in distress will make it much more likely that they will choose sympathetic action over avoidance.

Obviously, it's good for society as a whole for parents to help their children develop the emotional strength necessary to move beyond their own anxiety and toward active attempts to help those in need. It's also, however, good for the children. As we'll discuss in Chapter 5, children who voluntarily help others, especially those in genuine distress, are highly valued by their peers. After all, who wouldn't prefer a friend who can be counted on to help in a crisis over one whose typical reaction is simply to run for cover? The researchers who discovered this important individual difference between sympathizers and avoiders have also uncovered one way that parents can influence their child's reaction to feelings of empathy. The news flash includes highlights.

N E W S   F L A S H !

To Help or Not to Help, That Is the Question— Even for Three-Year-Olds, Scientists Say

Tempe, Arizona. With not a cloud in the sky to mar their outing to the park, two moms sit contentedly on a bench watching their three-year-old sons, Marco and Christo, at play. Suddenly the calm is shattered by a sharp cry from over near the swings, where the two boys had been busily engaged with a neighbor's child, eighteen-month-old James. Next thing they know, Marco and Christo are running toward them as fast as they can, while poor James sits crying forlornly on the ground, blood pouring from his nose.

It's at this point that, were they there, researchers Nancy Eisenberg and Richard Fabes from Arizona State would have popped out their clipboards and pencils, ready to record the outcome. What they would have witnessed is Marco hurriedly explaining that James had fallen off the swing and grabbing his mom's hand to drag her back to James's side, while Christo grabs his own mom's hand, holds tight, and begins sucking his thumb.

"Both children are reacting empathically to their friend's plight," Eisenberg explains. "It's just that their way of dealing with their concern is very different. Marco is focused on helping his friend feel better, while Christo is focused on helping *himself* feel better." Marco is a sympathizer and Christo is an avoider.

But would Marco and Christo behave this way in other situations? The answer, according to the researchers, is probably yes. The reasons lie, they say, in how the boys' parents have reacted to the children's own negative feelings during their short lives. Specifically, Eisenberg, Fabes, and their colleagues have discovered that children whose parents encourage them to freely express their feelings of vulnerability (sadness, fear, and anxiety) while at the same time restricting expressions of emotions that are clearly hurtful to others (anger and aggression) are more prone to develop sympathetic action as their primary reaction when feelings of empathy are aroused.

In contrast, parents who aren't willing or able to let their young children express any negative feelings, including feelings of vulnerability, are more likely to have children whose empathy leads to comfort-seeking for themselves. In other words, raising a child to have the proverbial stiff upper lip can yield some unexpected, and unfortunate, results.

Predicting Success

The work of Eisenberg, Fabes, and their colleagues provides good news to parents by demonstrating that there are some concrete steps they can take to help their children make the most of their inborn potential for empathy. Acknowledging a child's expressions of sadness, fear, and anxiety works to this end. Why? One possibility is that doing so helps diffuse a child's anxiety on a daily basis, with the result that anxious feelings in general aren't all that scary. So, when an emergency arises, these children aren't as likely to be overwhelmed by their own anxious feelings and, therefore, are better able to deal constructively with the situation. In other words, the knee-jerk "Oh no, oh no, OH NO!" reaction to seeing someone in distress is tempered by the fact that, in children whose parents routinely listen to them, anxieties don't tend to spiral out of control in day-to-day life.

Other researchers have added to the list of factors that contribute to the development of empathy, many of which, like the ones uncovered by Eisenberg and Fabes, are in parental hands. Although the following list provides general guidelines, more specific tips can be found at the end of the chapter.

TEMPERAMENT: IT'S AN EASIER ROAD FOR SOME THAN FOR OTHERS

Baby Orchid's Special Challenge. Given how we've described the difference between sympathizers and avoiders, it shouldn't come as a surprise to learn that children who are temperamentally cautious and inhibited are more likely to fall in the avoider category. In contrast to high-activity children like Baby Dandelion and easygoing children like Baby Sunflower, it doesn't take much to overwhelm Baby Orchid's fragile sense of comfort with her surroundings. As a consequence, encountering someone in distress is more likely to trigger in Baby Orchids high levels of anxiety and the need to seek comfort by avoiding the situation altogether.

Baby Holly's Special Challenge. Baby Holly, the "Irritable" child, may also find it hard to respond constructively to emergency situations. The upset is still there, but instead of dealing with it by running away, Baby Holly may react to her emotional feelings with resentment and even anger. It's not unusual, therefore, to see children with Baby Holly's prickly temperament reacting with aggression instead of sympathy.

Baby Orchid and Baby Holly may face particular challenges when it comes to expressing empathy in a constructive manner, but that doesn't mean that other children are guaranteed members of the sympathizer's club. No matter what a child's temperament, the ways parents interact with her will play a major role—for good or bad.

PARENTING PREDICTORS OF SUCCESS

A Parent's Role as Model. One of the most consistent findings in the research on the development of empathy is that a parent's own level of empathy makes a huge difference in how empathic his or her child is likely to be. Children tend to imitate the big people in their lives, whether it's trying to swing a tennis racket like Mom or trying to push a lawnmower like Dad. Empathy is no exception to this rule. With this in mind, parents need to pay very close attention to how they treat other people who are in distress. *And* they need to be on the lookout for their own use of those pesky "defense mechanisms" that function as excuses for ignoring someone's plight.

What will make an even bigger impression, however, is how parents treat their *own child's* distress. As Eisenberg and Fabes, along with many other researchers, have shown, children who receive empathic reactions to their feelings are more likely to react that way toward others.

A Parent's Role as Teacher. Modeling is a form of teaching, of course. But research shows that children also benefit from their parents' overt efforts to teach them about emotions, including empathy. As we discussed in Chapter 3, children have lots to learn about how people feel and what makes them feel that way. In the case of empathy, children need to be helped to understand the nature and cause of the distress they are witnessing. Sometimes, as with James in the news flash, the cause is obvious: He fell off the swing and got hurt. Even in these

One of the strongest predictors of empathy in a child is whether she was treated empathically herself when she needed comforting. Hugs and kisses in such situations do more than just pacify a child. They also model how one should react to a person in distress.

situations, however, parental description is a way to open a dialogue so that the child's own feelings about the event can be explored. Remember, very young children not only have trouble putting names to other people's emotions; they also need help identifying their own.

On other occasions, the causes of distress won't be so easy for a child to understand without parental explanation. "Oh, poor Annie. I bet she's sad because her mom is leaving." In these cases, the parent's words are critical because they help hone the child's knowledge of the emotional complexity that makes us human. They also open the door to another valuable lesson: *how* to help. Talking about what might and might not be done to solve a problem is extremely valu-

How Would You Feel If . . . ?

Max, the neighbors' overly friendly Labrador retriever, lopes toward two-year-old Timmy, who quickly takes shelter behind his dad's leg and begins to cry. His dad, Jim, following in the footsteps of generations of dads with sons, says, "Don't be such a scaredy-cat. He's not going to hurt you!" Do those words help? No. In fact, research shows that sympathizing with a child's fears is an important ingredient in the recipe for creating empathy. Perhaps the next scenario might make that dad react differently.

New York City born and bred, Jim decides to take Timmy and the rest of his family to Idaho for an exciting week on a dude ranch. While his family is still eating breakfast, Jim wanders out to the corral. As he approaches the gate, it suddenly swings open and a large, semiwild horse comes bounding out directly toward him, rearing up at the last moment. Jim jumps back quickly, slips, and finds himself in the dirt looking up as the horse's hooves come down, too close for comfort. As Jim lies in the dirt, shocked and shaken, the resident cowboy comes sauntering out and drawls, "Hey, city boy, don't be such a wuss. He ain't gonna hurt you!" Jim pulls himself up and stumbles back to the house, humiliated and angry.

We can only hope Jim makes the connection. Have you?

able. Like any of us, children who feel they know how to help are much more likely to do so.

A Parent's Role as Disciplinarian. We'll be touching on the question of how best to discipline children in many chapters of *Baby Hearts*. What makes the topic appropriate here is the unfortunate fact that some of the distress young children witness has been caused *by* them. Snatching away a toy can result in another child's tears. Hitting another child with a ball thrown in anger can cause an injury. And, of course, biting another child when frustrated is a sure-fire way to get wailing started.

Whatever else a parent does in response to such actions, the research on empathy is clear about three things:

1. The need to understand and acknowledge *why* the child did what he or she did, thereby modeling empathy
2. The need to explain to the child the consequences of his actions in terms of the harm caused to the victim's physical and psychological well-being
3. The need to start a discussion, either immediately or after emotions have cooled, of how the child might repair the damage he caused

Researchers call this manner of dealing with misbehavior induction, and they contrast it with two other strategies, withdrawal of love ("I don't want to have anything to do with a child who would do such a thing. I am *so* disappointed in you!") and power assertion ("You're getting a whipping for that, young man!"). Both of these strategies backfire in the effort to build empathy and its by-product, sympathetic action, because they increase a child's own anxiety and fail to present an empathic model for the child to emulate. What's more, they certainly don't help the child understand why he did what he did, the consequences to someone else, what he might do to repair the damage, how to avoid similar situations in the future, *or* the most important fact of all—that the behavior wasn't acceptable to the parent, but the child still is.

A Parent's Role as Cheerleader. In our descriptions of the steps a child goes through on the way to making empathy an automatic reaction, we emphasized the importance of the child incorporating the idea of herself as an empathic person into her developing self-concept. Well, clearly, this doesn't happen overnight, and it certainly doesn't happen without input from the adults around her. That's why research shows that parents who congratulate their children for behaving empathically and make statements to their children about their empathic "nature" tend to have children who behave more and more empathically as they get older.

> The walks and talks we have with our two-year-olds in red boots have a great deal to do with the values they will cherish as adults.
>
> —Edith F. Hunter, writer

Words of Wisdom and Tricks of the Trade

The general strategies just described (modeling empathy, being a cheerleader, etc.) provide a broad blueprint for how you can help your child develop into a kind and caring individual. Here are a few more specific tips designed to make your job even easier.

SOME HOW-TOS FOR MODELING EMPATHY

Modeling empathy toward others

◆ **Be a good neighbor.** Look for little ways to be helpful to others, let your child witness your kindness, and talk about what you're doing and why. Examples might include making a casserole for sick neighbors or friends, helping someone lift his luggage into the overhead bin on an airplane, offering your seat to an elderly person on the bus, graciously letting others go ahead of you in line when they are in a hurry, offering to help carry heavy parcels, putting change in the charity boxes at the grocery store checkout stand, staying in touch with grandparents, inviting lonely folks to share holidays, and so on.

◆ **Find "kindness projects."** Create big and little "kindness projects" to do either as a family or as a twosome. Big projects might include collecting items for poor families at Christmas, donating old toys to a charity, collecting canned goods for a local food closet, or volunteering to help the ASPCA house dogs and cats until homes can be found. Although toddlers can't assume much responsibility for such projects, they can be helped to contribute in small ways. Little projects might include taking flowers to a sick neighbor, drawing a picture to cheer someone up, or calling Grandma on the phone because it makes her happy. In each case, be sure to talk about why what you're doing is important and how glad you are to have your child's help.

◆ **Expect the unexpected.** Monitor your reactions to unexpected events that involve people (or animals) in need, especially when your child is present. Make sure that you remain calm so that you don't add to your child's anxiety, and be on the lookout for any tendencies you have to rationalize not helping. ("No, we can't stop to help that dog. The ice cream will melt. Besides, someone else will come along.") Based on our own experiences, we can assure you that the extra time it takes to rescue a dog stranded on the highway or help reunite a lost child and his mother at the mall (and it can be considerable) will be worth it in the long run for the lasting impression it creates of how important and rewarding it is to care.

◆ **Practice what you preach.** Research shows that young children sense hypocrisy years before they can put it into words. Here's why avoiding hypocrisy is important. Once children detect a contradiction between what someone says and what the person actually does, children tend to dismiss that person as a useful guide to how to behave. So be careful.

Modeling empathy toward your child

◆ **Be reassuring.** Remember, in your child's eyes, you are a big, powerful person. That's why the simple words "It'll be okay," combined with lots of hugs and kisses, are so reassuring to your child. Use them liberally. Doing so will endear you to him and also provide specific words and behaviors he can use to comfort others. In addition, assure him that together you will figure out how to solve whatever problem has him so upset.

◆ **Acknowledge negative feelings too.** Be aware of the importance of acknowledging *all* your child's feelings—even the negative ones. Acknowledging, after all, is not the same as condoning. If your child has done or is about to do something hurtful, by all means express your concern, but do so in a calm way, beginning with statements such as "I can see you're upset" or "You certainly seem angry." An added advantage is that these words may start a dialogue that can distract your child from whatever less-than-admirable behavior she had in mind.

The most important question in the world is, "Why is the child crying?"

—Alice Walker, American novelist

◆ **Help your child cope.** If the emotions your child is expressing are ones that Eisenberg and Fabes would label feelings of vulnerability—sadness, anxiety, fear—indicate that you understand and sympathize with her, provide whatever comfort is needed, and once things are back on an even keel, explore with her what might help her feel better in the future.

SOME HOW-TOS FOR TEACHING ABOUT EMPATHY

When other people's feelings are the issue

◆ **Use animals to practice being kind.** Kindness is at the heart of empathy, and a good way to introduce very young children to the concept is through involving them with the care of animals. Children are naturally attracted to animals and seem to easily grasp the dependence of many animals (particularly pets) on the love and attention of humans. If your child is too young for a big pet (such as a dog or cat) or other circumstances rule them out, try installing a bird feeder outside or an aquarium inside. (There's a reason every infant/toddler classroom includes a fish bowl.) If none of these alternatives is feasible, make it a point to visit friends with pets. Be sure, however, that the pets in question can be approached safely and that their owners understand your goal.

Very young children are naturally drawn to animals. Parents can use this attraction to teach children the importance of being kind. Teaching children to be gentle with pets is a good first step toward helping them develop empathy.

◆ **Take advantage of books.** Characters in books can be especially useful for teaching about empathy. Look for situations where expressions of empathy would make sense—for example, where a character is sad or hurt. Start a dialogue by asking questions ("What do you think Eeyore is feeling? Why do you think he feels that way?"). When appropriate, think of analogous situations from your child's life and help your child reflect on the similarities in feelings. ("Do you re- member when you lost your balloon? Do you think that's the way Eeyore feels?") Accept whatever answers are given as a starting point, remembering that the goal is to get your child thinking rather than worrying about whether he is right or wrong. If your child is still too young to answer such questions, ask them anyway, then supply the answers yourself. Doing so sets the stage for future dialogues when language skills are sufficiently advanced.

◆ **Talk about solutions.** Don't forget to talk about possible solutions to problems— strategies for *how* to help. Whenever unfortunate situations crop up at home, have your child help you think of what to do. ("Oh, dear! The dog tore that page of the newspaper before Daddy could read it. How do you think Daddy will feel? What could we do to help?") Also, reassure your child that when someone is hurt, coming to you for help is always an option.

When your child's own feelings are the issue

◆ **Help identify feelings.** Help your child identify the feelings underlying his emotional reactions to things. Point out that feelings can be complicated and that people sometimes can feel two things at the same time. Maybe his anger at a playmate is a result of having his feelings hurt, or maybe his anger when you leave him with a new babysitter is fear of the unfamiliar. It's good to start alerting him to such possibilities, but don't expect him to fully understand these complexities until he's five or six.

◆ **Establish a happy/sad routine.** Remember the "happy/sad" bedtime routine we suggested in Chapter 3? It provides a great opportunity to talk about the causes and cures of negative feelings like sadness, anger, and fear as experienced by *both* of you.

◆ **Watch for defense mechanisms.** As your child starts to be able to verbalize experiences, be on the lookout for the defense mechanisms that provide us all with excuses not to help. For example, point out the injustice of accusing the vic- tim of somehow bringing the torment on herself.

◆ **Encourage your child to use signs.** And finally, don't forget that toddlers who are too young to use words to talk about emotions and express empathy can use signs to do so. (See the box on page 89.)

SOME HOW-TOS FOR BEING A CHEERLEADER

◆ **Acknowledge good deeds.** Watch for baby steps in helping behavior, sharing, or sympathizing and express your pleasure with quiet words and hugs. Resist going overboard, however. The goal is for your child to *internalize* the desire to be helpful, not merely do what's right in order to earn your praise.

◆ **Use positive adjectives.** To help the internalization process along, attribute good qualities to your child's character when you talk with her. ("That was a nice thing to do. You're a very kind girl and I'm proud of you.") It's also helpful to enable your child to overhear you telling someone else how proud you are of the kind of girl she's becoming. Remember, children tend to live up to the labels we use; we might as well make them good ones.

5

I've Got a Friend:
Developing Healthy Friendships

N E W S   F L A S H !

"Imitation Is the Highest Form of Flattery"—for Toddlers Too

Durham, North Carolina. Eighteen-month-old Jared hasn't had much experience with other kids. With no older brothers or sisters at home and only his much-beloved mom, Cathie, for a playmate, Jared isn't quite sure what to make of the little blonde in the pink dress sitting across the table from him. Apparently his mom and her mom have decided to have coffee—although no one has asked Jared's opinion on the matter. So, warily keeping an eye on the intruders, Jared resumes his all-time favorite restaurant activity—banging the table with his spoon. Suddenly a broad smile spreads across his face, his eyes begin to twinkle, and he giggles. Why the abrupt change? Despite being only nineteen months old herself, his tablemate has already learned the way to a man's heart—at least a toddler man's heart—and has picked up her own spoon and joined the drum brigade.

Jared's delight comes as no surprise to developmental psychologist Carol Eckerman and her colleagues from Duke University, who have discovered that toddlers, just like the adults around them, are flattered by being imitated. "When someone imitates our actions, the message conveyed is one of approval. They like what we're doing enough to do it themselves," explains Eckerman. That's apparently why even very young children are more likely to interact with someone who is imitating them. They look more at the other person's face, smile more, and repeat the actions in an effort to establish an ongoing social game. As an added bonus, Eckerman and her colleague Sharon Didow have recently discovered that having their actions imitated by other children also inspires toddlers to engage in more sophisticated conversations. Sharing activities, they suggest, provides a common focus that makes it easier for these fledgling conversationalists to stay on track with their comments.

Why Getting Along with Peers Is So Important

Because of the careful observations of researchers like Carol Eckerman, we now know that imitative exchanges such as those Jared and his new friend were enjoying are more than just fun. It is within peer interactions that young children find opportunities for practicing their emerging social skills. To develop friendships, young children must learn appropriate ways to initiate play, enter ongoing playgroups, respond to a peer's initiations, and resolve conflicts. Peer interactions also create opportunities for toddlers to practice language skills, discover their ability to influence other children, begin understanding turn-taking, learn to share, and start to appreciate their existence as separate people—something developmental psychologists call a sense of self. Some of this can be accomplished through interactions with parents and siblings, but not all of it. Because peers are a child's developmental and social equals, issues like dominance need to be resolved between them, egocentrism is less likely to be tolerated, and responsibility for feelings is in the children's own hands.

As children get older, peers become even more important, often functioning as rich sources of emotional support—helping children deal with life crises, protecting them from the slings and arrows of not-so-helpful peers, providing a sense of security that promotes exploration and adventure, bestowing feelings of belonging and worthiness, and teaching valuable lessons about how to deal constructively with conflict. In fact, research shows that when children have good friends, their increased self-confidence enables them to do better in school and predicts healthy adult relationships. There's no doubt, therefore, that peer interactions provide opportunities for experiencing much that is good.

However, it doesn't require a Ph.D. in developmental psychology to know that peer interactions can also be the source of much that is *not* so good—of feeling different, ostracized, rejected, and lonely. And, unfortunately, negative ex-periences with peers in childhood can have serious repercussions in adulthood. For example, researchers Catherine Bagwell and Andrew Newcomb from the University of Richmond, along with colleague William Bukowski from Concordia University, report that eleven-year-olds without close ties to at least one "best friend" were significantly more likely to be depressed and harbor self-doubts twelve years later, at age twenty-three! That's why it's so important for parents to help their children get launched into the world of peers in the best possible way. Learning how to do that is what this chapter of *Baby Hearts* is all about.

> You are the bows from which your children as living arrows are sent forth.
>
> —Kahlil Gibran, poet

MORE IMPORTANT—AND MORE DIFFICULT—THAN EVER

Neighborhood Friends. Getting along with other children has always been important. But recent changes in the society at large have made getting along not only more important than ever before but also more challenging. Take, for example, the parental plea we know so well from our own childhoods: "Go outside and play!" In contrast to the wild games of hide-and-seek and vacant lot baseball that we enjoyed, children today are less likely to hear a parent say that phrase and, even if they do, are significantly less likely to find someone to play *with*. Why? As you scan the following factors, think about which ones are likely to affect your own child's opportunities to interact with others in the natural setting of the neighborhood.

◆ **Decreases in family size.** Although currently on a small upswing, the average number of children per family dropped dramatically at the end of the twentieth century (25 percent in one generation—from 2.44 in 1965 to 1.85 in 1998). As a consequence, there are fewer children both inside and outside the house for children to play with.

◆ **Increases in the number of working parents.** With more parents in the workforce, fewer children spend their days at home, and fewer parents are available to supervise play in the neighborhood.

♦ **Increases in perceived danger.** With increased attention to child abduction and molestation cases, fewer parents than in generations past permit their children to roam the neighborhood looking for playmates.

♦ **Secluded backyards.** With primary play spaces moving from front yards to fenced-off backyards, it's harder than ever for a child to spontaneously join a group of peers in play. Ringing a doorbell is much more intimidating than simply slipping into the action.

♦ **Increases in home-based entertainment.** With the seductive allure of TV, video games, and computers as competition, playing outside—particularly when few playmates and only limited freedom are offered—is less attractive than ever before.

Child Care Friends. Instead of the old-fashioned way of learning to interact with other children, approximately 40 percent of today's children under age three are thrown into such interaction (whether they like it or not) in the context of either part- or full-time child care. Fortunately, research shows that if the quality of the child care is high, the opportunity that child care settings provide to interact with other children can facilitate social development. The critical ingredient is the presence of highly skilled caregivers trained to help peer interactions go smoothly. Such people know how to handle disputes, encourage sharing and cooperation, and protect tender spirits. They also support a child's social development in another important way. If your child feels totally comfortable with her caregivers, then it's a bit like having *you* there as a buffer, freeing her to venture forth into interactions with others knowing there's a secure home base to run back to if feelings get out of control.

On the downside, reports from a large-scale study by the National Institute of Child Health and Human Development indicate that if the quality of care is not high, the result is likely to be more rather than fewer problems socializing with peers when the child gets to elementary school.

What does all this mean for your child? Whether her first years are spent at home (where the challenge may be having too few children to learn from) or in child care (where the challenge may be having too many children to learn from), there's lots you can do to help her make other children a blessing in her life rather than a burden. Just stay tuned.

The hardest part of raising children is teaching them to ride bicycles. A father can run beside the bicycle or stand yelling directions while the child falls. A shaky child on a bicycle for the first time needs both support and freedom. The realization that this is what the child will always need can hit hard.

—Sloan Wilson, American author

Steps Along the Way

Like every other facet of development, your baby's social world advances one step at a time. The changes reflect growing cognitive and motor skills, as well as a developing appreciation of other children as unique sources of fun.

◆ **2 to 4 months.** Fueled by their innate attraction to human faces and the same preference for "babyish" characteristics found among adults (round face, large eyes, small nose), babies begin to be interested in each other as early as two months. In addition to the face, there is often the added allure of unusual sounds, movements—and even smells.

◆ **6 to 9 months.** Now that they are able to sit up and see well at longer distances, their interest in other babies is much more apparent. They actively try to get each other's attention—smiling, babbling, and even laughing when they succeed.

◆ **9 to 12 months.** By now children have enough control over their bodies to be capable of small bouts of imitating each other's activities. However, they don't yet have the cognitive ability to truly understand that, in doing so, they are creating a partnership.

◆ **12 to 18 months.** Although they react more quickly and appropriately to one another, at the beginning of this period children still seem to view each other as interesting and somewhat controllable "toys" rather than as parts of a team. Toward the end of this period their play becomes truly "social" in that they smile at each other, hand each other toys, and generally seem to enjoy each other's company. Imitation is clearly a real "glue" in keeping interactions going.

◆ **18 to 24 months.** With a dawning sense of themselves as separate entities, toddlers seem truly aware for the first time of the coordinated roles that they and their playmates each play in their exchanges. They enjoy cooperating in the creation of "games," and imitation becomes mutually enjoyable, both children recognizing that what they are doing *together* is really "cool."

◆ **24 to 30 months.** Language becomes an important part of play, enabling toddlers to explain actions to each other and make suggestions. Rather than just imitating each other, they now are able to assume complementary roles, such as chaser and chasee in tag. The downside of this is that they also begin to recognize what they *don't* like about interactions, such as the need to share toys. Conflicts begin in earnest.

◆ **30 to 36 months.** As their ability to imagine things grows, so also does their enjoyment of playing "pretend" with each other. The scenarios are far from complex (such as Mommy and Baby), but still require cooperation and language. More than just fun, pretend play provides opportunities to learn to negotiate roles and rules, compromise, take turns, deal with other's feelings, and work out emotional issues. It's not surprising, therefore, that preschoolers who are good at pretend play tend to be popular with their peers.

Pretending that they are shopping for groceries is par for the course in peer play during the third year. Language now plays an important part, as does turn-taking and compromise. That may be why children who are good at pretend play are popular with their peers.

Baby Hearts in Action:
Two Friends Grin and "Bear" It

When Linda was little, her family routinely spent the summers in a cabin in New York's Allegheny State Park. The summer when she was three, she became best friends with a feisty five-year-old named Sharon and, as the literature predicts, tried to imitate everything Sharon did. All that was fine until the day a bear appeared in the campground, resulting in Linda's mom describing to the girls how bears hibernate in the winter. Inspired by what she had just heard, Sharon decided that she and Linda would pretend to be bears and find a place to hibernate. They snuck pillows and a blanket out of the cabin and settled down in a "cave" beneath a tarp covering a woodpile, giggling at how no one knew where they were. Unfortunately, that was true. Despite hearing their names called with more and more desperation, first by their moms and then by neighbors and a park ranger, the girls kept hiding and giggling. They finally emerged an hour later, ready to boast about their success as hibernating bears. Instead, as you might suspect, they found themselves in the center of a storm of tears and relief mixed with recriminations. As it turned out, it was Linda's last adventure with her friend—a decision made by her mother upon overhearing Sharon whispering to Linda, "Tomorrow let's be bees and find a hive to hide in!"

When Things Go Right . . . and Wrong

In their efforts to discover how parents can foster good interpersonal skills in their children, researchers have found it helpful to identify children who would qualify as success stories and children who would not. They do so using a variety of strategies called sociometric measures ("socio" meaning "with others," "metric" meaning "for measurement"). These strategies include observing children interacting with each other, asking children with whom they do and do not enjoy playing (and why), and interviewing adults who have opportunities to observe children in group settings (parents and teachers).

One thing these measures disclose is that children grade each other on two different dimensions. The first and most obvious is social preference. This dimension speaks to the degree to which other children do or do not look forward to inter-acting with a given child. If other children tend to do so, then the target child is high on this dimension.

The second, somewhat less obvious dimension is social impact. This term refers to the tendency of other children actually to have an opinion about the target child. In other words, a child may be well liked by those who notice him (high on prefer-ence), but simply not be noticed by very many kids (low on impact). Using these ways of analyzing the data, researchers have identified four categories of children.

POPULAR KIDS

Children, even toddlers, in the popular group are high on both the preference and impact dimensions. Other children *do* notice them, and the vast majority look for-ward to interacting with them. In other words, this is the child who seems to be a magnet for other kids: Wherever he goes, you can be sure others will follow. As we will discuss later, Baby Sunflower has an especially good chance of falling in this cat-egory, as does Baby Dandelion—at least if his zest for life is paired with self-control.

What distinguishes these kids from their peers? Children in the popular cate-gory tend to have these characteristics.

◆ **Advanced understanding of emotions.** The better able a child is to under-stand what makes people (including himself) happy, sad, angry, and so on, the more likely he is to be able to correctly read those emotions in other children.

◆ **High levels of empathy.** Simply being able to identify what another person is feeling is only half the battle. One also has to *care*. Empathetic children do care and, as a result, are more likely to express sympathy and try to help other children in need. Needless to say, that endears them to the children they help.

◆ **Well-developed "emotional self-regulation" skills.** These children have learned how to monitor and control their *own* emotions so that they don't completely un-wind when things get dicey. They think before they act, they are patient rather than impulsive, and they are willing to put the good of the group above their own desires.

◆ **Good language skills.** Being able to understand what others say and to com-municate your own thoughts clearly is a real boon to socializing with others—at *any* age. Research consistently shows that good language skills predict social competence as early as the toddler period.

◆ **Well-developed conflict resolution skills and a genuine interest in cooperating rather than controlling.** Figuring out how to resolve conflicts without coming to blows is particularly important during early childhood when one's peers aren't as likely to be able to do so. Kids who learn early on the advantages of cooperating with rather than controlling other people are appreciated by *everybody*—parents and teachers included.

◆ **A generally calm and friendly demeanor.** Basically, popular children tend to be temperamentally easygoing. They look on the bright side, expect the best of others, and are open to new people and new experiences.

Sharing doesn't come naturally to children. Here we see fourteen-month-old Kaia objecting to Gabriel's attempt to play with her toy. At this age, children are anything but subtle, preferring a direct approach—such as pulling on Gabriel's shoulder to get him to stop.

Sharing: When Self-Sacrifice Is the Name of the Game

"Now, Katherine, be nice and share with Josie." Sound familiar? Getting children voluntarily to give up control over something they value is not easy. Because it involves self-sacrifice, sharing doesn't come naturally and needs to be consciously fostered. Children have to be encouraged to share by caregivers who convince the child that the benefits of sharing outweigh its costs. Here's what sharing looks like over the first three years.

◆ **8 to 12 months.** Infants spontaneously share food with adults and hand them toys. Both actions are motivated by a desire to keep interactions going. In peer interactions, they will give away toys fairly easily. Even if a toy is actually snatched away by a peer, they usually don't understand enough to get upset.

◆ **12 to 24 months.** Willingness to share toys with other children actually increases during this period, as they learn that this is a good way to initiate or maintain play. This generosity reaches a peak at twenty to twenty-four months and then, unfortunately, begins a sharp decline that continues unless parents intervene. Why the decline? Twenty to twenty-four months is about the time when toddlers begin to experience self-awareness, an understanding of oneself as separate from other people. This knowledge is what fuels the frequently heard exclamation, "MINE!"

◆ **24 to 36 months.** Two- to three-year-old children will, however, usually share under two conditions: (1) when asked to by an adult they respect, or (2) when they perceive a direct benefit to themselves for doing so. This benefit often takes the form of keeping interactions going smoothly. They may at first refuse a peer's request, hoping he or she will give up, but then give in once it becomes clear that a conflict is in the offing. Obviously, there are dramatic individual differences among toddlers as to where this line is drawn, in part due to differences in how much conflicts bother them. For a child with an easygoing temperament, sharing for the sake of peace might be more attractive than for a child with a hair-trigger temper.

BOTTOM LINE FOR PARENTS?
Model sharing, suggest sharing, and reward sharing with love and praise. Suggest taking turns when you and your child play together or when conflicts arise between children. Do not, however, resort to bribery. Tangible rewards tend to backfire because kids continue to expect them rather than appreciating the intangible reward of your approval.

REJECTED KIDS

Rejected children are not faring nearly as well in the social arena as their popular peers. On the two dimensions researchers use, rejected children tend to be low on social preference (other children actively avoid interacting with them), but at the same time high on social impact (they are definitely noticed). Although all rejected kids have these characteristics in common, closer examination reveals two very different subcategories:

1. Rejected-aggressive kids. Unless help is on the way, rejected-aggressive children are in danger of getting into real trouble as they grow older. Why? Take a look at the characteristics that can be identified by age three:

   a. Strong desire to dominate, with force if necessary
   b. Inability (compared to peers) to manage their own emotions, positive *or* negative
   c. Little interest in or ability to cooperate
   d. Tendency to begin interactions from a hostile stance
   e. Strong tendency (compared to peers) to focus on self without regard to others' needs or desires

These children, in other words, are the classic bullies of literature and lore, making themselves unpopular by aggressively exerting their will over others regardless of the consequences. Unless helped to develop self-control and empathy for others, Baby Dandelion's high energy and devil-may-care attitude make him especially susceptible to falling into this category.

2. Rejected-withdrawn kids. In contrast, the children in the rejected-withdrawn subcategory are the classic victims, often picked on by bullies and deliberately snubbed by others. Rejected-withdrawn children know their peers don't like them, but simply don't know what to do about it. They tend to be...

   a. Immature and unskilled socially compared to their peers (lacking strategies for initiating, joining, or maintaining play with others)
   b. Insensitive to emotional nuances of interactions (unable to read or respond to peers' signals)
   c. Physically unattractive or different
   d. Desirous of acceptance, well aware of rejection, and therefore, often depressed

These children also need help. If they don't receive it, they are likely to continue to be the target of bullies, to feel lonely and isolated, and to suffer low self-esteem and depression even into adulthood. Unfortunately for Baby Orchid, her retiring and easily wounded temperament, especially when these traits keep her from gaining social skills, make her particularly vulnerable to falling into this category.

NEGLECTED KIDS

In addition to popular and rejected children, researchers have also highlighted a category called neglected children. The good news is that children in this category aren't particularly high or low on the social preference dimension. In other words, kids don't actively reject them. On the other hand, they don't notice them much either. As a result, neglected kids are on the periphery of activities but don't suffer nearly as many emotional consequences as rejected children. Neglected children tend to be . . .

◆ Shy around others; hesitant about initiating or joining activities
◆ Quiet rather than talkative
◆ Comfortable being in the periphery (although not terrified by being included); definitely not keen on being the center of attention

Sounds a lot like Baby Orchid, doesn't it? Baby Holly's prickly nature also can result in her being tagged with the neglected label because of the discomfort she naturally feels when confronting new social situations.

Fortunately, under the right circumstances, children in this category can find acceptance and enjoyment among their peers. It's just harder for them to come across the right circumstances on their own. Should they find even a single good friend, they can skate through childhood in relative comfort.

AVERAGE KIDS: THE REST

Researchers seldom resist the urge to categorize everyone, but in the case of social development they have. The truth is that not all children fall into these neat categories, some because they change from situation to situation, some because they just are in the middle on the two dimensions of social preference and social impact. Researchers refer to the approximately one-third of children who fit this description as average. And compared to the alternatives of rejected-aggressive and rejected-withdrawn, average isn't a bad place to be. (For parents interested in reading more about these categories, as well as what they portend in the later years, we recommend exploring the excellent work of three researchers: Steve Asher from Duke University, Bill Hartup from the University of Minnesota, and Jeff Parker from the Pennsylvania State University.)

N E W S   F L A S H!

Scientists Say, "Let the Games Begin—Early"

Los Angeles, California. It may look like a normal day in this Southern California child care center, but there's something new on the scene. Two young women are standing as inconspicuously as possible at the edges of the classroom, wearing earphones and armed with clipboards and pencils. As you look closely, you'll see them watch a certain toddler intently for five minutes, pausing every twenty seconds to make a note, and then, as soon as the five minutes are up, moving their gaze to another toddler.

What's going on? Researchers Carolee Howes and Catherine Matheson from UCLA can tell you. The unusual visitors to this toddler classroom are graduate students helping Howes and Matheson gather important information about how thirteen- to fifteen-month-old children interact with each other and whether the complexity of their play at these young ages predicts anything important about their futures. (In case you're wondering, the earphones play tones that tell the observers when the target times have elapsed, and the notes they take identify the type of play in which the observed child was engaged during that period.)

After following these same children for four years, the researchers had their answer. The results indicated that the way thirteen- to fifteen-month-old toddlers interact with playmates predicts social competence as judged by teachers at ages four and five. Specifically, the more these children engaged in games where they had to take turns or switch roles, such as rolling balls back and forth and playing peekaboo, the more sociable, less aggressive, and less withdrawn they were as preschoolers. Why? Games like these with complementary roles encourage children to play cooperatively rather than independently, thereby providing practice in negotiating rules, resolving conflicts, and paying attention to another person's feelings—all skills that pay off handsomely in social situations for years to come.

What Predicts Success?

Thanks to Howes and Matheson, parents now have a little bit more to go on in their quest to help their children develop good social skills. At least they know that it helps to encourage what we like to call "it takes two" games. Are there other discoveries like this that parents should know about? There sure are. Here are a few of the most important factors researchers have identified as contributors to social skill development, along with a quick reminder of the general role you can play in each case. (More specific tips and advice are included at the end of the chapter.) Many of the predictors correspond to characteristics found among popular children.

TEMPERAMENT: MAKING BOUQUETS WITH SOME FLOWERS IS EASIER THAN WITH OTHERS

Remember those four flowers that we used to represent the four basic inborn temperaments? They included Baby Sunflower (the "Easy" baby), Baby Holly (the "Difficult" baby), Baby Orchid (the "Slow-to-Warm" baby), and Baby Dandelion (the "Active" baby). These temperamental qualities clearly influence a child's style of interacting with other children and, therefore, long-term sociability. Here's how the four temperamental styles tend to play themselves out.

◆ **Baby Sunflower.** Nothing like getting off to a good start. All the characteristics that qualify a child for the title "Easy" baby are directly applicable to the wider social world. After all, if being easy to please, moderate in reactions, and generally good-natured endear a baby to parents, why wouldn't the same be true for peers? Having a pleasing temperament at birth isn't a guarantee, of course, but it sure starts the ball rolling in a positive direction. The best thing for parents to do is simply to make sure Baby Sunflower continues to view the world through rose-colored glasses.

Linda's son Kai, on the left, is thrilled at having made a new friend. Somewhat shy in social situations, Kai found that he could genuinely enjoy them if he had at least one buddy by his side.

◆ **Baby Holly.** Unfortunately, the "prickly" temperament of the "Difficult" baby puts a child at risk for difficulties interacting with other children. The problem arises because the tendencies to be hard to please and easily upset, which often test the patience of parents, are especially difficult for young children, lacking in social savvy themselves, to deal with. Mom may be willing to walk on eggshells around Baby Holly, but it's a safe bet that Baby Holly's peers won't be. The best way for parents to help their own Baby Holly is with patience, a calm disposition, and lots and lots of love from the time she's born. This is easy to say, but often very challenging to do. Parents need to keep in mind that the overall goal is to help Baby Holly learn to *trust* other people, and building that trust inevitably starts with learning that one's parents can be counted on to stick it out—even when the going is rough. (See Chapter 2 for specific tips on helping your baby develop a strong attachment. Specific tips for helping Baby Holly develop friendships follow at the end of this chapter.)

◆ **Baby Orchid.** Parents have a particularly important and direct role to play in helping Baby Orchid warm up to opportunities to interact with other children. Any unfamiliar situation can make Baby Orchid cautious, but add the rough-and-tumble that naturally arises when two or more toddlers convene and you're almost guaranteed to find Baby Orchid tenaciously holding on to Mom's or Dad's leg! What to do? Let's start with what *not* to do. There is nothing but additional trouble to be gained by forcing "Slow-to-Warm" children into the fray before they are ready. Trust us on that. Instead, acknowledge their feelings and look for ways to ease them into interactions. Provide lots of practice by arranging one-on-one playdates in the familiar turf of your home. Have the same children visit more than once so that Baby Orchid gets to know what to expect from particular kids. Remember, "Slow-to-Warm" children value being able to predict events, so the more they know in advance about an upcoming interaction, the faster they will thaw out. (For many more tips on how to deal with "Slow-to-Warm" children, see Chapter 7.)

◆ **Baby Dandelion.** Really active children like Baby Dandelion find themselves at a genuine fork in the road when it comes to dealing with peers. Things can either go in a very positive direction or in a very negative direction—and which road is taken is heavily influenced by parents. Basically, the high energy levels of the Baby Dandelions of this world, if balanced by as much self-control and sensitivity to others as they can muster, make them much-sought-after playmates. Their energy is intoxicating, their excitement contagious, and their zeal for trying new things is inspiring. If they haven't been helped to temper their exuberance, however, then their tendency to unwind situations to the point of chaos can make them very *un*popular among their peers. The best way to prevent this negative outcome is for parents to help Baby Dandelion develop the ability to regulate (control) his emotions and impulses as soon as possible. (See Chapter 10 for specific tips on promoting effortful control.)

OTHER PREDICTORS OF SOCIAL ACCEPTANCE

Emotional "Savvy." In Chapter 3 we talked about the importance of helping children understand what emotions are about—what causes them, how to identify their own, how to control them, and how to interpret emotional cues from

A Clever Study of Nature and Nurture

Question: Is "sociability" inherited? If Mom and Dad prefer to stay to themselves rather than socialize with other people, is it likely that their children will inherit that bias?

Answer: Researchers Denise Daniels and Robert Plomin say the answer is yes—and no. Before you roll your eyes and mutter "What else is new?" consider how they came to this conclusion. What Daniels and Plomin did was look closely at a very special group of children—adoptees. Children who are adopted actually have two sets of parents: their biological parents, with whom they share genes (and from whom they inherit traits), and their adoptive parents, with whom they share an environment. By determining how sociable the children turned out to be and then comparing the results to how sociable the two sets of parents were, the researchers were able to show that both nature and nurture have a role to play. But most encouraging was the additional discovery that the influence of the adoptive parents was the stronger of the two. The children were somewhat similar in sociability to their biological parents but even more similar in sociability to their adoptive parents. In other words, as we are fond of saying, "Biology is *not* destiny." A child's specific experiences in life make a difference in how sociable or unsociable he turns out to be.

others. Research consistently shows that children who are good at these things are significantly more likely to be rated popular by their peers. Fortunately, as we also point out in Chapter 3, there's a good deal that parents can do to foster emotional savvy even during the first three years.

Empathy. It's all fine and dandy to be able to identify what one's peers are feeling, but it also matters a great deal whether you *care*. Children who do care, who not only read emotions well but also genuinely want other children to feel good rather than bad, are highly valued by their peers. (See Chapter 4 for tips on promoting the development of empathy.)

Language Skills. As soon as children begin to talk, they start trying to communicate with each other—using words to initiate interactions, structure play, and express feelings. Children with good language skills, therefore, generally make more interesting playmates. They are also less likely to be aggressive. If a child can express needs and desires in words (or signs), he is less likely to resort to hitting and biting. As a result, he is also much less scary to be around and will tend to be more popular with his peers. Parents who are interested in fostering social skills, therefore, can indirectly help things along by encouraging language development. (See our book *Baby Signs* for information about the positive effects of signing on learning to talk.)

Sheer Exposure. Just as you can't learn to play tennis without swinging a tennis racket, a child can't learn to be socially skilled without opportunities to interact with other children. Experiences with siblings help, but because the power structure usually is determined by the relative ages of the siblings, a child also needs exposure to the more equal status relationships provided by children outside the family. (See the box on page 125 for tips on planning playdates.)

Language tends to play a larger role in little girls' friendships, in part because they tend to develop language skills faster than little boys. These two playmates, labeled "the little chatterboxes" by their parents, are no exception.

Parenting Style. Parents who direct every move, speak for their children, hover conspicuously over their interactions, jump in to resolve conflicts at the first hint of trouble, and criticize rather than encourage are likely to have children who find social interactions difficult and unrewarding. The trick is to support but not control, listen and suggest but not command, provide interactions with other children but not be intrusive, and let your child speak for herself—as long as what is said isn't hurtful toward others.

How Would You Feel If . . . ?

It's not unusual these days for busy parents of toddlers to use drop-in babysitting services at gyms, malls, resorts, and churches. It's also not unusual for toddlers to protest, clinging to Mom's or Dad's leg for dear life while the parent tries to "peel" the child off and get out the door. Are these parents being knowingly cruel? No. As harried parents look around, what they see is a room with great toys, kind caregivers, and lively playmates—all of which is true. But what the toddler sees may be very different. To help you understand what such a situation can feel like to a toddler, consider this scenario.

Imagine you are visiting a friend in Paris. Fortunately, she speaks English because your French is limited to "croissant," "crepe," and "poodle." Your friend is a great hostess and you're having a wonderful time until she suddenly turns her car into the driveway of a house you've never seen before. Still chatting about the hike to the top of the Eiffel Tower that has left you tired and sore, she hurries you through the front door and into what is clearly a cocktail party already in high gear. Then things go from bad to worse. As you look around at all the strangers speaking French, she suddenly announces, "I've got to run an errand and I need you to stay here until I get back. Look at all the nice people and all the yummy hors d'oeuvres. I'm sure you'll have a great time. Now, be sure to be nice to everybody. Bye!"

Admit it. Suddenly being in the midst of strangers who don't know either you or your language is unlikely to be your idea of a good time. Now don't you have a bit more sympathy for your toddler?

Words of Wisdom and Tricks of the Trade

Here are a few tips to help you help your child conquer the wider world of children with ease and enthusiasm.

KNOW YOUR CHILD

◆ **Typical reactions to novelty.** Think about how your child deals *in general* with novelty and identify any other temperamental qualities that might affect his ability to interact with peers. Forewarned is forearmed.

◆ **Typical reactions to other children.** Observe your child carefully in a variety of situations where other children are present. Does she react differently with familiar kids compared with unfamiliar kids? Familiar settings compared with unfamiliar settings? With one other child compared with many children? Use these observations to decide if there are any areas in which she might need a little help to expand her comfort zone and how you might best provide it.

KNOW THYSELF

◆ **Reflect back on your own childhood.** What kind of experiences with peers did you have as a child? Can you see yourself representative of any of the categories recent research has identified? Remembering your own peer experiences may provide insights into why you react to your child's social experiences the way you do.

◆ **Talk with your spouse.** Do you and your spouse agree about whether a problem exists? If not, it may be because of differences in how you each view the importance of interactions with other people. For example, a father who prefers to be on the periphery of groups may be less concerned about a child who seems to be falling into the neglected category than a mother who enjoys being the belle of the ball. Talking things over can help ease concerns and/or spur parents to unified action.

PROVIDE OPPORTUNITIES TO PLAY WITH OTHER CHILDREN

◆ **Choose your neighborhood carefully.** When deciding where to live, give serious consideration to the availability of potential playmates for your child. Having friends close by will simplify your life.

◆ **Take advantage of classes.** Join classes that cater to parents and children together, such as exercise, music, or Sign, Say & Play™ classes.

◆ **Arrange playdates.** Whether your child is enrolled in child care or not, arrange playdates. The beauty of arranging for someone else's child to come to your own house to play is that you get to hand-pick the child, select the activities, and monitor the play. The beauty for your child is that it all takes place on familiar turf with her best friend (you!) available as a safety net.

How to Make the Most of Playdates

Inviting other children to your home to play with your child is an excellent way to foster friendships. You're not going to reach this goal, however, if the interactions are dominated by tears and tantrums. Here are some tips for creating a successful playdate.

◆ **Choose the playmate carefully.** Choose the playmate with your *child's* needs in mind, not your own. Just because you enjoy a child's parent doesn't mean his or her child is an appropriate choice.

◆ **Match your child.** To the extent you can, look for playmates who are a reasonable match to your child in energy level, play preferences, language skills, and emotional and cognitive sophistication. Doing so will make it easier for the children to interact in a manner that makes your child want to repeat the experience.

◆ **Foster ongoing relationships.** When you find a playmate that your child enjoys, keep the relationship going. Toddlers who know each other well tend to play at more mature levels, perhaps because they no longer need to waste time on the "preliminaries" and have learned to trust each other.

◆ **Keep dates brief.** Keep the playdates relatively short at first. That way you increase the chance that the children will end the session *wanting* to get back together. One hour is a reasonable length to begin with.

◆ **Make toy and activity plans in advance.**

  ◆ **Have the playmate bring toys.** Have the visiting child bring along some of her own toys so that both children can have the experience of sharing with others and enjoying new toys.

box continues on next page

BE A GOOD ROLE MODEL

◆ **Be sociable yourself.** Children are sponges, soaking up information from watching the big people around them. Take advantage of this tendency by making it a point to interact frequently with other people in your child's presence. Invite other families for backyard barbeques, attend church picnics, join family-oriented clubs, start a neighborhood get-together, and so on.

- ◆ **Decide on "off-limits toys."** Have older toddlers decide what they absolutely do *not* want to share and have them put those items away.

- ◆ **Provide some identical toys.** Try to provide at least a few identical toys so the children can imitate each other's play behaviors. Watch for evidence of imitation and congratulate them. For example, "Josh stacked three blocks and you stacked three blocks. That's great!" The other advantage, of course, is that children are less likely to fight over something when they each have their own version.

- ◆ **Supervise, but indirectly.** Research by developmental psychologists Gary Ladd and Beckie Golter found that children whose parents watched from afar were better liked than those whose parents intruded on their play.

- ◆ **Use distraction.** If the children begin to fight over a toy, try to distract them before it escalates and threatens to unwind the whole situation. If necessary, put the toy away, explaining why you have done so.

- ◆ **Suggest "it-takes-two" games.** As your toddler gets a bit older, be on the lookout for activities that involve imitation but still take two children to play. Rolling a ball back and forth, playing on a teeter-totter, or a game of follow the leader are age-old favorites that fit the bill. In such cases, the name of the game is cooperation plus imitation, and the lesson learned is that playing with others is both more fun and more effective than playing alone. Gradually move on to games that require complementary roles—where each person has a slightly different role to play (examples are tag, hide-and-seek, pretend scenarios, builder and knocker-down).

- ◆ **Teach turn-taking skills.** Take an active role in helping children take turns when they are playing with each other. Verbalize the principles ("First it's Jesse's turn and then it's your turn.") Be sure to notice when they manage it themselves, and pour on the congratulations.

◆ **Model specific social skills.** Watch your child to see if he is having trouble in specific situations and model behaviors that might be helpful. For example, if your child has trouble joining existing groups of children, partner with him occasionally and demonstrate appropriate ice-breakers. Talk about what you did later in the day.

USE YOUR OWN PLAYTIMES TO ADVANTAGE

◆ **Play imitation games.** Look for opportunities to imitate your child's actions. Even a two-month-old makes interesting noises and faces. If she makes a raspberry sound with her mouth, try it yourself and watch her response. If she sticks out her tongue, follow her lead. Continue creating imitation games as she grows older, being sure to narrate the fun with words yourself until she can take over. ("First me, then you.") Adding words will help your child's language development and also make it clearer to her what the rules of imitative exchanges are. Playing with her in this way will show her the pleasure to be had in imitation games and allow her to practice her partnership skills.

◆ **Initiate turn-taking games.** Help your child learn to play and enjoy turn-taking games by initiating them yourself. Or encourage an older sibling to do so. Be creative. Games as simple as "I tickle you, you tickle me" or "I put the diaper on my head and you take it off" are good lessons in cooperation and mutual enjoyment.

◆ **Encourage pretend play.** Keeping in mind that being good at pretend play is a social asset, look for opportunities to initiate this kind of play for the two of you.

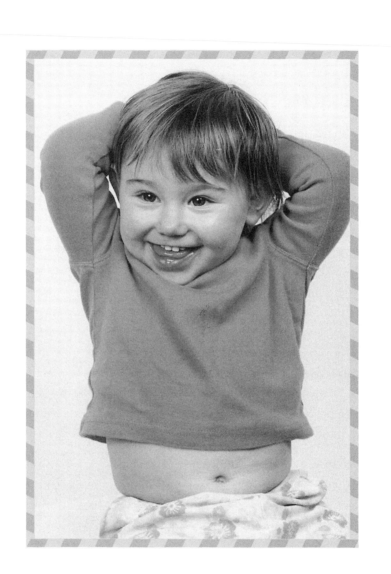

6

I Can Do Anything:
Having Self-Esteem and
Self-Confidence

N E W S   F L A S H !

What's Trivial to You May Mean Triumph to Your Baby

Rahway, New Jersey. It may not be quite as headline-worthy as a hole in one on the golf course or winning the Pillsbury Bake-Off, but to three-month-old Malcolm, the ringing of those plastic bells over his head is music to his ears in more ways than one. Yes, the sound is lovely, but lovelier still is the satisfaction of having been the one who figured out how to make it happen. You heard right. Malcolm may be a tiny baby, but that doesn't mean he's not able—no, eager—to solve simple problems. And how did he do it? Well, the truth is he did have a little help from researchers Carolyn Rovee-Collier and her colleagues at Rutgers University. They are the ones who suggested to Malcolm's mom, Alisha, that she take a soft ribbon and simply tie one end to the bells and the other end to Malcolm's foot. "At first when he moved his foot and the bells began to ring, he looked startled," says Alisha. "But within minutes it was off to the races. He just kept kicking that foot over and over, hardly taking his eyes off those bells long enough to blink!"

Rovee-Collier's discovery that babies as young as two to three months find great satisfaction in solving simple problems came as no surprise to Stanford psychologist

Albert Bandura. It fits perfectly with his theory that feelings of accomplishment, one of the hallmarks of self-confidence, are as important to babies as they are to adults. The entire first year, in fact, is a prime time for the development of what Bandura calls a sense of self-efficacy. This is essentially the I-did-it! sensation that accompanies having made something desirable happen. Anyone who's watched a baby work hard to roll over, sit up, or finally crawl knows what he means.

Besides learning to control his body, how does an infant come by such self-affirming experiences? There are two important sources, both under the control of parents. The first of these, like Malcolm's bells, involves providing infants with age-appropriate activities and toys that challenge them to figure how to make something happen. The second potential source involves interactions with people. When baby smiles at Dad and he smiles back, baby feels not only happy but also successful. When baby signals he's hungry and Mom delivers the needed food, the result is not only a full tummy, but also a sense of self as an effective agent. According to Bandura, both "people mastery" experiences like these and "task mastery" experiences like Malcolm's lay an important foundation for future self-confidence and self-esteem.

Why Self-Esteem Is So Important

Lately the word *self-esteem* has been the victim of bad press. Ever since the 1970s, when educational experts in California pronounced it a high priority, an increasing number of voices have expressed the suspicion that "pandering" to a child's self-esteem is responsible for the "fact" that the younger generation just isn't measuring up to our expectations. (Of course, what younger generation ever does?) Frequently cited sins include increased laziness, contentment with shoddy performance, lack of ambition, and inflated egos. Will global warming be the next addition to the list?

As we hope to make clear in this chapter of *Baby Hearts*, no matter what these pundits say, healthy self-esteem is *not* synonymous with self-centeredness, arrogance, or a tendency to expect the world to be delivered on a platter. Nor does its development require shielding a child from disappointment, frustration, or failure. That's neither possible nor desirable. On the contrary, feeling good about themselves helps children deal constructively with life's small setbacks and simply get on with things. In general, children high in self-esteem greet new challenges with enthusiasm and take pride in achieving goals. As a result, when coupled with other goals of good parenting—like the development of empathy, emotional self-regulation, and moral values—high self-esteem results in children who are more, rather than less, likely to live productive, emotionally satisfying lives. They have more friends, do better in school, think more creatively, suffer less frequently from depression, and generally feel more optimistic about life. What parent wouldn't want a list of attributes like this to describe his or her child? How their children evaluate themselves should be high on every parent's list of concerns.

PIECES OF THE PUZZLE

Although it's convenient to speak in global terms about self-esteem—as if there were one "number" that adequately describes where a child lies on some self-esteem meter—the reality is much more complicated. Instead of one number, there are lots of little numbers, each reflecting how confident or nonconfident a child feels in regard to specific subareas of her life at a particular point in time. In broad terms, the pieces of the self-esteem puzzle traditionally are said to include these confidence areas.

♦ **Task-related confidence (feeling capable and competent).** Beginning soon after birth with the task mastery described in the news flash, this category gradually expands to include almost any activity related to the general theme of "This is how the world works." As children get older and begin formal schooling, this category is the one that will include self-esteem in the realm of traditional academics. (Task-related confidence covers such a broad array of skills that we had no trouble filling an entire book—*Baby Minds: Brain-Building Games Your Baby Will Love*—with tips for fostering this aspect of your child's self-esteem during the critical first three years.)

♦ **Physical confidence (feeling adept physically).** We all know children who would rather climb the bookshelves than sit and read the books. Chances are very good that these children are starting off high on the physical dimension of self-esteem. As the years go by and their bodies mature, children high on this dimension of self-esteem may be drawn to athletics, dance, or other activities that require good coordination.

♦ **Social confidence (feeling comfortable with others).** This component of self-esteem includes a child's feelings about how well or poorly she fares when required

A child can feel good or bad about herself in regard to a variety of domains, one of which is called task-related confidence. Here seventeen-month-old Michaelan reflects this kind of pride in having accomplished her goal of stacking three big blocks on top of each other.

to interact with people outside her immediate family. Feeling comfortable in this arena is absolutely critical to a child's emotional well-being. That's why the whole of Chapter 5 was devoted to helping your child develop healthy friendships.

♦ **Emotional confidence (feeling worthy of love).** If any of these subcomponents is closer than the others to the "core" of a child's self-esteem, it's this one. In contrast to social confidence, with its emphasis on people outside the family, emotional confidence results directly from interactions inside the family—and particularly with parents during the earliest years of a child's life. What's at stake in these interactions is nothing less than whether a child feels *lovable*. As we explained in detail in Chapter 2, if children do feel lovable, it's inevitably the result of enjoying a secure attachment bond with their parents—or, in other words, having a secure emotional home base from which to explore the wider world.

Baby Hearts in Action:
There's Even Pride in Being *Almost* There

Sometimes self-esteem comes in strange packages. An incident with Linda's daughter, Kate, provides a good example of an unexpected source of pride.

Linda, an ardent supporter of breastfeeding whenever possible, had managed to nurse Kate well into her second year. The time eventually came, however, to begin the process of weaning her. Linda took it slowly, cutting back first one feeding and then another until, just as Kate turned two, she was down to one feeding before bed. Soon thereafter, they went to visit Kate's grandmother, who, over dinner, asked how the process was going. "Very well," answered Linda. "She's practically weaned"— whereupon Kate stood up proudly in her chair and echoed the good news, announcing to one and all, "Yup! Me practically beaned!"

Steps Along the Way

Although development within each of the four domains just described proceeds at different paces, a few developmental milestones are relevant to them all. These milestones mark important transitions in the ability to experience pride, be aware of failure, and understand the nature of competition. Here are the highlights.

◆ **Birth to 18 months.** The first year and a half of life is really an age of innocence when it comes to issues of self-evaluation. The reason is simple: Children don't *do* any. You'll see what we mean as we review the three separate issues: pride, failure, and competition.

　　◆ **Pride.** Like little Malcolm who enjoyed mastering his bells, children for the first eighteen months solve problems for the pure joy of doing so. (Don't you wish it stayed that way?) Although it's clear from the smiles on their faces that they are happy when they succeed, they don't expect reactions from other people and don't seek them out in any purposeful way.

　　◆ **Failure.** Because they are motivated solely by the internal desire to master a task, their inability to do so is more accurately described in terms of frustration rather than failure. Unlike older children, children of this age have no sense of embarrassment or shame, only brief annoyance, and they quickly move on to other activities.

- **Competition.** Children in this early period have no sense of competition. Until the end of this period they aren't even cognizant of their existence as independent entities separate from other participants in activities. Think about it. If you aren't even aware of Johnny as a separate individual with behaviors of his own, how likely is it that you're going to worry about whether he'll beat you or not? Not very.

- **18 to 36 months.** Everything changes with the dawning of a sense of self—the awareness of oneself as an individual separate from all those other people out there. For the first time, children begin to care about how other people view their behaviors. This change, obviously, has important implications for how children experience both success and failure.

  - **Pride.** Children still are motivated mainly by a desire to master challenges, and their new sense of self results in a strong desire to exert their independence by finding and conquering as many challenges as possible. Whether it's putting on their own shoes or fastening their own car seat belts, the common theme is "Mommy, I'd rather do it *myself*!" In contrast to the former period, however, they now also seek recognition for their successes from others (almost always adults). For example, instead of just smiling when they succeed, they often also purposefully make eye contact, sometimes arching their eyebrows as if to ask "Did you see that? Isn't that cool what I just did?" The pleasure they feel when you agree constitutes the seeds of true pride.

  - **Failure.** On the downside, their new sense of self and the accompanying awareness of other people also make them sensitive to the fact that failures on their part are sometimes met with disapproval. As a result, an inability to complete a task may lead them to turn away and avoid eye contact with their adult partners. (Notice that peers still aren't heavy players in these evaluative situations.)

  - **Competition.** Children of this age still are enjoying comparative freedom from the competitive spirit that lurks around the developmental corner. Although interested in their own successes and failures, they remain oblivious to the successes or failures of others. They see the people around them, particularly adults, as sources of approval or disapproval but not as rivals. This all changes when peers become a more salient part of their everyday landscape.

"Is That a Red Dot I See Before Me?"

Throughout *Baby Hearts*, you will see reference to an important change that takes place between eighteen and twenty-four months in children's knowledge of themselves. Researchers refer to this change as the dawning of a sense of self. What they mean is that the child is finally awake to the knowledge of his existence as an actual entity in the world, a person who is totally separate from, but capable of interacting with, other independent people. But how do researchers determine when this invisible line gets crossed? After all, eighteen- to twenty-four-month-olds aren't very good at filling out questionnaires.

Developmental psychologists Michael Lewis and Jeanne Brooks-Gunn have found a way that they call the "Rouge Test." The idea is that without a sense of self, individuals won't understand that they are actually looking at *themselves* when they look in a mirror. Instead, they'll perceive the reflection to be someone else. In other words, they won't show evidence of self-recognition. What Lewis and Brooks-Gunn do to test a toddler's self-recognition is remarkably simple. They instruct children's mothers to surreptitiously leave a spot of rouge on their child's nose while casually wiping the child's face. Then the mothers place their child in front of a mirror, and the researchers watch to see if the child notices the rouge *and touches her nose*. If she does, then she must be relating the image to herself.

Interestingly, cultural anthropologists have found that this method works even with children who have never seen mirrors. And the findings are the same: Self-recognition clocks in between eighteen and twenty-four months, in large part, scientists suspect, the result of advances in neurological development.

◆ **3 to 4 years.** An important development takes place around three years of age in the way children think and talk about themselves. Researchers call it the beginning of the categorical self. By age three, children have been around other people enough to have noticed the various ways that people differ from one another—the categories into which their characteristics fall. Except for a few very basic psychological dimensions, like "good" versus "bad," most of these categories are based on easily observed characteristics, such as age, gender, size, physical attributes, and activities. These dimensions provide the labels children can now

The young baby in this photo is enjoying playing with the baby in the mirror, but without the sense of self that develops between eighteen and twenty-four months, he doesn't realize that baby is him.

apply to themselves. For example, a three-year-old boy might say, "I'm a big boy," or "I'm a ballplayer." For the first time, children are thinking about themselves in comparison to others (for example, babies, girls, and non-ball-playing children). These social comparisons, however, tend to be descriptive rather than evaluative, although we do see the first hints of *self*-evaluation in the three areas of pride, failure, and competition.

- **Pride.** The description of self in terms of observable characteristics enables children to carry around in their minds specific expectations for themselves. They have internalized crude standards and feel good when they meet their goals. This feeling good after having done well is the mark of genuine *pride*. Children can give *themselves* a pat on the back even if no one else is around to do it.

- **Failure.** Again there's a downside. Not only can children of this age feel genuine pride; they also can feel genuine shame. If they haven't lived up to the simple standards they have set for themselves, they feel bad—even if there are no witnesses.

- **Competition.** With the advent of crude social comparisons comes the first hint of competition. Children begin to view peers, with whom they are spending more and more time, as rivals. How do we know that competitiveness has begun? Simply by comparing the facial expressions of children who come in first in some event with those who come in second. The smiles of the winners are definitely bigger than the smiles of the losers.

◆ **5+ years.** Think about the play activities that children enjoy in kindergarten and the early elementary school years—tag, races, hopscotch, jacks, board games, two-person video games, little league, and gymnastics—and you'll begin to get a sense of the growing role played by comparison to peers in determining a child's self-esteem. What do all of these activities have in common? Somebody wins and somebody loses. Influenced in part by entry into formal school with its emphasis on grades, children are shifting away from what researchers call learning goals, in which the goal is mastery for its own sake, to performance goals, where the emphasis is on outdoing everybody else. This shift has obvious implications for pride, failure, and competition.

- **Pride.** If a child's self-esteem is off to a good start in the four domains listed at the beginning of this chapter, then pride will be a common emotion. What is changing is the proportion of time generated by besting someone else (performance goals) rather than doing something well for its own sake (learning goals). Wise parents strive to support the latter goals rather than the former as frequently as possible.

- **Failure.** Because children's activities are more and more likely to be governed by performance goals where winning is all, failure is not only more obvious than at earlier ages, but also harder to take. Indeed, once a winner has been declared in a contest, children tend to give up immediately rather than continue striving to see what they themselves can accomplish. What's more, if a child is *never* the winner in a domain where success is synonymous with beating everyone else (grades, spelling bees, gymnastics contests, etc.), there is a good chance he will simply stop even trying to do well. As evidence of the importance of success, psychologists H. W. Marsh and K. T. Hau recently proved that it is, indeed, better to be a big fish in a little pond (that is, the best out of a few) rather than a little fish in a big pond (far from the top out of a big group).

◆ **Competition.** Competition is clearly what performance goals are all about. Although cultures vary in what is gained by winning or losing a contest (see box on page 144), there are few children in this world who don't start incorporating the results of competition into their self-concepts after age five. Whether it's about who wins a game, who has the biggest birthday party, who sells the most cookies, or who ends up with the most candy at Halloween, the bottom line is that children, like all the rest of us, inevitably find ways to compete. Wise parents make sure the criteria for winning are positive ones when competition is inevitable (who's the kindest rather than who's the most intimidating) and support learning goals with their emphasis on effort and self-satisfaction whenever possible.

NEWS FLASH!

Foster Pride by Letting Directing Credit Go to Baby

Los Angeles, California. We all know parents who overmanage their children, parents who cram their children's schedules with everything from acrobatics to zoological expeditions. What these children lose, according to developmental psychologist Deborah Stipek and her colleagues at UCLA, is not only free time, but also the opportunity to pick their own goals and decide which are worth tackling. It turns out that giving children a chance to choose their own goals is important even for infants and toddlers, especially if parents want their children to develop pride in their accomplishments. In one of Stipek's studies in particular, children ages thirteen to thirty-nine months were observed playing with their mothers. The researchers discovered that when children in this age range were allowed to choose their own goals during play, they were much more likely to revel in their own successes. They showed pride in their accomplishments, calling attention to their success and smiling and clapping for themselves. Children whose mothers were more intrusive, directing their activities toward parent-determined goals, were less likely to display positive emotions and more likely simply to look up at their mothers when they accomplished something (as if to ask "Did I do okay?"). The difference, of course, is that the children whose mothers were less intrusive weren't looking to others for validation. In contrast, they appeared to know instantly when they had something to be proud of.

Predicting Success

As Deborah Stipek's work demonstrates, researchers have uncovered facts about the very earliest stages of self-esteem that can help parents get their children off to a good start. Here are some other predictors of success.

A SECURE ATTACHMENT BOND

All researchers agree that the single most important thing you can do to foster high self-esteem and self-confidence in your child is to ensure that his relationship to you is steeped in love, affection, and trust—in other words, forge a secure attachment bond. As we pointed out in Chapter 2, a child who feels loved, protected, and important to his parents just naturally develops a positive view of himself and an optimistic perspective on the world. New people, new places, and new challenges aren't nearly as scary when one *expects* things to go well and has a secure home base to which to retreat on the off-chance that they don't. The security of that home base also means that failures don't jeopardize the love a child receives; parental love is steady and unconditional. Feeling assured on that score lowers anxiety that might interfere with a child's doing well.

APPROPRIATE RESPONSES TO SUCCESS AND FAILURE

Research shows that everyone's self-esteem, toddlers' included, is based on how they answer these two questions:

1. Do I have the *ability* to reach this goal?
2. If I really make an *effort*, will I reach this goal?

These two questions may sound the same, but they're really not. For example, you may approach learning to play golf with confidence because you feel you are good at sports. Or you may not think you have any natural talent but are willing to work hard, confident that your efforts will pay off.

Obviously the best outcome is to have a child feel that the answer to both questions is yes. Unfortunately, that doesn't always happen. So how do you, as a parent, work toward the goal of having your child feel both competent and willing to work hard? It's simple:

1. You hone your parenting skills (improve your *ability*).
2. You really make an *effort*—in this case to watch what you say and do when your child succeeds or fails. (Sound familiar?)

The advice we're about to give to help you hone your parenting skills is based on the work of many researchers, but in particular on discoveries made by psychologist Carol Dweck from Columbia University. After she assessed children from preschool age to middle-school age in many different situations, two groups of children stood out—those children who tended to say yes to both questions and those who tended to say no to both. These tendencies, moreover, were apparent in children as young as four years old. Having categorized the children, Dweck then looked to see what kinds of parenting each group had experienced.

The moment I decided to follow instead of lead, I discovered the joys of becoming part of a small child's world.

—Janet Gonzalez-Mena, educator

Mastery Orientation. Dweck described the first group—the "yes" sayers—as "mastery oriented" because they approached a broad range of challenges with every intention of mastering them. Children in this group typically attributed success to basic competence ("I'm pretty good at that sort of thing") and failure not to a deficit in ability, but to factors that would be easy to fix—like working harder. They also believed that one's basic competence wasn't fixed for all time but could be increased little by little through working hard.

And what kind of parenting strategy predicted this outcome? Just what you might expect. When these children succeeded at something, their parents praised both their ability ("Wow! Good job! You're sure good at climbing") *and* their willingness to work hard ("I was proud of how hard you worked to get to the top!"). Even more important, however, was the fact that these parents were also warm and affectionate in the face of failure, going out of their way to assure their children that trying again, perhaps in a slightly different way, could make all the difference. In other words, they communicated that failure was caused by something the child could fix.

Learned Helplessness Orientation. The second group of children—the "no" sayers—reacted very differently to their successes and failures. If they "happened" to succeed, they tended to treat it as a fluke, as the result of outside help, or as a consequence of working hard that one time. It didn't seem to enter their heads that they might be inherently good at things. In other words, they didn't seem to experience the pride that comes from viewing themselves as competent. The result was that they seldom *expected* to succeed and, therefore, often didn't—thus

Baby Hearts in Action:
The Case of the Revolving Sweater

The old adage "If at first you don't succeed, try, try again" has been a touchstone for Susan's adorable granddaughter Leanne since the day she was born. Here's one of the most memorable examples of her tenacity in Susan's own words, one that clearly shows the importance of achieving a goal as a cornerstone of self-esteem:

"Of course, there are many I-do-it stories involving Leanne. Perhaps the funniest was when, at eighteen months, she tried to put on her sweater by herself, got one arm in, and then turned around and around in circles trying to get her other arm in. Unfortunately, as she turned, her sleeve turned with her body and stayed exactly the same distance away. We kept offering help, but she would not let us touch her and insisted 'I do it!' She finally got so dizzy that she fell down. Even then she persisted. Fortunately, now that the sweater couldn't move, she finally succeeded—and from down on the floor we all heard, once again, her favorite phrase, but this time full of pride: 'I do it!' "

contributing to a general feeling of helplessness in the face of challenges and the descriptor "learned helplessness" coined by Dweck.

And what kinds of parental reactions to success and failure had these children received? Certainly different ones from those experienced by the first group. Just as their children eventually learned to do, these parents greeted success with surprise, saying things that suggested it was due to temporary factors such as luck, outside intervention, easiness of the task, or hard work this one time. Missing here, obviously, is any reference to a belief in the child's basic competence. When these children failed, things got even worse. Finally their parents mentioned ability—but only to throw it into question. Sometimes the message was downright mean, expressing clear irritation at the child's failure ("See? I knew you wouldn't be able to do that!"). Other times, however, the parent meant well but still ended up emphasizing the failure instead of the potential for future success ("Don't worry. Lots of kids aren't good at climbing"). Whether mean-spirited or not, the two messages both imply that there's not much point in trying again, that effort is irrelevant. That's the kind of message you should make every effort to avoid. If you've failed to avoid them in the past, our message to you is the same as your message to your children should be: *Try, try again!*"

REALISTIC EXPECTATIONS

Expecting more out of children than they are capable of delivering—and the resultant disappointment that is hard to hide—is another sure-fire way to start children doubting their own self-worth. That's why just reading this book is a step toward fostering healthy self-esteem in your infant or toddler. The more you know about what is typical in development, the more realistic your expectations will be. Knowing, for example, that some children are just naturally more cautious than others can prevent you from communicating disappointment when your child doesn't jump into things with both feet. Similarly, once you understand that exerting independence—including some forms of outright defiance—is a natural part of a toddler's emotional journey, the more likely you are to deal with such occasions with patience and appropriate actions instead of anger and frustration. Your ability to deal firmly but affectionately with your child under these conditions will help her learn more constructive approaches to problems and, in this way, contribute to the development of her self-esteem.

How parents react to a child's failure can have a huge impact on self-esteem. Giving this discouraged little boy a hug, assuring him that you're proud of him for trying, and encouraging him to try again is the best tactic. Wrong tactic? "I knew it would be too hard."

Words of Wisdom and Tricks of the Trade

The research we've already discussed has provided lots of general guidance to help you support development of self-esteem and self-confidence in your child. Here are some additional, more specific suggestions for how to develop your child's positive expectations about herself (while keeping your own expectations in check!).

◆ **Know thyself.** Keeping in mind that infants and toddlers are keen observers of the adults they love, take a close look at your own attitudes and interactions with others. Ask yourself these questions:

◆ Do you expect your children to live out your dreams? Sometimes this tendency translates into having very rigid ideas of what successes count and

"Who Am I?": The Answer Depends on *Where* You Ask It

Thanks to recent advances in communication technologies, it's easier than ever before for scientists around the world to talk to each other. As a result, we are learning more each day about interesting differences among cultures in how they perceive the world, what values they hold dearest—and how they translate all this into raising their children. One fascinating difference uncovered by psychologist S. D. Cousins involves children's self-concepts.

Japanese and American teenagers were first asked to fill out a "Who Am I?" questionnaire. The questionnaire included two lists, one a list of individual attributes (traits that set one apart from others, like "I am smart" or "I am good at sports") and the other a list of relational attributes (descriptors that define one's relationship to other people, like "I am a daughter" or "I am a student"). After first rating themselves on all the items, the teens were asked to go back and circle the five items out of the whole questionnaire that they felt were most critical to defining who they were. The results revealed a striking difference between the groups: While the American kids showed a slight preference for the individual attributes, the Japanese kids showed a very strong preference for the relational attributes.

Why? Unlike American culture's emphasis on helping children develop personal strengths and weaknesses, Japanese culture tends to emphasize the connection between a child and the group to which he or she belongs. The first, individualistic perspective is typical of most Western cultures; the latter, collectivistic perspective is more prevalent among Asian cultures. An interesting question is what shape this fundamental difference in perspectives will take as the world shrinks and people from different cultures have more and more opportunities to interact.

what successes don't count. Remember, your child is a separate individual with different talents from yours—and a completely different world within which to find his place.

◆ Do you often compare your child to siblings or other people's children? Particularly with infants and toddlers, this is a very hard habit to break—*but try!* Otherwise, there's a good chance your words, facial expressions, and behaviors will communicate your worry and disappointment.

- Do you have realistic expectations for your child? As we said earlier, not knowing what's normal can create unnecessary tension between you and your child.
- Do you model self-esteem and self-confidence? Remember, even infants as young as nine months of age are watching your facial expressions to see how *you* are reacting to situations. Because children naturally imitate the important adults in their lives, being confident yourself is important.
- Do you model a try-try-again attitude toward mistakes and failures? Again, remember that the eyes of children are on you.

- **Support your child's general emotional development.** How your child feels *in general* plays a role in his feelings of self-worth. So...
  - **Forge a secure attachment bond.** Reread Chapter 2 for how you can foster this critical contributor to high self-esteem.
  - **Help your child interpret and express his own emotions.** If you can establish a calm dialogue around an instance of success or failure, your child will be in a much better position to listen to what you have to say about it. Reread Chapter 3 for help in developing your child's understanding of emotions.

> **F**eelings of worth can flourish only in an atmosphere where individual differences are appreciated, mistakes are tolerated, communication is open, and rules are flexible—the kind of atmosphere that is found in a nurturing family.
>
> —Virginia Satir,
> family therapist and author

- **Use playtimes well.** When you play with your child, try to be supportive but not intrusive.
  - **Let your child take the lead.** Remember Deborah Stipek's discovery that the challenges children choose for themselves are more likely to generate pride when conquered than any challenges you choose for them.
  - **Resist the temptation to finish the job yourself.** Try to resist jumping in and doing a task for your child. Doing so sends the message that you didn't think she was capable on her own. Support her efforts with hints or suggestions, but avoid detailed instructions.

Child-chosen challenges are most rewarding, research shows. Case in point: Pride shines in fifteen-month-old Emma's eyes at having accomplished a task few adults would have guessed would be significant: flinging balls around. To Emma, however, it's definitely worth shouting about.

- ◆ **Encourage try-try-again activities.** These are toys and activities that even children recognize will require multiple attempts and many failures along the way. Some examples include puzzles, games of catch, hide-and-seek, treasure hunts, and physical skills like learning to ride a bike, balance on a beam, or roller skate.
- ◆ **Maximize success experiences.** The more success your child can experience, the better. Here are some ideas for increasing the odds.
  - ◆ **Be sure challenges are at the right level.** Research has revealed that having a wide variety of age-appropriate toys and activities available to a child is a strong predictor of healthy self-esteem. Activities that are too easy are not satisfying, and those that are too difficult are frustrating. Many commercial

toys, such as busy boxes, provide challenges at just the right level of difficulty for babies and toddlers.

◆ **Appreciate the "I do it!" phase.** At some point your toddler will start wanting to do things herself: get a button into a buttonhole, put on a shoe, feed herself. Appreciate this exciting change and make time for it. Recognize that it's going to take longer to get ready now that your child is "helping," and build the extra time into your schedule.

◆ **Appreciate the significance of *tiny* triumphs.** Too many parents fail to appreciate that what looks like trivial play (getting the washcloth stuffed into the toy boat) is really challenging "work" to a child. Take time to notice your child's little successes and let him know you think he's pretty clever.

◆ **Let your child make choices.** By providing several alternatives from which your child can choose ("Do you want the red one or the blue one?"), you provide a real boost to what psychologist Albert Bandura called self-efficacy (see page 130). After all, we want our children to grow up able to think for themselves, not simply dependent on what other people (such as their peers) tell them to do. Providing controlled practice in deciding between alternatives early in life gets the ball rolling in a positive direction.

◆ **Assign little chores.** Toddlerhood may be the only time in life when children *want* to help around the house. Doing so makes them feel grown-up and important. Take advantage of their eagerness and choose simple tasks they can do. But remember, at these ages enthusiasm is likely to disappear unless you remain engaged in the activity too. Try allowing them to:
  ◆ help give items to the cashier in the grocery store
  ◆ take their empty plate to the kitchen
  ◆ put toys away
  ◆ carry library books to the checkout counter
  ◆ water outside flowers with a watering can
  ◆ wash the car

◆ **Review accomplishments at bedtime.** Add another feature to your "happy/sad" bedtime ritual (see Chapter 3, page 77) by talking about what made you each proud during the day.

◆ **Praise your child's successes in others' hearing.** Even as adults, hearing a superior tell someone else how well she thinks we're doing is especially ego-boosting. There's something about a statement being made in public that gives the words increased credibility ("I guess she really *means* it!"). The same dynamic works for kids. So, in addition to praising your child to his face, make a point of praising him to other people when he is in a position to overhear your enthusiastic comments.

◆ **Watch your reactions to failure.** As Carol Dweck's work on learned helplessness makes clear, parents (and teachers, for that matter) can crush a child's sense of worth by the way they handle less than stellar performances.

   ◆ **Be careful not to attribute failure to a lack of ability.** Avoid any implication that you didn't have faith in your child. Let him know you were proud of him for trying and encourage him to try again, perhaps suggesting a slight change in strategy.

   ◆ **Work hard to find a silver lining.** When your child is discouraged, look hard to find something good that has come out of the situation and point it out. Perhaps she learned something along the way, made new friends, or simply worked up a good appetite. This is one way for children to learn that failing isn't a catastrophe.

◆ **Be careful how you criticize.** Nobody's perfect—and especially not infants and toddlers. Criticism has a legitimate role to play in raising children. It's *not* good for children always to receive praise or to be lavishly praised for completing simple tasks that took no effort. The result will be false expectations about how others will view their behavior. However, how you deliver criticism matters too. Follow these rules:

   ◆ **Criticize the behavior, not the child!** This is one of two absolutely critical rules. The second is:

   ◆ **Never leave your child with the impression you love her any less.** If necessary, post reminder signs in every room of the house.

   ◆ **Balance criticism with praise.** Even adults respond more openly to criticisms that are prefaced by legitimate praise of some kind. Well, the same is true of young children. ("You certainly worked hard to get your toys put away. That was great! Next time, though, try to get them stacked more neatly so it will be easier to find what you're looking for.")

   ◆ **Avoid using the terms "You always . . ." and "You never . . ."** These phrases are extremely accusatory—and seldom true.

   ◆ **When improvements are needed, deliver the news with love.** Although it's very unlikely to be an issue in the first three years, there will certainly be

One look at this little girl's face and you know that she feels pretty good about herself—and we bet it would be true even if she wasn't wearing a crown!

times in the future when you feel your child really is capable of doing a better job and needs to try. In such cases you won't be doing your child a favor by pretending that her effort was an A+ when it was not. Your child needs to know you have standards. What you can do to make the news more palatable is explain exactly why you feel it's important for her to try to improve and assure her that you're confident she can do better because she's both competent and capable of working hard.

the "big five" challenges to healthy emotional development

Pick up almost any newspaper these days and you'll find at least one disturbing article reminding you how wrong a child's development can go.

EXTRA! EXTRA! READ ALL ABOUT IT...

School Shooting Leaves Two Dead

New School Building Torched by Vandals

Gang Violence Erupts at Theater

Eight-Year-Old Convicted of Murder

Headlines like these represent just a few of the issues that strike fear into a parent's heart. And as if those articles aren't bad enough, turn the page and you're likely to find additional ones highlighting the internal problems that too many children face, such as depression, anorexia, and this-that-or-the-other phobia.

With so much bad news about kids surrounding us, it's natural for parents to wonder how to keep their children on an emotionally and behaviorally stable path.

A century ago the advice to parents was quite simple: "Spare the rod and spoil the child." Fortunately, thanks to the contributions of many researchers both in the United States and abroad, there is increasing recognition that building a kinder and gentler world requires kinder and gentler parenting. But at the same time there is also strong evidence that kinder and gentler parenting simply must *not* mean the absence of standards and discipline. In other words, what's required is that parents find the appropriate middle ground between these two extremes. Finding this middle ground, however, isn't always easy, especially in the day-to-day world of specific children and specific situations. And so, their hearts definitely in the right place, modern parents are looking for advice on how to do it right—and especially how to do it right when it comes to handling the scary parts of raising children.

What are those scary parts? We believe that the list contains a "big five" set of issues, each one a topic that has the power to keep parents awake at night worrying about what to do. The next five chapters of *Baby Hearts* focus on each set of issues. The five include:

- ◆ Fear and anxiety (Chapter 7)
- ◆ Shyness and withdrawal (Chapter 8)
- ◆ Anger and defiance (Chapter 9)
- ◆ Hostility and aggression (Chapter 10)
- ◆ Shame and guilt (Chapter 11)

In each case we draw from research studies conducted in laboratories around the world in our search for helpful insights about causes, consequences, and cures. Our hope is that these chapters will enable parents to feel more confident that they are doing the very best they can to lead their children through the inevitable maze of challenges that are part of any family's life.

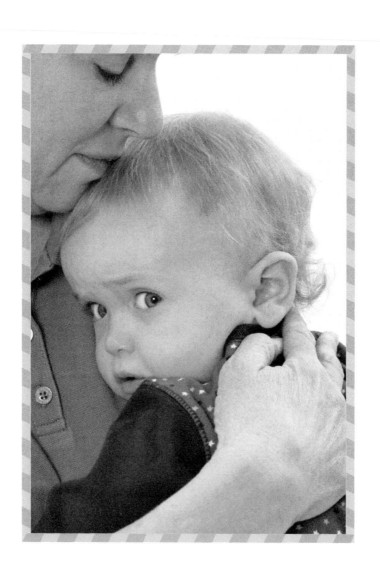

7

Monsters and Meanies:
Addressing Fear and Anxiety

N E W S   F L A S H !

Scientists Catching On to How Babies Catch Fear

Denver, Colorado. Like most babies his age, twelve-month-old Jake loves going up and down stairs. With the strong arms of his mom or dad to catch him if he needs help, Jake routinely negotiates the four stairs at home, the five stairs at Grandma's house, and the two stairs at day care. That's what makes his refusal just now to back down one small stair to reach his mother so unusual.

In fact, the thirty-centimeter stair separating Jake from his mom isn't a stair at all, only an illusion created in the Child Development Lab at the University of Denver. Researchers Jim Sorce, Bob Emde, Joe Campos, and Mary Klinnert have cleverly extended a plate of glass out from a step high ledge so that it looks like a stair, but is really a solid glass surface—what the researchers call a visual cliff. They've done so to make a specific point: Because babies don't know everything they need to know about the world around them, they routinely take their cues about what's dangerous or not dangerous from their parents. One look at Jake's mother, therefore, and the mystery of the boy's reluctance is solved. Following the researchers' instructions, Jake's mom is looking back and forth between the illusory stair and Jake with an expression of absolute horror on her face.

"We call what Jake's doing 'social referencing,'" explains Jim Sorce. "Jake is using another person he trusts as a reference to help him decide how he should feel about the situation. In this case, his mom's facial expression of fear has indicated he should be afraid too, and so he refuses to budge."

The larger message of this research and the many studies that have followed it is that babies catch more from their parents than just colds and flu. They also catch fear. Parents consciously and unconsciously communicate their emotions—both sensible and not so sensible—to babies in many ways. Sometimes it's through a facial expression like Jake's mom's look of horror. Other times it's through a change in the parent's tone of voice, a sudden intake of breath, or even just increased pressure around the baby's waist. These are all ways that parents communicate anxiety and fear. That's why, researchers tell us, phobias—those relentless fears that don't make much sense—often run in families. Mom's fear of spiders all too easily becomes Junior's fear of spiders too. In other words, because of social referencing, the old adage "Like father, like son" (along with every other gender combination) rings all too true.

From Healthy to Harmful

Fear and anxiety, when they work the way they are supposed to, are handy tools in the human toolbox. Without them, our ancestors might have kept trying to pet those cute saber-toothed tigers or cuddle with those twenty-foot pythons—with the end result that none of us would even be here to talk about it! Fortunately, the fight-or-flight response of our sympathetic nervous system mobilizes us when our senses perceive and our brains interpret a situation as dangerous. What this system leaves a bit up in the air, however, is the definition of "dangerous," and that's where people—including children—differ substantially from one another.

All parents face the challenge of finding the right balance between creating a healthy fear of dangerous things and making their child unrealistically afraid and anxious about the world. Yes, it's important for a child to be wary of strange dogs, but not to the point of becoming rigid with fear at the sight of one down the street—or the street itself even *without* the dog. The same can be said in regard to strangers, heights, crowds, spiders, snakes, or even novel situations and ideas. Individuals who grow up with generalized feelings of fear and anxiety simply don't find life much fun.

Nor do the people around them. Having an overly fearful child in a family can make *everybody's* life miserable. Parents vacillate between being supportive and frustrated, reassuring and accusatory; siblings feel neglected and resentful; and the whole family feels put-upon by the need to maneuver daily life around the targets of the child's fears. In short, when fearfulness goes from being healthy to harmful, life for child and family alike goes from being normal to being a nightmare.

Fortunately, over the past decade researchers have discovered a number of important factors that contribute to creating overly anxious and fearful children, as well as useful techniques for defusing these emotions. Little Jake's social referencing, the sneaky route via which parents unwittingly contribute to the problem, is just one example. How to take advantage of this new knowledge as you struggle to walk the fine line between healthy and unrealistic caution is what this chapter of *Baby Hearts* is all about.

When and Why the "Scaries" Begin

Even newborn babies experience fear—or at least the physical features of it. The triggers for them are few in number and totally devoid of psychological meaning, namely, loud noises and sudden loss of support. Drop a dish next to your newborn's infant seat or almost drop *her* and she will experience the same jolt of adrenaline you experience when someone jumps out of a closet at you yelling "Boo!"

ANXIETY ARRIVES

For most babies, fear continues to be this uncomplicated throughout two-thirds of the first year. But as the infant mind grows more sophisticated, so also does the fear response. Starting at about eight months, babies begin to be able to remember the faces of the special people in their lives. This wonderful achievement, however, has a double downside—two forms of fear that for the first time have psychological as well as physical causes and consequences. These include separation anxiety (feelings of intense discomfort when the loves of a baby's life are out of sight) and stranger anxiety (feelings of fear when an unfamiliar person enters the picture). The first of these, separation anxiety, usually begins around eight months, peaks between fourteen and eighteen months, and then gradually becomes less and less intense. The second, stranger anxiety, is shorter lived, peaking between eight and ten months and then gradually decreasing over the second

Little Sean misses his mommy, but having his favorite toy, Woofie, to hold on to makes him feel better. Such comfort toys, as they are called, help children cope with separations from their favorite people.

year. Both are perfectly normal fears reflecting progress in an infant's mental ability and emotional relationships. That isn't much consolation, however, when your babysitter is trying to calm your frantic ten-month-old.

THE LIST GROWS LONGER

Things really begin to heat up in the second year. In fact, it's the unusual child who doesn't develop an interesting variety of at least temporary fears during the toddler and preschool years. Here are some of the most typical candidates:

- Monsters ("Mom! Things are beginning to go bump in the night!")
- The dark ("I sure *wish* out of sight was out of mind!")
- People in masks and costumes ("Who *is* that masked man!?")

- ◆ Vacuum cleaners ("If it can suck up dirt, why not me too?!")
- ◆ The bathtub drain ("There but for the grace of a little circle of metal go I!")
- ◆ The toilet ("Just how much can one flush flush?")
- ◆ Animals (big teeth, big feet, big noise = big fear!)

In the years that follow, from kindergarten through elementary school, children's fears become increasingly complex. As children begin to understand time and perhaps experience the loss of a pet or grandparent, the permanency of death can create fear and anxiety. As they start to understand the really serious consequences of illness, they become increasingly concerned about their own health. As they face the social and academic challenges of elementary school, social and

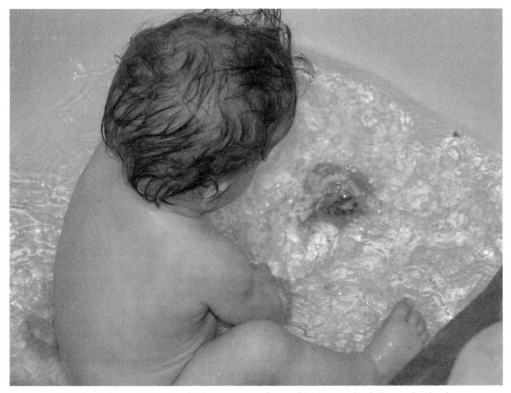

Toddlers' fears—like the fairly common fear of being sucked down the bathtub drain—are often so unrealistic that parents find them hard to take seriously. It helps for parents to realize that a toddler's life is full of pretty implausible things—like TVs, telephones, and elevators!

school phobias can begin to arise. As they become more aware of the violent potential of Mother Nature, fears of natural phenomena such as earthquakes, storms, and tornados can take root. And as they begin to pay closer attention to human relationships, marital conflict can contribute mightily to a fear of divorce with its threat of abandonment.

A LITTLE KNOWLEDGE IS A DANGEROUS THING

Why the significant increase in fear after the first birthday? Again, much of the responsibility can be traced to changes in the child's mental skills. Unfortunately, however, these changes aren't balanced by nearly enough knowledge of how the

How Would You Feel If . . . ?

It's easy for parents to say there's nothing to be scared of, but it's not always easy for toddlers to take them at their word. The world, after all, is full of totally unfamiliar animals, vegetables, and minerals. And that doesn't even include all the strange people who tower over them as they make their way through a forest of legs. To help you understand things from a toddler's perspective, imagine this.

In a situation straight out of Rod Serling's *Twilight Zone*, you suddenly wake up on another planet. The odd thing is that this planet is very similar to Earth with the exception that everything but you is three times as large as it should be. Somewhat dazed, you carefully drop to the floor from your five-foot-high bed, stop off at the bathroom (where you almost fall into the toilet), make your way *very* carefully down the stairs (each of which is two feet high), and eventually make your way outside. And what greets you? You mean besides the five-foot-high dog with the twelve-inch tongue and four-foot-long tail that swishes so hard it knocks you down? Several people see your dilemma and run to your aid, scooping you up into the air—actually *ten feet* up into the air—into their five-foot-long arms. "Don't be afraid," they say. "It's a *nice* doggy!" Hmph.

You get the idea. A significant part of what toddlers find so disconcerting about their world is the mere fact that it's so big and they're so small. Now, don't you feel a bit more sympathetic?

Whoa! It's a long way up there! Part of the reason toddlers are prone to fear is that they feel so little in comparison to most of the other elements in their world. Understanding their perspective can help parents feel more sympathetic.

world actually works. The result is fear of things that you and I know from experience aren't likely to happen—like getting sucked up by vacuum cleaners or flushed down the toilet. We may know the laws of mechanics that make such things impossible, but our toddlers and preschoolers clearly don't. To them the world is full of weird things—garage doors that go up and down with the press of a button, people who sing, dance, and talk on a little screen in the family room; and doors that close on one part of a store only to open a few seconds later elsewhere. In a world where these things are possible, who's to say that there isn't a monster under the bed?

Here are some of the other reasons why the list of fears inevitably grows longer between years one and five:

◆ **The wonderful—and not so wonderful—world of imagination.** Toward the middle of the second year, the toddler brain begins to be able to do something that sets humans apart from other animals: create ideas and images that have little, if any, basis in reality and then ponder those ideas and images at will. This is a fancy way to say that children begin to use their imaginations. The good news is that this ability enables them to have fun pretending to be firemen or ballerinas; the bad news is that this same ability enables them to imagine bogeymen and monsters.

◆ **Figuring out what's real and what's not.** Toddlers face a particularly interesting challenge when it comes to distinguishing fantasy from reality. Their new awareness of their own thoughts and dreams doesn't come with an automatic recognition that these are all in the head. Ask your toddler if you'd be able to watch his dream if you came into his room while he was dreaming and he's likely to say yes. Very young children think of their dreams as taking place in real time and space, which is one reason they find nightmares so upsetting. Movies and televi-

Sweet Dreams? Not Always

Although we know that newborns experience rapid eye movement (REM) sleep, the type of sleep that accompanies dreaming in adults, researchers have not yet figured out how to determine exactly when infants and toddlers begin to dream. By the time children are two and a half to three, however, most provide clear evidence to their parents that the bridge to dreamland has been crossed. Unfortunately, this evidence takes two less than positive forms: garden-variety nightmares and a type of dream specific to young children called night terrors.

◆ **Nightmares.** The brain depends on stored visual images to fuel dreams, so as the toddler's memory capacity improves, so does the stockpile of material dreams can draw from. The result is the onset of both good dreams and nightmares. Unfortunately, children's understanding of what dreams actually are—that they are only in one's head (others can't see them) and only a product of one's imagination (not real)—is severely limited at these early ages. That's why it's so important to take their distress seriously. Parents should respond with physical comforting, assurances to the children that they are safe, and information about the fantasy nature of their nightmares.

sion pose similar problems. Even a quick look at weekly TV listings is likely to yield a very scary cast of characters and frightening plots. The difficulty they have distinguishing between fantasy and reality is illustrated nicely in a clever study by Paul Harris of Oxford University. Three-year-olds were shown a closed box and asked to imagine that it contained either a bunny or a monster. All of the children acknowledged that they were "just pretending," but when it came to staying alone with the box, those who were imagining a monster were too scared to do so!

◆ **Down memory lane.** Another reason why fears are fewer in number before age one is because very young infants live by necessity in the here and now. The downside of this is that they don't get to relive the happy moments of their short lives—the delightful games of tickle, the warm and snuggly moments in Mom's arms, the giddy back-and-forth of their swing. The upside, however, is that very young infants also can't remember the scary moments. Unfortunately, due to

---

◆ **Night terrors.** While nightmares tend to occur in the later portions of the night, a second form of bad dreams called night terrors tend to occur in the first few hours of sleep. Witnessing a child in the throes of a night terror is, pardon the word, terrifying. The child is likely to be screaming and crying while thrashing around, clawing the air, or even walking. Part of the parent's own terror comes from the sense that her child is really and truly frightened. The other part comes from the fact that there is nothing the parent can do to help. Trying to hold children during night terrors is likely to result in more distress rather than less, and trying to wake them is usually futile. They remain in a sleep state throughout. The best course of action is to do what's necessary to keep children out of physical danger and simply wait the terrors out. Eventually (after five to thirty minutes), children will simply settle themselves down. What's more, they will not remember a thing about the event in the morning.

What causes bad dreams? Just as we do not understand the sources of our own bad dreams, no one knows much about the childhood versions either. However, pediatricians do warn that nightmares and night terrors are more likely to occur when children are overtired, sick, or under stress. They also caution that professional help should be sought if night terrors last beyond age six.

much improved memory capacities, toddlers and preschoolers definitely *can*. This means that a single harrowing experience with a dog, clown, or merry-go-round can haunt them for days, weeks, months, or even years to come.

◆ **Smack dab in the center of the universe.** A young child's world revolves around the only things he truly knows—his own wants, needs, and experiences. For the first four or five years, he's even fuzzy on what's happening to the rest of his family, let alone the world at large. As a result, young children are of necessity among Earth's most self-centered creatures. This egocentrism, as psychologists call it, contributes in an interesting way to fear and anxiety. Should the news of a disaster happening to someone else actually break through into their awareness—such as a house fire, robbery, or airplane crash—toddlers and preschoolers see no reason to believe it won't happen to them next. This is the reason why some children with no personal connection to New York City or Washington, D.C., were seriously traumatized by the horrific images of the September 11 terrorist attacks. Without the larger perspective on events that comes with increased experience, toddlers and preschoolers automatically take things personally and assume the worst.

◆ **On the go.** One final reason toddlers and preschoolers are more vulnerable than infants to developing fears is the simple fact that they get around better. Not much scary can happen when you're confined to a highchair or crib, but let your world expand to include the yard, the park, and the neighborhood, and the chances of encountering something unexpected and scary increase markedly.

Those at Special Risk

The progression we've just described is a fairly normal one, at least in terms of the types of fears parents can expect. What separates the normally fearful child from the overly fearful child, therefore, is not the absence of fears during childhood but, rather, the range of situations that produce fear, the length of time they last, and the degree to which they interfere with a child's daily life. In other words, it's not unusual for a three-year-old to be afraid of the dark, but if the fear expands to include riding in the car at night, lasts for years, and/or prevents the child from ever getting a restful sleep, then the fear has crossed the line from normal to problematic.

Research has revealed that some children, unfortunately, are especially vulnerable to developing levels of anxiety and fear that interfere with everyday life.

Baby Hearts in Action:
A Stitch in Time . . . Should Remain There

When Susan was five years old, she was hospitalized for a hernia operation. The surgery itself was uneventful, and everyone—including Susan—was breathing a sigh of relief until it came time to take the stitches out. Thinking he was being reassuring, the doctor explained what he was going to do and that it wouldn't hurt at all. However, no sooner had he finished his statement than Susan burst into tears, suddenly terrified about what was going to happen. "I promise you, Susan, it's not going to hurt," he said again, with Susan's mom and dad echoing the doctor's assurance as convincingly as they could. But to no avail. Susan just kept sobbing and trying with all her might to keep the doctor at bay. Despite her efforts to resist, the doctor finally succeeded in getting the stitches out, whereupon Susan looked first at her stomach and then up at the doctor in clear surprise. It was only when she said in amazement "There's no hole!" that the adults finally understood the cause of Susan's alarm. Based on her limited experiences with sewing, taking *out* stitches inevitably reopened whatever hole had been closed when they were put *in*. You see, it wasn't the pain Susan was worried about; it was the prospect of her insides spilling out once the stitches that held her tummy together were gone. Clearly, adults aren't always as smart as they think they are!

Knowing what these "red flags" are can help parents ward off some fears and deal more effectively with others should they arise.

CHILDREN WHO BEGIN LIFE FEARFUL: BABY ORCHID

In Chapter 1 we highlighted four different inborn temperaments, including Baby Orchid, the "Slow-to-Warm" child. We know a good deal more about the origins of Baby Orchid than we used to thanks to the work of developmental psychologist Jerome Kagan and his colleagues from Harvard University. His research with infants and toddlers revealed a biological "nudge" in the direction of increased fearfulness and caution among about 20 percent of four-month-olds. These infants were much more easily startled and distressed by unexpected objects and events than their peers, and most (75 percent) of them stayed this way into the second year and beyond. In other words, about 15 percent of toddlers and preschoolers come by their increased fearfulness through no fault of their own or anyone else's. They are simply predisposed by their "hair-trigger" amygdalas (the switchboard in the limbic brain that dictates our emotional responses) to react with great wariness to new experiences. In other words, they see potential danger where their more adventuresome peers see none.

But something else happens as these children begin interacting more and more with the environment, something that contributes greatly to their increased vulnerability to specific fears. Because they approach things with the *expectation* that something bad might happen, they are also quicker than their peers to judge that it actually has. For example, let's say Blackie, a boisterous Labrador retriever, jumps up on two toddlers, one a Baby Orchid and the other a Baby Dandelion (the temperamentally "Active" baby). Even though their experiences are identical, their take-away messages are likely to be very different. Whereas Baby Dandelion, although startled, quickly regains her composure and begins to giggle, Baby Orchid is quite likely to react with fear and crying. And then, since we take forward into our next experiences our *perceptions* of events rather than the events themselves, Baby Orchid's encounter with Blackie goes on to color her perceptions of the next dog, and the one after that, and on and on. The result? A serious fear of dogs that, if it begins interfering with her daily life, can even cross over into the realm of a true phobia.

Fortunately, many parents of children with a biological nudge in the direction of fearfulness instinctively try to monitor and even moderate their child's exposure to potentially scary objects or events. Research by developmental psychologists Jennifer Urbano Blackford and Tedra Walden at Vanderbilt University has revealed that many of these parents are careful not to look frightened themselves when something unpredicted happens. Instead, they tend to emphasize positive reactions to things, exaggerating their facial expressions and tone of voice to communicate their pleasure and downplay their concern. Given the tendency for children to look to their parents for advice on how they should react to the world (social referencing), this is *exactly* the right thing to do. It's not a guarantee that the child won't react with fear, but it increases the probabilities at least a bit.

If only all parents were this insightful. But they're not—a fact which brings us to the next category of vulnerable children.

CHILDREN WHO "CATCH" FEAR FROM THEIR PARENTS

Some parents, unfortunately, contribute mightily to their children's fearfulness by approaching their own lives with a generalized sense of anxiety and dread. The mechanisms by which they transfer their fear to their children include the fairly subtle operation of social referencing, where children take their cues from their parents' own reactions to things. But the mechanisms also often include outright warnings of dire consequences, prohibitions against taking chances, and accusations of foolhardiness for being too bold.

Here's an example from a fascinating research study by developmental psychologists Mary Main and Erik Hesse from the University of California, Berkeley. A twelve-month-old infant and his mother are in a university playroom awaiting the return of the experimenter. The playroom is equipped with age-appropriate toys, and the little boy soon ventures over to a pile of toy cars, taking one and beginning to *vroom-vroom* it across the floor. His mother's response? Instead of something normal, like "You sure make it go fast!" this mother pleads, "Don't go so fast! There will be an accident and everyone will be killed!" See what we mean? There's nothing subtle about this mother's message of fear and dread.

Main and Hesse found that this kind of extreme reaction was typical of a group of mothers who had themselves lost a significant figure early in their own lives and had, for whatever reason, never come to terms with the event. Clearly, the experience had led them to view the world as an unpredictable and dangerous place, a perception they were both consciously and unconsciously now passing on to their children.

It's not only parents with loss-induced fearfulness like the ones Main and Hesse describe who transfer their own fears to their children. Many adults find themselves so shaken by the day's headlines describing terrorist attacks, child abductions, natural disasters, and freak accidents that they end up narrowing their children's worlds too far in their efforts to keep them safe. Unless parents

> Our children are watching us live and what we are shouts louder than anything we can say.
>
> —Wilfred Peterson, author

Children who enjoy secure attachment bonds with their parents are less vulnerable to prolonged fears, in part because they know they can trust their parents to protect and comfort them when they are afraid.

are careful, the result can be children who are too frightened to accurately assess risk and end up unnecessarily fearful and anxious. The best remedy to this situation, of course, is a safer world. Lacking that, parents should at least pay more attention to the general messages they send their children about the world outside the home.

CHILDREN WITH INSECURE ATTACHMENTS

The plight of the mothers in Main and Hesse's study who had suffered a loss during childhood reflects a third source of high anxiety and fearfulness in children—the absence or disruption of a strong bond with one or more of a child's major caregivers. In fact, these mothers make the case in a dramatic way. The disruption in attachment that they had experienced years earlier had left them feeling overwhelmed by life, seeing threats practically everywhere they turn, and frantic in their efforts to protect their children.

Why did this happen to these women? What is it about not maintaining a secure attachment that makes a person vulnerable to lifelong anxiety? As we discuss in more detail in Chapter 2, the answer lies in the role parents play as buffers between babies and the huge, complex world around them. Because they are totally helpless, babies are completely dependent on their caregivers to alleviate all forms of distress, whether caused by hunger, cold, wet diapers, loneliness, boredom, or fear. When they experience these things, babies signal their need for help by crying. If Mom and/or Dad typically respond quickly and appropriately, then babies learn to trust that help is on the way. It's this trust that keeps anxiety at a low level. But if, instead, babies cry and nothing happens, then they begin to anticipate that they *won't* receive the help they need. The more often this happens, the more anxious babies become any time their tranquility is threatened.

> My father used to play with my brother and me in the yard. Mother would come out and say, "You're tearing up the grass." "We're not raising grass," Dad would reply. "We're raising boys."
>
> —Harmon Killebrew, baseball player

It's a lot like the adult experience of waiting every day for the same bus. If the No. 9 bus to City Hall typically arrives at our stop right on schedule, then we don't experience much anxiety while we wait. However, if the bus's arrival is totally unpredictable, then we can't help but worry. Our time at the bus stop, instead of being filled with pleasant thoughts, is spent on pins and needles. What's even worse is if the bus fails to arrive on time so consistently that we simply give up and try walking to work on our own. Doing so can be both wearying and scary, two words that also describe what children experience when their parents are so undependable that their only option is to garner whatever resources they can in order to face the world on their own.

CHILDREN WHOSE FEARS MASK OTHER TROUBLING FEELINGS

Sometimes the anxiety children experience is really covering up feelings that make them even more uncomfortable. The most common culprit is anger. Children who experience angry feelings but are taught implicitly or explicitly that such feelings are unacceptable frequently turn their discomfort into something more private—anxiety. So, for example, a child who is angry at the intrusion of a new baby into the cozy cocoon he calls home may unconsciously transform his anger into some form of fear. It might be as easily interpreted as a return to intense separation anxiety, or it might be so distant from the actual source of distress that its emergence is a true mystery—such as a fear of shadows or umbrellas.

Feeling anger toward parents is especially anxiety-provoking for children. The obvious worry is that, were such feelings expressed, they might alienate the very people children depend on for protection. What a fine mess that would be! As a consequence, children who repress anger toward their parents frequently displace that anger onto something else (the poor frog cornered in the field) or add anxiety and fear to the cauldron of their emotions. The psychological assumption seems to be that it's better to be anxious than to risk losing the love of one's parents.

The Whatever You Do, *DON'T!* List

Based on extensive clinical experience, psychiatrist Alicia Lieberman has identified eight factors that, if children experience them frequently, often lead to the development of excessive anxiety and fear.

1. Lengthy separations from important attachment figures without the comfort of trusted substitutes
2. Frequent, unpredictable changes in who cares for the child
3. Threats of abandonment ("Watch it, or I'll call the police and they'll come take you away!")
4. Generalized criticism that leaves the child with no idea how to win back the parent's approval ("You're a rotten kid!" "Can't you do anything right?!")
5. Blame directed at the child for endangering the parent's mental or physical health, even in jest ("You're driving me crazy!" "Another day like this and I'll kill myself!")
6. Frequent harsh punishment, either emotional or physical
7. Role reversal where the child becomes the nurturer and the parent the fragile one
8. Rigid standards, especially if unattainable

N E W S   F L A S H !

Fears Fade Once Infant Is in Charge

Minneapolis, Minnesota. Twelve-month-old Jeremy has just run crying to his mother. The apparent cause? A very noisy mechanical monkey introduced into a playroom at the University of Minnesota by developmental psychologist Dr. Megan Gunnar. Far from trying to torture children, however, Dr. Gunnar is actually testing a theory that suggests a way for parents to help children cope with the multitude of scary things they are likely to encounter in the world.

The basic idea becomes clearer when the next child enters the room. In sharp contrast to Jeremy, twelve-month-old Samantha reaches out with enthusiasm toward the monkey. What made the difference? Control. Half the children in Dr. Gunnar's study, including Jeremy, had no control over when the monkey would make noise, while the other half, including Samantha, were given an easy way to start and stop it. "Instead of crying and protesting," Dr. Gunnar explains, "the children who could control the toy were delighted with it, taking great pleasure in making the noise happen. The noise, of course, was the same. All that differed was the baby's sense of being in charge."

The bottom line of Dr. Gunnar's research is that objects and situations become less frightening to infants and toddlers, just as is true of adults, if they feel they have some control over what's happening. Fortunately, there are many ways parents can increase their child's feelings of control. A child who is wary of animals can be taught how to behave when they come close and/or how to pet them. A child who is afraid of the stairs can be taught how to hold on to the banister. A child who is afraid of the dark can be given a flashlight. A child who is afraid of monsters—and impervious to all there's-no-such-thing arguments—can be given a can of "Monster Spray" (actually available in some retail stores). And a child who is afraid of the vacuum cleaner can be shown the on/off switch. Once parents understand the basic principle that control helps alleviate fear, their anxiety about their children's fears begins to decrease. Why? Because the knowledge makes them feel more in control too.

Words of Wisdom and Tricks of the Trade

Even if your child's fears and anxieties are among those likely to be outgrown, they still don't feel good *at the time*. That's why we advise all parents to take such discomfort seriously and do what they can to relieve their child's suffering. Gunnar's work on the importance of perceived control has been extremely helpful to parents in this regard. Fortunately, hers isn't the only line of research that has paid off. Here are some other strategies that scientists have found effective in dealing with childhood anxiety and fear.

KNOW THYSELF

The discovery of the power of social referencing (the tendency for infants to monitor their parents' reactions for clues as to how they themselves should behave) highlights the critical role of parents' own fears and anxieties in inspiring negative emotions in their children. Keeping this in mind, list your own fears on a sheet of paper. Think about each one and objectively decide if it is a fear you want or do not want your child to share. Be aware that some of these will come to mind easily (heights, spiders, dogs), but others will be more subtle in nature, requiring deeper reflection (meeting new people, tackling a sports activity, or trying new foods). For any fear you do not want your child to share, try to pinpoint ways you may be consciously or unconsciously communicating your fear to your child. Write these down. Perhaps you tense up and stop smiling when a new person approaches, wring your hands when your toddler starts up a slide, or pull your head back and briefly frown when a new food is set in front of you. You may not even be aware of how subtly you communicate your fears, so ask family and friends to help. And, finally, if your level of overall anxiety is extremely high, seek the advice of your doctor for ways to relieve your own discomfort. Remember, doing so will benefit your child as well.

KNOW THE COMPANY YOUR BABY KEEPS

Make a list of other people who interact frequently with your baby. Are any of these people inadvertently communicating unreasonable anxieties to your child? All that's necessary, after all, is for the person to be someone a baby trusts. In a nonaccusatory way and using your own behaviors with your child as examples,

Children are like wet cement. Whatever falls on them makes an impression.

—Gaim Ginott, child psychologist
and author

talk with these individuals about how subtle the process of "catching" fears can be. Should you notice your child suddenly manifesting a new anxiety about something, considering these other possible sources of influence may help you figure out what's behind it.

DEALING WITH SEPARATION ANXIETY

Even though the "Where did you go?!" phase (eight to thirty months) is perfectly normal, it can be hard on baby and parent alike. Here are some tips that can make dealing with separation anxiety a bit easier:

◆ **Keep as much of your child's environment the same as possible.** Separation is easier on children if they are surrounded by familiar things. At the very least, make sure favorite "comfort" toys are available. And if she doesn't have any such toys, start promoting some to this status.

◆ **Leave your child with someone she knows well and trusts.** Have the substitute spend as much time as possible with the two of you in advance so the caregiver knows the baby's schedule, likes and dislikes, and special little games.

◆ **Leave some reminders.** Children do better if they are reminded of your love while you are gone. Leave pictures of the two of you together or an audiotape of you reading a story or singing a song.

◆ **Let your child miss you.** Encourage the caregiver to talk about you and to tell your child that it's all right to miss you.

◆ **Avoid being away overnight, if possible, through the first fifteen months.** By that point most children understand enough language and have enough sense of time to grasp the fact that you will return.

◆ **Prepare your child for longer separations.** When the time comes and you have to be gone, prepare your child by explaining the reasons for your absence and the length of time before you return. Use a positive tone of voice and facial expression. If your child "catches" your anxiety, he will feel more anxious himself.

◆ **Plan for reunion.** Provide something specific for your child to look forward to doing with you when you return—such as exchange big hugs and kisses, go to the park, make cookies.

◆ **Provide a representation of the time going by.** Use some kind of pictorial representation of the time passing and have those at home help her mark the days as they go by. For example, create a drawing of a path from left to right. Place a photo of your child on the far right end and one of you on the far left end. Represent the days you will be away by dividing the path into sections. Have someone move your photo from section to section ever closer to your child's photo as the days go by. The point where the two photos are joined signals reunion.

DEALING WITH STRANGER ANXIETY

The "Who the heck are you?!" phase (eight to twenty-four months) is also a normal part of the infancy and toddler years. Although it overlaps with separation anxiety in many ways, the two are distinct enough that a few specific tips apply.

◆ **Ask people to approach slowly and soothingly.** Sometimes this will entail an out-and-out "Slow down, Uncle Tony!" Strangers, no matter how well intentioned, who swoop into a baby's space end up overwhelming a baby with feelings of vulnerability. Because feeling overwhelmed is the exact *opposite* of feeling in control, the result is fear.

◆ **Provide a prop.** Providing the babysitter, unfamiliar friend, or relative with your child's favorite toy is another helpful ploy because it works to distract the baby from the newness of the visitor and defines him or her as having something in common.

◆ **Enthusiastically introduce the stranger.** Get into the habit of introducing people to your baby, expressing sincere delight. This may sound odd if your baby is just a few months old, but by about four months your baby will be sensitive to your facial expression and the tone of your voice. By ten months your baby will be purposefully monitoring these emotional cues.

◆ **Be patient and understanding.**

DEALING WITH OTHER FEARS

Here are some tips that hold true no matter what the source of your child's anxiety or fear.

◆ **Acknowledge.** One of the worst feelings at *any age* is to have one's thoughts and/or feelings simply dismissed as silly or inconsequential. The same holds true for very young children. That's why we advise parents to strike the phrase "Don't be silly!" from their vocabularies. Obviously, it follows from this that no one in the family should be allowed to tease the child. "Scaredy-cat!" taunts from an older sibling only make a child feel worse. Remember, even if the fear is unrealistic in everyone else's eyes, it's very real to your child. And, finally, don't use platitudes like "There's nothing to worry about!" when there really is.

◆ **Probe.** If you sense anxiety in your child, ask questions. If your child is too young to use words, observe closely and talk to other people who know your child well. The more you understand about the specific nature of your child's discomfort, the better position you are in to help. Besides, as any clinical psychologist will tell you, simply talking about fears helps defuse them.

◆ **Promise protection.** The other half of taking your child's fear seriously is communicating that you care very much about her feelings and will do everything you can to help keep her safe. The very fact that you—a strong and capable adult—are on her side is helpful in and of itself.

◆ **Provide information.** Many things that children worry about—both realistic and unrealistic—can be lessened or eliminated with additional information. For example, talking about smoke alarms to a child worried about a house fire can be very helpful, as can talking about the strength of the home's construction to a child worried about storms. Sometimes a demonstration is in order. If your child is worried about being sucked up by the vacuum cleaner, show him that it can't suck up a doll or a box. Use the same strategy for the bathtub drain and the toilet. The most important information you can provide, of course, is the constancy of your love, vigilance, and protection.

◆ **Don't force confrontations!** Here's a case where an exclamation point is in order. Making your child do something that strikes terror in her heart only makes matters worse. Typically, all it does is raise anxiety levels even higher and convince her that you don't care—neither of which helps down the line. We are not, how-

By providing love and support as Baby Emma encounters a petting zoo for the first time (top photo), Dad David is making it easier for Emma to eventually touch the animals on her own (bottom photo)—albeit with a lifeline still to Dad!

ever, advocating that a child be allowed to hide forever. Using all the tips we are recommending will communicate your support and *gradually* (and that's the critical word) enable your child to conquer her fear.

◆ **Use the power of touch.** A systematic program of research by psychologist Tiffany Field, director of the Touch Research Institute at the University of Miami School of Medicine, has demonstrated that physical touch has a powerfully positive influence on human emotions—*whatever* the age of the person. In particular, she and her colleagues have discovered that affectionate touching and massage reduce stress hormones. (See page 47 for some tips on infant massage.) Even something as natural as a good cuddle can go a long way toward reassuring a frightened child.

◆ **'Fess up.** Talk about your own fears and how you've dealt with them over the years. It helps children to know that being afraid is nothing to be ashamed of— that everyone is afraid sometimes. Adding the bit about how you overcame your fears reassures your child that he can do so too.

TIPS FOR WHEN YOUR CHILD IS AFRAID OF . . .

Given the right—or actually, the *wrong*—circumstances, children can become afraid of just about anything. For example, a child in one of our research studies, for some unknown reason, developed a fear of basketballs. (His mother eventually solved the problem by somehow shaping and frosting cupcakes to *look* like basketballs.) More typical examples include the bathtub, monsters, and the dark. Here are some ideas for coping with these common fears.

◆ **The bathtub.** In addition to showing him that big things can't go down the drain:
  ◆ Play games or have picnics in the tub without the water.
  ◆ Bathe with your child.
  ◆ Provide traditional pool toys like water wings or rings.
  ◆ Try a shower using an umbrella to make it fun.
◆ **Monsters.** In addition to the standard Monster Spray:
  ◆ Check it out. Showing her the empty closet reassures her that you are truly concerned.
  ◆ Rent the wonderful film *Monsters, Inc.* and talk about it with your child.

Taking It One Step at a Time: Systematic Desensitization

One tried-and-true method for helping children get past their fears or phobias has the rather intimidating name, Systematic Desensitization. The idea, however, is very simple. Here's how it works.

STEP 1: HELP YOUR CHILD DEVELOP A "FEAR HIERARCHY"

Most things that people fear come in more and less fear-producing forms. With this in mind, suggest various ways your child might encounter the feared item, presenting them in pairs and asking your child to say which would be scarier. ("Sarah, would you be more scared if you stood close to a dog or had to pet a dog?") Take notes and you'll soon have a hierarchy from least scary to most scary something like this:

1. Hear the word "dog."
2. Say the word "dog."
3. See a picture of a dog.
4. Touch a picture of a dog.
5. Handle a toy dog.
6. See a dog playing with someone behind a fence.
7. See a dog playing with someone *not* behind a fence.
8. Stand next to a dog on a leash.
9. Stand next to a dog *not* on a leash.
10. Pet a little dog.
11. Pet a big dog.

STEP 2: CHOOSE AN INCOMPATIBLE BEHAVIOR

Some behaviors simply can't occur at the same time. Among those that are incompatible with fear are feeling relaxed, feeling interested, and feeling happy. The idea is to pick one and help your child practice feeling that way "on command." In Denise Chapman Weston and Mark Weston's book, *Playful Parenting*, for example, they suggest taping a piece of tissue or crepe paper to the bottom of a pair of toy eyeglasses and having the child practice deep breathing by breathing hard enough to make the tissue move. Other possibilities might be letting the child play with a favorite toy, eat a favorite food, watch a favorite video, or listen to a favorite audiotape.

STEP 3: SYSTEMATICALLY PAIR THE INCOMPATIBLE BEHAVIOR WITH ITEMS ON THE LIST

Starting with the least feared item in the hierarchy, have your child engage in the incompatible behavior in the presence of that item until he feels comfortable. Then move on to the next most feared version of the feared object and so on. For example, as you and your child sit watching her favorite video/DVD, periodically say something that includes the word "dog." Once she is comfortable with you saying the word, ask her to say it back to you whenever you say it. Make a game out of it by varying how you say the word—sometimes whispering it, sometimes saying it with a high-pitched voice, saying it rapidly, and so on. Once these two levels of the hierarchy have been conquered, simply continue down the list.

Whatever you do, *don't rush the process* or you may make things worse. It can take days, if not weeks, to take your child through the whole list—and you may need to repeat the sequence numerous times before the fear is gone for good.

One other tip: Books and movies that put the feared object in a good light are especially helpful. In fact, Linda recently got over a lifelong fear of spiders by reading Barbara Kingsolver's sympathetic portrayal of spiders in her lovely book *Prodigal Summer*. Linda still has a long way to go with snakes, however.

- ◆ Create a friendly monster using pillows, old clothes, or decorated dolls. It will be this monster's job to tell all the other monsters that your child is "already taken."
- ◆ Find soothing music that can take your child's mind off her worries.
- ◆ Clean out the closets and add lights.
- ◆ If your child is sure there's a monster under the bed, put the mattress on a solid foundation—or better yet, directly on the floor.
- ◆ **The dark.** In addition to the classic nightlight:
  - ◆ Provide an easy-to-use flashlight.
  - ◆ Mount photographs of family members where they can be easily seen or handled.

- Get your child used to having fun in the dark with activities like shadow play, "in-the-dark-art" (drawing things with the lights out), hide-and-seek under the covers.
- Cover the ceiling with glow-in-the-dark stars.

WHEN IT'S MORE THAN A FEW FEARS

Here are some tips for dealing with a child who suffers not from one or two specific fears, but from an overall, high level of anxiety.

- **Search for the source.** As we discussed in detail earlier in the chapter, some children are more vulnerable than others to high levels of anxiety. The first step, therefore, is to figure out as best you can which category or categories apply to your child. Is your child one of those who is biologically predisposed toward anxiety, or has something changed in her life that is proving too difficult for her to handle in normal ways? The answers will help you sort out your next steps.

- **Establish routines.** Here's a "next step" that almost always helps. Children who are prone to anxiety are desperate for predictability in their lives. One way to provide that predictability is by establishing daily routines whenever possible, such as standard mealtimes, naptimes, bathtimes, and bedtimes. Scheduling daily life this way may require putting your child's need for consistency ahead of other people's convenience ("We'll need to wait until after his nap"), but trust us, you and your child will *both* pay a high price if you don't. It's also soothing to a highly anxious child to have a standard order of events *within* each of these larger episodes, so that, for example, she can always count on bedtime beginning with a fresh diaper and jammies and ending with a good book, a cuddle, and one final kiss.

- **Seek professional help.** We are strong believers in the value of seeking professional help whenever you feel your child needs help in addition to your own. Doing so is especially important if your child's general anxiety or specific fears have grown to the point that they are interfering with the family's daily life. Your pediatrician is generally your best place to start. You might also solicit recommendations from family and friends or contact local mental health agencies. Frankly, we look forward to the day when every family, in addition to having a trusted pediatrician, will enjoy the benefits of a child developmental specialist to whom they can turn for comfort and counseling.

8

No Need to Hide:
Dealing with Shyness and Withdrawal

N E W S   F L A S H!

Shyness Starts in the Cradle, Scientists Discover

Cambridge, Massachusetts. Twenty-one-month-old Daniel is hard to find unless you look closely. That's because he's hiding behind his mother, clinging with apparent desperation to her skirt. Just a minute before, he had been happily playing with a set of toy cars on the floor of a playroom at Harvard University. All that changed, however, with a knock on the door and the entrance of a pleasant young woman named Heidi. For the next ten minutes it didn't matter what Heidi did to win his trust, Daniel stayed right where he was—two little eyes peeking out from behind his mother's skirt.

This actually wasn't Daniel's first visit to the playroom. Although he doesn't remember it, his mother brought him here when he was just four months old to be part of psychologist Jerome Kagan's study of the origins of inhibited versus uninhibited personality styles. On that first visit, Daniel had seen colorful mobiles and moving objects, heard a variety of sounds, and even smelled unusual smells on a cotton swab near his nose. His reaction? Daniel hadn't been any happier about those events than he was to see Heidi seventeen months later! Like 20 percent of the four-month-old American infants Kagan and his colleagues tested, Daniel reacted to these sudden, unfamiliar experiences by thrusting his arms and legs out, arching his back, and beginning to cry.

What's more, there's a fifty-fifty chance that even at age eight and older, Daniel will be continuing to struggle with what Kagan calls an "inborn nudge" in the direction of reacting to new things—and especially new people—with fear and trepidation. The reason lies buried deep in the part of Daniel's brain that allows humans, and other mammals, to feel emotions. Often referred to as the limbic brain, this system is dominated by the amygdala, the structure that analyzes information from our eyes, ears, and other senses and decides whether or not an object or event poses danger. Simply put, Daniel's amygdala, in comparison to an uninhibited child's amygdala, doesn't take any chances! "Better safe than sorry" is its motto, with the result that *anything* unexpected results in changes in the body that prepare it for flight: faster heart rate, shallow breathing, and great caution. As a result, babies with hair-trigger amygdalas like Daniel's are much more likely than babies with less sensitive amygdalas to grow up as cautious—even shy—adults.

Is there anything that Daniel's parents can do to help him reprogram his amygdala? The answer, according to Kagan, is a clear and resounding YES! "If adult caregivers prepare Daniel for novel experiences and gently encourage him to approach unfamiliar things," says Kagan, "it is quite possible that his inhibited style will not become a preserved habit." In other words, unlike some of Mother Nature's little gifts to us, biology is not destiny when it comes to shyness. Children like Daniel can indeed learn to appreciate and even enjoy the richness and variety that life provides.

Is Shyness a Problem?

All parents want their children to be comfortable interacting with other people and open to learning about the world. Not all children, however, fit this description. Some children, like little Daniel from the news flash, are easily frightened and upset by novelty from the moment they're born. As they approach their first birthday and become aware of other people, the situation becomes even more obvious. They grow especially wary of strangers, frightened of having to participate in unfamiliar social situations, and eager to find ways to escape. The most common term used to describe such children is "shy."

What causes parents and professionals to worry about shy children is not just the fact that they prefer solitude. When accompanied by feelings of contentment and the ability to interact confidently with others when necessary, such a preference may be different from the norm but not particularly problematic. The problem arises when it's clear that a shy child wishes she were different, would like to interact with others but can't, feels marginalized in social situations, and as a result of all this becomes more and more self-conscious and unsure. Such feelings can be *extremely* painful, often causing a child to withdraw into a shell, thereby increasing the chances even further that she will be openly rejected by her peers. If these feelings continue into adolescence and adulthood, the results often include . . .

- Self-imposed isolation and profound loneliness
- Clinical depression
- Marriage for the wrong reasons (for example, to the first person who shows interest)
- Lack of career advancement (These people are not among the "squeaky wheels" who "get the grease.")
- Anger and hostility toward the world

Clearly, no parent wants his or her child to suffer in these ways. The goal of this chapter of *Baby Hearts* is to share with you what research has revealed about the origins and developmental milestones of shyness and then provide you with research-based strategies for dealing effectively with a child biased in this direction.

Shyness from a Parent's Perspective

Before exploring in more detail what shyness means for a child's day-to-day life, let's stop and think about how it affects the big people who love her—and especially her parents. It turns out that helping a child conquer shyness helps them too.

HER PAIN IS YOUR PAIN

Even if parents of shy children aren't aware of the long-term consequences just listed, they are very much aware of the pain and discomfort their children are suffering. And it hurts. Try this. Imagine that your infant or toddler is already five years old and starting kindergarten. Day after day you go to pick her up only to find her hovering at the edge of the action with a knitted brow, scared expression, and tears in her eyes. See what we mean? If you're like us, you actually can feel a sudden ache grow in the pit of your stomach along with an overwhelming desire to rescue her.

There's no doubt that one of the reasons the human species has survived as long as it has is because Mother Nature has tilted the scale toward great empathy on the part of parents for the suffering of their very young children. The value of this lies in the fact that it motivates parents to *do* something to make their children's pain go away. Fortunately, as you'll see, there's a great deal that parents *can* do, especially in the first three years, to help shy children deal with their anxieties.

IT'S NOT YOUR FAULT

Another reason that parents of shy children suffer is because they are incredibly quick to blame themselves. Their inner voice may be chiding them with accusations—"It's because I started child care too early" or "It's because I started child care too late." Or possibly "It's because I didn't give her enough one-on-one attention" or "It's because I gave her too much one-on-one attention." In other words, there's usually no need for other adults to chastise the shy child's parents because they've undoubtedly beaten them to it.

It's this knee-jerk tendency to blame themselves that makes Jerome Kagan's work so important. The discovery of an inborn, physiological basis for fear of novelty in infants and toddlers means, quite simply, "It's not your fault!" If, like little Daniel, your baby has been easily upset by new things for as long as you can remember, chances are excellent that what you're dealing with is a personality *style* or temperament. Using the flower analogy from Chapter 1, you may have been given a "Slow-to-Warm" Baby Orchid or a "Difficult" Baby Holly. In either case, rather than being a reaction to what you've done or not done in your interactions with her, your child's shyness quite likely reflects a physiological tendency based on having a highly sensitive limbic brain. That said, what *is* in your hands is helping your child learn to live with her inborn nudge toward inhibition in a way that brings satisfaction and self-esteem rather than pain and loneliness.

Is Shyness Good or Bad? Depends on Where You're Born

A little boy hovers on the edge of the school playground, clearly wanting to join the other boys but a bit too shy to try. It's not the first time the boy has behaved this way, and the teacher, watching him struggle with uncertainty, thinks to herself... What? What does she think to herself?

Well, it turns out that it all depends on where this particular little drama is taking place. If the playground is almost anywhere in the United States, the teacher's thoughts quite likely go something like this: "Poor Christopher. Too bad he's so shy. It's going to be a real problem if it continues." Rightly or wrongly, in American culture shyness is usually seen as a liability, as a fault that needs fixing if a child hopes to be successful.

Were this scenario to take place within an Asian country—say Thailand—the teacher's reaction probably would be very different: "Ah, there's little Kydong. What a quiet, well-behaved boy. He will go far in this world." In sharp contrast to American culture where a carefree, lively personality is likely to win a child friends and adult admirers, Asian cultures regard reserved, unobtrusive behavior in children as a sign of maturity and a portent of future success.

The lesson here is an important one. Shyness is a problem only if the rest of a child's social world makes it so.

A Variety of Developmental Pathways

As with every other aspect of development, there are significant individual differences among shy children. These differences are important for parents to know about for several reasons. First, the more you know about *why* your child is shy, the better able you will be to help him deal with his anxiety. Second, knowing how your shy child *behaves* will help you better understand the reactions of others toward him. And third, because the different categories of shyness have distinctive *developmental pathways*, knowing which one best describes your child can help you predict more exactly what his specific challenges are likely to be and when they are most likely to arise.

American parents tend to worry if their children are shy more than parents in Asian cultures. In America, a lively personality is likely to win a child friends, while in Asian cultures, more reserved, unobtrusive behavior is preferred by both children and adults.

TO BE A CHILD IS TO BE SHY . . . SOMETIMES

But first it's important to point out that all children are shy at one time or another, especially during the first three years. The reason is simple. Human beings are built to be cautious in the face of unpredictable and potentially dangerous circumstances. That's what the limbic brain with its watchful amygdala is for, after all. It follows, then, that the less an individual understands about how the world works, the more unpredictable and potentially dangerous it will seem. And it's hard to find anyone less knowledgeable about the world than a very young child.

For example, all children develop a fear of strangers toward the end of their first year because they are both unfamiliar and unpredictable. What does a nine-month-old know about a new face approaching rapidly from across the room? Nothing. All he knows is that it's not Mommy—or Daddy, or any of the other people whose predictability he's grown to trust. What sets shy children apart, therefore, is not the fact that they exhibit a fear of strangers. All babies, even bold Baby Dandelion, our "Active" baby, will do so. (See Chapter 1 for descriptions of the flowers representing four inborn temperaments.) The difference lies in the amount of information shy kids require about specific strangers (and eventually, strangers in *general*) before they are willing to let down their guard.

TO BE A CHILD IS TO PLAY ALONE . . . FOR A WHILE

Another trait all children share is the tendency to play alone for a good chunk of the first three years. As we pointed out in Chapter 5, although infants and toddlers may be aware of other children sharing their space, it's not until the middle to end of the second year—or even into the third—that they begin playing together. It's at this point that a child's basic attitude toward interacting with other children becomes noticeable. Whereas Baby Dandelion and Baby Sunflower tend to seize the opportunity, Baby Orchid and *perhaps* Baby Holly are more likely to hold back.

There is a type of solitary play, however, that remains common—and is even highly encouraged by adults—throughout the preschool years. Psychologist Kenneth Rubin from the University of Waterloo in Canada, one of the world's leading experts on shyness, calls this solitary constructive play. What he's referring to is play that centers on creating or assembling something or that involves a degree of problem solving. Good examples would include putting puzzles together, stacking blocks, building with Legos, painting and doing other craft projects, and—most recently—playing computer games. By their very nature these tend to be single-child activities, and because they are considered educational, parents and caregivers actually encourage preschool children to spend time in this way. The good news is that doing so comes naturally to shy children. The problem arises when children continue to occupy themselves with such activities beyond the age that adults (at least *American* adults) view as appropriate and do so to the exclusion of nonsolitary activities.

THE BIOLOGICALLY WARY CHILD

We begin our description of the different subgroups of shy children with the group we've been highlighting all along. These are the children psychologist Jerome Kagan discovered are innately more cautious than their peers, the ones with the hair-trigger amygdalas for whom shyness is really a nature-given personality style.

Like little Daniel from the news flash at the beginning of the chapter, these kids are simply wired differently from others. For example, psychologist Nathan Fox and his colleagues from the University of Maryland have repeatedly found that, starting in infancy, inhibited children have more activity going on in the front of the right side of their brains than in the front of the left side of their brains. And because how a child is wired is at least in part a result of messages carried in his genes, it should come as no surprise to learn that this type of shyness runs in families. Although we don't understand the genetic base behind it, the fact that identical twins are more alike in shyness than nonidentical twins is a good indication that there *is* one.

Is This Your Child? The best way to tell if your child fits this category is to compare her reactions to three different situations:

1. Familiar objects, people, and places
2. Novel objects and places
3. Novel people

Baby Hearts in Action:
From Baby Orchid to Social Butterfly

Susan's granddaughter Emma was a Baby Orchid if there ever was one. "Slow-to-Warm" from the day she was born, Emma was a year old and would still wail in protest if anyone but Mom and Dad—including Grandma Susan—even tried to *touch* her.

Despite living six hundred miles away, Susan had faithfully traveled to see Emma at least once a month, always hoping that the baby would be glad to see her too. No such luck, however, until one day soon after Emma had turned fourteen months old. Susan came down the escalator at the airport to find Emma with her arms stretched in greeting and a huge smile on her face. From then on, "Mimi," as Susan is known to all her grandchildren, was clearly a favorite in Emma's eyes. It seemed like a miracle, but like many miracles, it was actually the result of patient and insightful parenting. What had happened?

It turns out that Emma had started going to day care. But rather than just drop-

The biologically wary child, as you probably already have guessed, reacts quite positively to #1 but extremely cautiously to #2 and #3. As long as these kids are on familiar turf and involved with familiar people and predictable objects, they are happy as clams. They explore with confidence, moving easily away from you, and then come happily back to you to share their new discoveries. In fact, when they are surrounded by all things familiar and predictable, you'd never know they were any different from other kids. But let something new intrude and they react swiftly with caution and fear.

The Mix of Nature and Nurture. This form of shyness starts off biologically driven, but unless parents lend a helping hand, it can very easily transform itself into a fear of social interaction fueled by a realistic concern about how others perceive and treat these shy children—or at least how they *think* others perceive them and will treat them, should they try to participate. Sadly, it's what psychologists call a self-fulfilling prophecy: The biologically wary child starts off afraid that people will hurt her even though they really wouldn't. But over time, the child's avoidance becomes so much more obvious and inappropriate

ping her off and hoping for the best, Emma's mom, Amy, had gone to great lengths to help Emma slowly warm to the idea. For the entire first week, Amy stayed at her side, introducing her to the staff and other children with a big smile on her face to show Emma that Mom thought these folks were all pretty special.

Amy spent the second week there as well, but purposefully left Emma's side for longer and longer periods of time. The strategy was working. Emma was voluntarily getting involved with the other children and letting the caregivers initiate play.

By the third week, Amy and the staff felt Emma was ready to take the plunge. Although Emma wasn't totally happy that week and the staff had to spend significant amounts of time comforting her, their patience paid off. By the fourth week, Emma was waving good-bye to Amy when she left! What's more, the joy Emma was finding in the care and companionship of the adults and children at day care was generalizing beyond the classroom to other people—including a totally delighted (and much-relieved) Mimi.

Siblings can vary enormously in terms of inborn temperament, including how bold or shy they are. Big sister Caroline's "Hello, world!" attitude seemed to characterize her from Day 1, as did little sister Katherine's classic "I'm not so sure" shy face.

that other people often begin having negative perceptions and treating her unkindly.

There are several reasons why this happens, and knowing what these are can help parents ward them off. Because biologically wary children are so afraid of new people, they tend to avoid them whenever given the option. As a result they...

◆ **Have fewer success experiences.** How do *non*shy children get over their fear of strangers? By accumulating rewarding experiences with unfamiliar adults and peers. In other words, they learn to expect such interactions to be fun rather than frightening. And here's where another self-fulfilling prophecy comes into play: If you *expect* to have fun, there's a greater chance that you actually will. In this way the ball keeps rolling in a positive direction. Unless their parents intervene, biologically wary children may never learn this lesson.

◆ **Fail to learn how to interact.** Certain "tricks of the trade" help children initiate and maintain contact with other kids. How do you join a group that's already playing? How do you invite someone to play with you? How do you handle conflict? Nonshy children learn these tricks in the course of playing with other kids, either through trial and error or through imitating behaviors they see working for others. Because they avoid interacting with new children, biologically wary children fall further and further behind in knowing how to do so.

> A torn jacket is soon mended; but hard words bruise the heart of a child.
>
> —Henry Wadsworth Longfellow, poet

◆ **Develop negative "self-talk."** In his excellent book on parenting shy children, psychologist Ward Swallow points out that children who hover on the edges of interactions or avoid them altogether often do so because of the negative tone of what they are saying to themselves, such as "They don't like me," "I know they won't let me play," or "I won't know how to do things right and they'll laugh at me." With all that going on in the background, shy children find themselves paralyzed with fear, unable to take the chance to prove that they are wrong.

THE BIOLOGICALLY SOLITARY CHILD

The term "biologically solitary" refers to children who have never met an object they didn't love but who simply aren't that interested in people. In the extreme, this tendency can be a sign of a serious developmental problem such as autism or Asperger's syndrome, but in its milder forms it's just a personality style. These are the kids who are fascinated with how things work, who take things apart just to put them back together, who develop their own pretend scenarios that enable them to use objects creatively, and who, basically, find their fellow humans less intriguing in comparison.

Is This Your Child? The biologically solitary child has a profile in terms of familiar and unfamiliar events that's quite different from the biologically wary child. Rather than distinguishing between familiar and unfamiliar, these children tend to distinguish between objects and people. It's not that they dislike or are particularly afraid of people (at least when they are young), it's just that, given their druthers, they'd rather spend their time with familiar *or* unfamiliar objects. That's *not* to say, however, that these children don't develop strong attachments to Mom and Dad. The biologically solitary child, just like *every* child, revels in being loved, needs to be able to trust Mom and Dad, and enjoys sharing discoveries with the important people in his life.

The Mix of Nature and Nurture. You may be wondering why these children are even included in a list of "shy" profiles. After all, they are the ones who make the choice to be on their own. And that's true at the beginning. However, a similar thing happens to biologically solitary children as we described happening to biologically wary kids. Although they start off content, they gradually begin to suffer the consequences of being different.

When does this happen? If their solitary play is mainly of the "constructive" variety—that is, putting things together or playing computer games—then their preference for solitude won't attract attention until early elementary school, just as tends to be the case for biologically wary children. However, if biologically solitary children also really enjoy what Rubin calls "solitary dramatic play"—elaborate pretend scenarios that don't involve other kids *even when other kids are available*—then their behavior begins to stand out earlier, and even in preschool they may begin to be rebuffed by other children if they do seek interaction.

And because biologically solitary children choose not to play with other children when they are very young, they end up being handicapped in the same ways as biologically wary children. Unless gently guided into social interactions at early ages, they don't accumulate success experiences, they don't learn *how* to interact, and eventually they develop destructive self-talk that prevents them from attempting to interact with others even when they want to. End result? Shyness. Ironically, these feelings also can lead to fits of aggression and hostility as children reach a point of discomfort where lashing out feels better than continuing to withdraw.

Look on the Bright Side

One way to balance your anxiety over your child's shy temperament is to remember that being shy usually comes with some very nice side benefits. In fact, the human race probably wouldn't still be here were it not for the talents shy people tend to develop. Children with hair-trigger amygdalas definitely face challenges, but those challenges also tend to make them . . .

◆ **Keen observers.** Because they are so concerned about what other people think about them, shy children work harder than most children at being able to read subtle emotional cues in other people's behavior and expressions.

◆ **Natural empathizers.** Because they are keen observers and know all too well what it is like to suffer, shy children often develop greater empathy for others than their peers.

◆ **Good imaginers.** Because they spend more time on their own, shy children often create inner worlds of great richness.

◆ **Loyal friends.** Because shy children often have trouble making friends, once they have one, these kids are incredibly loyal. They understand how precious a good friend truly is and go to great lengths to be the very best friend they can be.

◆ **Affection givers and seekers.** Because shy children see their parents as safe harbors, they tend to make their parents feel loved and needed. Like little puppies that lick their owners' faces when rescued from the pet store, shy children tend to shower their parents with affection. (In fact, parents need to make sure that they aren't unconsciously supporting shy behavior out of a desire to maintain this abundance of affection and dependence.)

THE "SHY-THROUGH-HARD-KNOCKS" CHILD

A third group of shy children arrives at that designation not because they are biologically predisposed in some way, but because their early experiences have conspired against them. Among Jerome Kagan's sample of uninhibited "bold" children, 12 percent had become highly fearful by twenty-one months. This fearfulness, like the anxiety felt by the biologically wary children, stands in the way of developing appropriate social skills and success experiences. With the ball continuing to roll in a negative direction across the preschool and into the elementary school years, they too eventually fit the profile of the shy (or reactively aggressive) child. According to Kagan, their amygdalas have actually *learned* to be hypervigilant.

What "hard knocks" are we talking about? Basically it's anything that teaches a child that the world is a scary place and that people can't be trusted. The following are the most typical causes.

◆ **An attachment gone awry.** As we discussed in Chapter 2, the importance of the relationship between a baby and her major caregivers in the first years can't be overstated. If, instead of a secure attachment, a baby reaches toddlerhood with an insecure attachment, then the inability to trust her caregivers starts to generalize to other people.

◆ **Traumatic loss.** Infants and toddlers don't understand *why* they may have lost

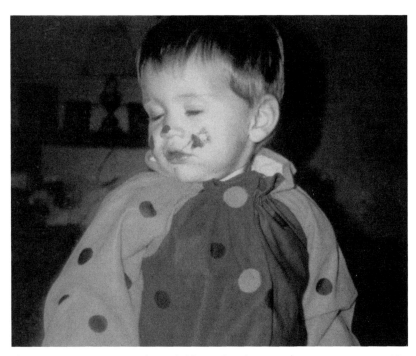

There are many reasons why a child may be shy. Some are serious issues, like physical disabilities or family problems. Others are much less serious—like having to wear a silly clown costume on Halloween!

someone important to them—for example, through death, divorce, or a hired caregiver who moves on. All they know is that the person they depended on is *gone*. Unfortunately, the feeling of having been abandoned can create a fearfulness that interferes with their ability to trust people for years to come.

◆ **Dramatic transitions.** As we said earlier, children thrive on predictability. When things suddenly become dramatically unpredictable, even temperamentally bold infants and toddlers may have a hard time adjusting. The resulting generalized anxiety may start to include a previously unseen wariness of people. Forewarned, however, is forearmed. Parents can do a great deal to smooth their child's passage through transitions such as the birth of another child, enrollment in child care, beginning of kindergarten, a move to a new home and neighborhood.

◆ **Being "different" mentally or physically.** Unfortunately, the playground isn't known for being the most accepting environment for children who are obviously different from the norm. It could be a physical or mental handicap, a different color skin, or even just unusual clothes. Whatever the source, a prolonged negative reaction from other children can cause even biologically bold children to turn shy. Parental alertness to sudden changes in a bold child's behavior is the first step toward addressing the problem.

N E W S   F L A S H !

Being at a Loss for Words Scares Toddlers Too

Guelph, Ontario. It's lunchtime in the Psychology Department at the University of Guelph, and graduate student Laura Johnson is talking with a friend. "I'd love to go to the party at Professor Evans's house," she says, "but I never know what to say!" Ironically, following this conversation, Laura returns to the Child Development Lab where she continues to help psychologist Mary Ann Evans demonstrate the connection between shyness and language ability. It turns out that, just as is true for adults, shy children often avoid social situations altogether rather than stand awkwardly in silence. And with good reason, it seems. In study after study Dr. Evans finds that children as young as thirty-six months who are shy also tend to be less facile with language than their more outgoing peers. Because their language skills are no match for their more verbal playmates—or for the unfamiliar adults who try engaging them in conversation at the grocery store—they quickly learn to withdraw completely or to rely on their parents rather than risk being judged as inadequate or dumb.

What's a parent to do? Fortunately, researchers specializing in language development have uncovered a number of ways parents can support their child's development of this critical skill. Here are just a few of their recommendations.

- Talk to your baby from the day he's born.
- Ask lots of questions even if you have to answer them yourself for a while.
- Encourage him to communicate with signs before he can say words.
- Take your baby along on outings that can stimulate his interest in naming things.
- Start early reading books together.
- Limit the amount of time your child spends passively watching TV and videos.
- And above all, praise every attempt he makes to communicate.

Words of Wisdom and Tricks of the Trade

As the news flash makes clear, doing everything you can to give your child a good start in learning to talk is one way to increase the chance that she will enjoy interacting with people. Fortunately, research on the development of shy behavior provides many additional tips for helping shy children—even those who are biologically nudged in that direction—to become more self-confident in social situations.

SEE THINGS THROUGH YOUR SHY CHILD'S EYES

In his book *The Shy Child*, psychologist Ward Swallow points out that the most important first step parents of a shy child can take is to make every effort to understand what the world looks like though their child's eyes. Here are a few things that doing so is likely to reveal.

- **Shy children are really and truly *scared.*** In fact, in many cases it's no exaggeration to say that they are paralyzed with fear. This truth is often hard for parents, particularly outgoing parents, to understand because what strikes terror into a child's heart can look perfectly benign or even fun to an adult. The reality, however, is that shy children suffer from a form of tunnel vision. In their eyes the threatening aspects of a situation loom so large that the positive ones are literally invisible. When a shy child hovers at the edge of a group clinging to her parents, she's not being manipulative; she is truly frightened—as frightened as her parents might be if required to step to the podium in front of a thousand angry strangers. Keeping that in mind can increase both your compassion and your patience.

◆ **Even asking for help is hard.** For a shy child, even something as simple as ordering food at McDonald's can be terrifying. With that in mind, it's easier to understand why shy children won't ask their teacher to repeat something, won't ask another child's parent where the bathroom is, or won't even ask a store clerk to help them find their mommy. As strange as it seems to adults, to shy children, the benefits simply don't outweigh the imagined costs.

◆ **The stomachaches can be real.** Because younger shy children lack the ability—and older shy children often lack the *freedom*—to talk about their fears, their discomfort often moves underground, manifesting itself in the form of very real physical symptoms. This is even more understandable once you remember that a shy child's fear is caused by a physiological reaction in his brain—the same part of the brain that connects directly to his stomach, sweat glands, respiratory system, and heart. Why is this important to know? Because all too often parents jump to the conclusion that the shy child is faking illness to avoid the problem. Being accused of such malingering in the face of real distress only makes it harder for the child to trust the parent to help him deal with the anxiety he's feeling. Next we turn to specific ways to deliver such help.

BE YOUR CHILD'S SECURE HOME BASE

In order to take the risks necessary to overcome shyness, a child must know that you're a secure home base to which she can retreat if the going gets too rough. This means building a relationship steeped in love, acceptance, and absolute trust. (See Chapter 2 for guidance.) And remember, offering a secure home base means not discounting fears, withdrawing love when someone falters, applying negative labels like "shy" or "inhibited," or making children doubt themselves. Always and everywhere be your child's biggest fan.

Baby Hearts in Action:
When Silence Is Golden

Here's an extremely important tip for parents of shy children: Be careful not to an-swer for your child when the two of you are in social situations. This is a very easy habit to get into and a very hard one to break. Although your heart is in the right place—you want to spare your child discomfort—you are both denying him the chance to practice his conversational skills and sending a message that you don't think he's up to the task.

Despite all her experience as a developmental psychologist, Linda had to learn this lesson the hard way when her wonderful son, Kai, was already twelve years old. Like Kai, Linda had been extremely shy as a child. As a result, she had become ex-quisitely sensitive to Kai's own tongue-tied embarrassment when asked questions by strangers and was all too quick to put him out of his misery by speaking for him. This is exactly what happened on the day they were touring the Capitol in Washing-ton, D.C.

Having been suitably impressed at the grandeur of it all, they stopped at a sou-venir stand so Kai could add to his key chain collection. As Kai was scrutinizing his options, the salesperson, a pleasant, twenty-something young man, said in a friendly tone, "Well, hi there! What's your name? You look to be a junior high student. Am I right?" Hesitating only an instant, Linda quickly answered, "His name is Kai and he's in seventh grade"—whereupon the nice young man turned to her and said quite firmly, "Well, excuse me, but if he's in seventh grade, I think he's probably old enough to tell me so himself." Linda knew immediately how right he was, and now she tells this story in all her developmental psychology classes as a lesson in how tricky parenting can be.

What should Linda have done instead? In general, a much better strategy is to smile and signal approval of your child's own attempts to converse with others. If the message your child conveys isn't adequate, let the other person ask clarifying ques-tions rather than rushing in yourself to fill in the gaps. Remember, practice makes perfect in this domain too. So try practicing *not* talking so your child can practice talking.

START EARLY MAKING STRANGERS INTO FRIENDS

It's never too early to start introducing your child to other people. Doing so can gradually convince her that unfamiliar folks are sources of pleasure rather than pain. Daily life is full of situations that will allow even infants and toddlers to see you interacting in a positive way with unfamiliar adults and children. Don't push your child to contribute, but look for ways to sneak in some direct interaction—for example, having your child help you hand items to the cashier at the grocery store. Here are some other promising venues.

◆ Children's sections of bookstores and libraries
◆ Central areas in shopping malls
◆ Restaurants
◆ Play areas at fast-food outlets
◆ Playgrounds and beaches

And don't overlook the silver lining of trick-or-treat day. Halloween provides young children with one extremely positive interaction after another.

> Parents need to fill a child's bucket of self-esteem so high that the rest of the world can't poke enough holes in it to drain it dry.
>
> —Alvin Price, author of *How to Boost Your Child's Self-esteem*

KNOW THYSELF

If you have a tendency toward shyness yourself, work hard on managing it with confidence and good humor. Infants and toddlers learn by watching other people, and, as we explained in more detail in Chapter 7, can even "catch" their parents' fears. Be aware of your facial expressions and body language when interacting with store clerks and friendly strangers. Linger to talk to people after a school event rather than rushing home. Chat with friends you encounter in the grocery store. We don't mean to imply, however, that you must keep your own anxiety a complete secret. It actually can help to talk about it with your child. Your goal should be to show your child that enjoyment can come *despite* initial concerns—and that if you can accomplish this, so can he.

MAKE YOUR HOME A HUB OF ACTIVITY

In the box on page 121 we described a study by researchers Denise Daniels and Robert Plomin who found that adopted children's shyness was more strongly influenced by the level of social activity they experienced in their adoptive homes than it was by their biological parents' shyness. Take your clue from this study and invite family and friends to your home regularly. Shy children are much more accepting of novelty when they encounter it in a safe environment—and nothing feels as safe as home sweet home. Associate holidays—when children generally are anticipating good things—in your child's mind with having guests. Stop worrying if the house looks "perfect," and encourage people to just drop by instead of waiting for carefully orchestrated visits. Have older siblings invite their friends over. Bring new neighbors, exchange students, and business colleagues over to play games, watch movies, or just chat. Remain aware, however, that shy children need a safe place to retreat (their bedrooms, for example) if they start to feel overwhelmed.

Handle all this wisely and you will increase the likelihood that your child's future memories of home will be characterized by a comfortable hustle and bustle rather than the endless ticking of the hall clock or the droning of the TV.

ARRANGE ONE-ON-ONE PLAYDATES

After making as sure as you can that the chemistry is right, arrange for playdates with one other child and his or her parent. Keep the dates very short at first, gradually increasing the length when and if a relationship between the children grows. If your child is struggling to cope with a larger group of children (during child care, for example), target one of the children within the larger group as the playdate candidate. Having even one "buddy" among her classmates will make a tremendous difference to your child's sense of comfort. (See Chapter 5 for guidance on making the most of playdates.)

An older child can help a younger shy child become more confident. The older child's slightly more sophisticated play can build the shy child's repertoire of skills.

PREPARE YOUR CHILD IN ADVANCE

As we are fond of saying, forewarned is forearmed. The more information your child has about an impending social experience, the more in control she will feel. And with increased control comes decreased fear (see the news flash on page 173). Drive by the house where a birthday party will be held and talk about what is likely to happen, focusing, of course, on fun things like cake and ice cream. Don't settle for generalities; whenever possible provide details—such as who is likely to answer the door, what other children will be there, and what activities are planned. (Ask ahead of time.) All this applies in triplicate when introducing your shy child to a new classroom, organized Mom and Baby activity group, or hospital stays.

REMAIN ON SITE FOR AS LONG AS IT TAKES

Expect to have to spend whole days with your child when helping him make the transition into a child care setting, gradually easing yourself from being right by his side, to being closeby, to being across the room. Any quality child care program will welcome such a strategy, and if it doesn't, you should seriously consider finding another one. It's true that helping your child in this way is time-consuming. However, it's an investment upfront that will pay off big time in the months to come. If your schedule absolutely won't permit you to do it all yourself, ask another trusted adult (like Grandma) to share the burden. As we explained in Chapter 4, that's exactly what Susan did to help her grandson become comfortable with his new nursery school.

BUILD SOCIAL SKILLS THROUGH PRETEND PLAY

We strongly recommend psychologist Ward Swallow's book *The Shy Child,* for great ideas on how parents can help young children solve specific social problems through pretend scenarios and role-play. Among the most valuable tools parents have in this regard is humor. In describing how a parent could help his child deal with a cookie-snatcher at snack time, for example, Dr. Swallow has parent and child play the "what-if?" game: "What if your cookie came to life when Jason grabbed it, and it bit his thumb?" Getting your child giggling is a good way to ease into a serious exploration of options.

FIND THE BALANCE BETWEEN PUSHING AND PROTECTING THAT'S RIGHT FOR YOUR CHILD

Although we prefer the word "nudging" to "pushing," the basic dilemma is the same: At what point should you stop encouraging your child to spread his wings and allow him back into the safety of the nest? Unfortunately, there is no one correct answer to this question. It all depends on your own knowledge of how much stress your child can take at any particular point in time. Here are some rules of thumb that may help you decide.

◆ **Outright pushing seldom works.** The end result is usually increased anxiety because your disapproval gives the impression that even his home base is in danger.

◆ **Be sure you're acting in your child's best interests rather than your own.** Sometimes parents push when they shouldn't simply because they need to be on their way. The realities of life these days make a few such occasions unavoidable. When they happen with some consistency, however, a child begins to lose faith in his parent, a situation that only increases the child's anxiety.

◆ **Don't expect too much too soon.** Just as no adult learns to be a good golfer in a day, no shy child changes into a social butterfly (or even a caterpillar!) overnight. Success comes in baby steps, one challenge at a time—and each one, no matter how tiny, is worthy of praise. A simple "I was proud of the way you asked Jasmine to help you" can work wonders to boost a child's self-esteem and motivate her to go even further next time.

Finally, remember that shyness is not a disorder that needs to be "fixed." Your child is not "broken." True, a tendency toward being wary in social situations is a personality style that may pose certain challenges, but so does being extremely gregarious, opinionated, or physically active. Your goal needs to be to equip your child with whatever tools he'll need to cope with whatever life has in store for him. And what's the most important tool he can have in his toolbox? The knowledge that you will *always and forever* be on his side!

9

Tempers and Tantrums:
Handling Anger and Defiance

N E W S F L A S H !

Hanging In There with Difficult Babies
Pays Off Down the Line

London, England. Phoebe and her fifteen-month-old son, William, are a good example of some exciting research coming out of the University of London. Although clearly happy together now, it hasn't always been this easy. Far from it. From the moment he was born, William had seemed upset with the world. He would cry at the drop of a hat and was really hard—even at times impossible—to soothe. To make matters worse, he didn't seem to know the meaning of the word "sleep." In short, for months there was almost none of the cuddling and cooing the movies had led Phoebe to expect from a baby. "At first I thought there was something really wrong with him. And then I thought there was something really wrong with me!"

Everyone has heard it said about a problem child, "He was like that from the day he was born." The implication, of course, is that the outcome is inevitable, that the path from screaming, impossible-to-soothe newborn to difficult, impossible-to-control child is a direct one. Fortunately, Ian St. James-Roberts and his colleagues at the London University Institute of Education are proving that it's not.

How do they know? The researchers followed the development of persistent criers like William, as well as normal, easy-to-soothe babies, from age six weeks to fifteen months. The results were clear and very encouraging. Mothers of highly negative six-week-olds who held and interacted with them the most were rewarded by a change from negative to positive behavior at fifteen months. Sadly, the reverse was also true. Easy babies whose mothers did not hold and interact much with them at six weeks tended to shift in the other direction, becoming identifiably negative in their behavior at fifteen months. Finally, negative babies whose mothers had not shown patience and perseverance at six weeks continued to be difficult and negative into their second year.

"Phoebe's worry that there was something 'wrong' with her or her baby is very common," says St. James-Roberts. But no one is really to blame. Like millions of other new mothers, Phoebe was simply facing the challenge of dealing with an infant whose nervous system was wired in a way that made him highly irritable. Fortunately for William, Phoebe found the reserves of patience and persistence that he needed to help him deal with his volatile temperament.

Phoebe's final comment sums up the good news: "It's so satisfying to find out that all those hours spent walking, holding, and singing to William actually did make a difference!"

The Whys and Wherefores of the "Terrible Twos"

There certainly is good news in the research results coming from the University of London. In fact, the last decade or so has provided lots of good news like this—information that can help parents increase the chance that they and their child will survive the tough times with bonds of affection and good humor still strong. And tough times there certainly are. As Phoebe can attest, the first months can be very challenging. Unfortunately, more challenges still lie ahead. While more commonly associated with the teen years, "anger" and "defiance" are also the hallmarks of the second and third years of life.

This period is commonly, if somewhat numerically inaccurately, referred to as the terrible twos. The popular image of the child during this time is of a stubborn and unpredictable whirlwind with a hair-trigger temper and the ability to hold her breath until she turns blue. This stereotype of young toddlers as little tyrants is unfortunate because often it causes parents to overreact, to see manipulation where there is none, and to attempt to exert control with an enthusiasm uncomfortably akin to crushing the opposition.

That said, we must admit that the stereotype does contain a kernel of truth. Research by developmental psychologist Zeynep Biringen and her colleagues at the University of Colorado reveals a rise in conflicts with parents as they begin to impose necessary restrictions on toddlers' behavior. Add to this their increasing notions of themselves as individuals (sense of self) and their developing ability to express themselves verbally, and you have a picture of why toddlers find themselves more and more deeply embroiled in the important developmental task of launching their quest for independence. How parents support their child's efforts on this critical journey in the first three years has a significant influence on their child's tendencies toward anger and defiance throughout life. The goal of this chapter of *Baby Hearts*, therefore, is to point out the truth of the old adage, "An ounce of prevention is worth a pound of cure." By acquainting new parents with recent research on the psychological sources of anger and the environmental situations that contribute to persistent defiance, we hope to help everyone avoid serious problems later.

THE SILVER LINING: UNDERLYING EMOTIONAL ADVANCES

What parents need more than anything else to deal constructively with a toddler during the terrible twos is *patience*. But where are those reserves to come from? While we can't give you two of the main ingredients, sleep and free time, we can provide a third important contributor: understanding. By recognizing the positive advances that are fueling a baby or toddler's behaviors, you increase the likelihood that you will react without the hostility and punitiveness that are guaranteed to make things worse—*much* worse. So, here are the upsides of the terrible twos in more detail.

◆ **Birth to 2 months.** To understand the changes you see in the average one- to three-year old, you need to appreciate how far he's come. As we described in Chapter 3, babies are born with a rather narrow range of emotions: distress, disgust, interest, and contentment. Nowhere in this list is anger. Unfortunately, this is about to change.

◆ **2 to 10 months.** It's during this second stage that the rest of the inborn, or "primary," emotions begin clocking in: joy, sadness, surprise, fear, and *anger*. You may be wondering what such young babies have to get angry about. After all,

Every Cloud Has a Silver Lining

The terrible twos get their name from the increased belligerence and noncompliance so typical of the toddler years. It helps to know that these negative behaviors reflect positive changes in what children are learning to do and how well they are learning to think.

- **2 to 10 months**
  - **Upside.** Babies are learning how to make things work, both toys and people.
  - **Downside.** They get frustrated and angry when actions they've learned to make things happen suddenly don't work anymore.

- **10 to 18 months**
  - **Upside.** Babies are finally moving around the world on their own and enjoying every minute.
  - **Downside.** They require more supervision and restrictions that result in more "testing of wills" with parents.
  - **Upside.** Babies are learning lots about how the world works by experimenting.
  - **Downside.** They get frustrated and angry when parents bring experiments to a halt.
  - **Upside.** Babies' thoughts are getting more sophisticated.
  - **Downside.** They get frustrated and angry when they can't communicate them.

- **18 to 36 months**
  - **Upside.** Toddlers are eager to do tasks themselves.
  - **Downside.** They get frustrated and angry when they don't succeed.
  - **Upside.** Toddlers have finally developed a sense of self, a prerequisite for healthy social interactions.
  - **Downside.** They get frustrated and angry when their bids for independence are thwarted.

So, the next time your toddler suddenly goes from trying to put her shirt on to kicking and screaming on the floor, try to be a bit more sympathetic. She's just trying to grow up—and it's not easy.

aren't parents at their beck and call, trying mightily to meet their needs? The answer may surprise you. Even babies as young as two months are able to—and even *eager* to—learn how to control things. They may learn how to kick their feet to make a toy move, how to shake a rattle to make a noise, and certainly how to smile to get Mommy to smile back. By analyzing facial expressions of young infants in laboratory situations, researchers have shown that if the expected responses suddenly stop happening, very often the result is anger. The brows draw together and point down, the eyes stare straight ahead, and the mouth is squared rather than frowning. Oh yes, and there's also likely to be an accompanying wail. Of course, some children tolerate such violations of expectations better than others.

◆ **10 to 18 months.** Two sources of anger are predictable around the end of the first year and into the second. Both relate to underlying advances.

- ◆ **Baby as explorer.** Around ten months of age, babies become fascinated with figuring out how things work—how objects land when they fall, whether they float or not, how easy or hard they are to throw, whether they make neat noises when you bang them together. This is all great—unless the items in question are Grandma's precious knickknacks. The result is increased conflict between baby and adult, with baby often chafing at the arbitrary (in his mind) curtailing of his experiments.

- ◆ **Baby as wannabe communicator.** Unfortunately, babies' minds develop well in advance of their mouths. In other words, just because babies can't talk doesn't mean they don't have lots to say. It's certainly wonderful that they have so much more thinking power, but not being able to communicate their thoughts and needs effectively becomes more and more frustrating as the months roll by, often resulting in angry outbursts and tantrums. (As you'll see in the next chapter, one of the main advantages of encouraging babies to use signs before they can talk is that their frustration levels decrease.)

◆ **18 months to 3 years.** We've described the next important advance many times already. Around eighteen months, toddlers experience an epiphany. They recognize, in a way they haven't before, that they are consolidated entities with minds of their own, that they are separate from everyone else. ("Ah-hah! I'm me!") This knowledge, in combination with greater strength, physical agility, and curiosity, creates in them a very strong push to prove their independence in these ways:

The video looked like a fun toy to twenty-month-old Shade, until he heard his father's warning that it was on the list of no-nos. Distracting toddlers with safe objects is a great way to head off tantrums while supporting their blossoming curiosity about the world.

- **Doing things themselves.** Content up to now to let parents take care of them, toddlers are suddenly—and stubbornly—keen on doing mundane tasks for themselves: feeding themselves, putting on their own shoes and socks, washing themselves, brushing their own teeth, buckling themselves into the car seat, and so on. If you stop to think about it, this is really good news. Unfortunately, parents don't always have the time or wisdom to accept and encourage these attempts. The result is anger and tantruming—sometimes on *both* the child's and the parent's part.
- **Expressing their own opinions.** Ask most parents of toddlers what their child's favorite word is and the likely answer is "No!" This shift toward what can seem like knee-jerk belligerence is really quite normal. In fact, many

scientists believe that having children begin to break away from parents at this point—to spread their wings and try to fly—is so adaptive for our species that changes in hormones have been built in to trigger it. In many ways it's a miniature version of what happens during the teen years as adolescents establish their own identities and fight for independence—and believe it or not, it's something to celebrate. Learning how to handle this aspect of your child's natural movement toward independence is one of the hardest yet most *important* tasks you'll ever face as a parent.

Anger and Defiance Without a Silver Lining

Unfortunately, for all too many children, the belligerence they display during these early years doesn't stem from such benign causes as those just listed—and doesn't go away with increased maturity. For example, as the research described in the news flash indicates, nonsupportive parenting measured as early as six weeks predicts negativity on the part of a child at fifteen months. These findings illustrate the common denominator researchers have identified among all the factors known to contribute to abnormally high and persistent levels of anger and defiance in children: anxiety about the steadfastness of their parents' love.

As we described in detail in Chapter 2, the nature of the relationship between baby and parent during the first years of life is critically important. Even though babies and toddlers aren't capable of remembering things in the same way adults do, research has proven that from Day 1 they are automatically laying down memories based on specific experiences with those who care for them. And just as is true of all of us, those memories color their expectations for the future.

If a baby's experiences are happy ones, based on many occasions where her distress, fear, bids for attention, and offers of affection have been pretty consistently satisfied in a timely fashion, then her expectations are for continued safety. The baby trusts her needs will continue to be met and brings a general openness to future interactions and a readiness to listen to and cooperate with her caregivers. Such a generally positive attitude doesn't eliminate anger and defiance completely during the toddler years, but limits it to the kinds we have listed—those with a silver lining. (And don't worry. At the end of the chapter we provide tips for how to deal with the typical, hot-tempered toddler in ways that don't make matters worse.)

However, if a baby's needs for attention and affection have not been met in a consistent fashion, if caregiving has been erratic, abusive, or neglectful—either emotionally or physically—then the baby's memory bank automatically fuels continued distrust, anxiety, and anger.

> Kids who have their needs met early by loving parents . . . are subjected totally and thoroughly to the most severe form of "discipline" conceivable: they don't do what you don't want them to do because they love you so much!
>
> —M. Bevan-Brown, M.D., psychiatrist and author of *The Sources of Love and Hate*

A child who brings this reservoir of negativism into the second and third years is a much bigger challenge than the typical toddler. What's more, if the inappropriate parenting style that gave rise to the child's heightened anxiety in the first place doesn't improve dramatically (and it seldom does without education or intervention), then the child's anxiety and anger just continue to grow, often at an even faster pace because the clashes between child and parent become even more contentious as the child gets older, stronger, and more defiant. As we'll see in the next chapter when we discuss aggression, it's a cycle that all too often plays itself out in the form of serious conduct problems and even criminal activity in later years. At the very least, the toddler who brings this extra burden of negativism into the terrible twos will be a challenge to one and all.

In general, then, less than optimal caregiving experiences lead a child to question the steadfastness of a parent's love. This questioning results in heightened anxiety, and the anxiety, in turn, often surfaces in the form of anger and defiance. But what causes critical lapses in the quality of caregiving? Why do parents sometimes fall so far short of what their children need that they put their children's futures at risk? Here are some of the most common storms the parent-child relationship has trouble weathering.

DIFFICULT TEMPERAMENTS

Baby Holly. Remember Baby Holly? The baby whose "sharp edges" are evident from Day 1? This is the baby whose inborn temperament earns her labels like "Difficult" or "Irritable." William, the fifteen-month-old in the news flash, was one of these. From birth he was easily upset, hard to soothe, and emotionally intense. Such babies can be incredibly difficult to parent well. As we explained in Chapter 2, parents with a Baby Holly on their hands need all the support they can get, especially in the form of time off to recover their equilibrium—and sleep! If they don't get good support and can't find sufficient reserves of patience and affection within themselves, they often become openly angry at their child. It's easy to see why. As one parent in our research expressed it, "I give him so much and get so little in return!" Unfortunately, the parent's anger causes the child to become more and more anxious and intense—a combination that often leads to high and persistent levels of anger and defiance as the child gets older.

The Baby Hollys of the world, because they are easily upset and difficult to calm down, can be hard on parents. When the result is anger toward the baby, it's all too easy for a vicious cycle to get started, with more and more anxiety and anger on both the part of baby and parent.

Baby Dandelion. And remember Baby Dandelion? The baby whose activity level is so high that he seems to be here, there, and everywhere all at once? There's no doubt about it; children born with this temperamental quality are also a challenge to parent, particularly as they become more and more mobile. In fact, the challenge can become so great that parents, out of frustration, go to one extreme or the other—either becoming destructively punitive or giving up control completely. Neither is good for the child. We'll have more to say about the special challenge Baby Dandelion represents in the next chapter when we discuss aggression. For now, it's enough to know that both parenting extremes—too much or too little control—contribute greatly to the development of anger and defiance.

What Type of Garden Will You Grow?

Just as children differ in their temperaments, differences we've highlighted by analogies to particular flowers, so do parents differ in their parenting temperaments. Researcher Diana Baumrind refers to these differences as parenting "styles" and has gathered a good deal of information on how children fare under the different strategies. The three main styles she describes include authoritarian parenting, authoritative parenting, and permissive parenting. An easy way to understand how these styles differ from one another is to carry our flower analogy a step further.

THE FORMAL FRENCH GARDEN AND THE AUTHORITARIAN PARENT
A formal French garden is typically very geometric in form with sharp corners and perfect symmetry. The flowers are kept within rigid boundaries of color and shape, and stragglers are dealt with severely. The dominant theme, in other words is "Control" with a capital c.

Likewise, authoritarian parents are intent on controlling their children through the imposition of rigid rules to which they expect strict obedience. Children are given little, if any, say in what happens to them, individuality is ignored, and disobedience is dealt with harshly. The parent's word, just as the French gardener's plan, is the *law*.

Unfortunately, children are not as easily controlled as flowers, and the result of authoritarian parenting is often far from beautiful. Baumrind's research has revealed that children reared under these conditions tend to be unhappy and unmotivated as young children and underachievers with low levels of self-confidence as adolescents.

THE ENGLISH GARDEN AND THE AUTHORITATIVE PARENT

Although the riot of color and texture that characterizes an English garden might make it *look* like the flowers rather than the gardeners are in charge, there really is an underlying plan. In contrast to the formal French garden, however, it's a plan that takes into account the natural qualities of the flowers, such as height and color, and allows them to grow freely within flexible boundaries. Similarly, authoritative parents do establish rules, but do so while taking their children's perspectives into account and providing rationales for why the rules exist. They are more flexible than authoritarian parents and more willing to admit to being wrong. Children raised in this way tend to thrive like the flowers in the English garden. They are self-confident and friendly as young children and motivated to achieve as adolescents. In addition, they develop the capacity to think for themselves rather than merely conforming to standards set by others or rebelling just for the sake of doing so.

THE WILD GARDEN AND THE PERMISSIVE PARENT

By "wild garden" we mean one where the seeds are simply thrown about without much thought to what goes where. The resulting flowers are allowed to grow in a haphazard way while the gardener simply stands back and observes. Like these gardeners, permissive parents pretty much let their children do as they please, imposing few demands and rarely attempting to exert control. Like the flowers, their children are allowed to run wild. Not surprisingly, children raised under these circumstances tend to be self-centered and impulsive. They often lack the discipline necessary to do well in school, and their tendency to flout authority continues to get them in trouble later in life.

Which kind of garden does Diana Baumrind's research favor? The English garden—and the authoritative parent—wins hands down!

MATERNAL DEPRESSION

As we point out in Chapter 2, mothers who suffer from depression for extended periods during a child's early years put their children at great risk for emotional problems through the development of insecure attachments. A significant part of the problem lies in the depressed mother's inability or unwillingness to engage in the lively face-to-face interactions that babies so enjoy. Depressed moms tend to behave like mothers in Ed Tronick's "Still Face" experiments (where mothers were asked to show no emotion for a short period), remaining unresponsive no matter how hard their babies work to engage them in reciprocal smiles, gurgles, and happy play. As a result, the babies of depressed mothers eventually give up trying, often becoming depressed and despairing themselves.

The problems between depressed mothers and their children don't get any easier as the children get older and in need of even more thoughtful parenting. Depressed mothers are easily overwhelmed by the need to discipline consistently and empathetically, with the result that they either lash out unpredictably or give up trying to control their children at all. In either event, the children are pretty much left in charge of their own behaviors and emotions, a state that leads directly to feelings of anxiety and insecurity. From there it's a quick and predictable jump to anger and defiance.

The message here is clear: Maternal depression is a very serious matter that demands attention. If you or someone you care about is suffering from depression, seek the advice of a physician or counselor. A child's future may be at stake.

> What is done to children, they will do to society.
>
> —Karl A. Menninger, American psychiatrist

MARITAL CONFLICT

Research shows that children—even very young children—are affected by conflict between their parents. The result is almost always increased anxiety. It's easy to understand the reasons why. Parents who are angry with each other...

- ◆ Often take their anger out on their children.
- ◆ Sometimes engage in frightening behaviors.
- ◆ Suffer from depression, which makes them less effective caregivers.

◆ Are often anxious or afraid of abandonment themselves, emotions that children of all ages can "catch." (See Chapter 3, page 61, for an explanation of social referencing.)

The pathway between the increased anxiety that marital conflict creates and increased anger and defiance on the part of the child is also easy to understand. In a volatile household where anger is routinely modeled, anger may seem like the safest and most familiar way to deal with fear. The best defense is a good offense, as they say.

All too often the assumption is that infants and toddlers are too young to be touched by marital conflict. As you examine your own family life, it's important to keep in mind that this is clearly *not* the case.

STRESSFUL LIFE EVENTS

Even under the best of circumstances, with parents who try their hardest, life can deliver serious blows to a young child's sense of security. And as always, it's a short hop from increased anxiety to anger and defiance. Knowing the sources of such negativity can help parents respond with compassion and patience. Some examples:

◆ **"Say hello to your new sister."** The arrival of another baby is a major event for a child and may cause him to worry about how life in general, and parental love in particular, is going to change. Parents often underestimate the impact a new baby has on an older sibling, a problem that the next box is designed to correct.

◆ **"Say hello to your new child care provider."** A very young child's sense of security is extremely fragile. If even a new babysitter can cause alarm, think what havoc the transition to a new child care environment can wreak! Of course, the problem is increased tenfold if the child care environment isn't well staffed and totally supportive. Unfortunately, many children spend their days simply trying to cope with care that is at best neglectful and at worst frightening. It's no wonder that such children often give vent to their anxiety through displays of anger and defiance.

◆ **"Say good-bye to your mother/father/grandma."** Whenever someone the

How Would You Feel If . . .

The following script represents a typical conversation between a parent and a first-born child when it's time to break the news about the impending arrival of a new baby brother or sister. We have substituted different players in the drama to help you see things through a child's eyes.

HUSBAND: I've got a wonderful surprise for you! Now, you know I love you very, very much, honey, don't you? And you know you've brought great joy into my life, right?

WIFE: I love you, too!

HUSBAND: Well, here's the surprise. I've enjoyed having my own little wife *so* much that I thought it would be nice for all of us to have *another* wife in the family! Won't that be wonderful?

WIFE: What!?

HUSBAND: Just think about it. You'll have another wife to play with and maybe even share your room with. And because you're such a good wife and know so much more than she will about *everything*, you can help me take care of her. The three of us can go on walks together and read books together . . . and everything! We'll all be one, big happy family! Won't that be fun?

WIFE: Hmph!

Now, don't you have more sympathy than before for kids who are getting this "wonderful" news?

Source: Adapted from A. Faber and E. Mazlish, *Siblings Without Rivalry* (New York: Avon, 1998.)

child is close to disappears, either for an extended period of time or forever, the child's world is turned upside down. The reason can be perfectly sensible to the adults around the child—a lengthy vacation or hospital stay, divorce, death, or relocation—but the child's sense of abandonment is neither sensible nor easy to overcome. This anxiety often surfaces as anger and defiance.

The arrival of a new baby in the family is harder on displaced older siblings than many parents realize. Recognizing the problem, today many hospitals offer sibling classes to help prepare older brothers and sisters for the Big Day.

NEWS FLASH!

"Please" and "Thank You" Key to Child's Compliance, Scientists Say

Ames, Iowa. Two-year-old Bethany is having a great time playing with all the toys that the nice lady put out on the rug before she left the room a few minutes ago. All that's about to change, however, as Bethany's mom, Alice, suddenly announces, "Bethany, it's time to clean everything up. Can you help Mommy put the toys in this basket?"

That "nice lady" may have left the room, but she's still interested in what's going to happen as Alice tries to get Bethany to comply with her request. In fact, she is watching and videotaping the action through a one-way window. The young woman is one of many research assistants working on an important project conducted at the University of Iowa by developmental psychologists Leon Kuczynski and Grazyna Kochanska. Their quest? To find out why some parents are able to win their child's cooperation while others are not.

And here's what they've found. Based on observing many parents and their eighteen- to forty-two-month-old children, they have discovered that parental behavior makes a big difference in both how and how often toddlers refuse a request. Although no parent should expect to have a completely compliant child, their research clearly indicates that parents can improve their odds by using positive strategies rather than negative ones.

On the positive side are parental behaviors like asking politely ("Can you please put the puzzle away now?"), providing clear but nonhostile reprimands ("There are still pieces on the floor. Please pick those up too."), explaining the reasons for your request ("We need to leave the puzzles where other children can find them."), giving choices ("Do you want to put the doll or the puzzle away first?"), and rewarding good behavior ("Thanks for doing that so nicely."). Among the "no-nos," according to Kuczynski and Kochanska, are using unclear requests ("Hey, didn't I say puzzle time is over?"), issuing commands rather than requests ("Stop playing with that puzzle and put it away."), giving arbitrary reasons ("Because I said so!"), focusing exclusively on lapses rather than acknowledging compliant behavior, and resorting to physical force.

Using the positive behaviors, the researchers say, won't turn a toddler into a perfectly compliant child (there is no such thing), but will decrease the amount of whining and angry defiance and will also increase the child's tendency to try to negotiate a settlement. Can a career in diplomacy be far away?

Words of Wisdom and Tricks of the Trade

Is a toddler who refuses to do what you tell him at age two destined to be filled with feelings of anger and defiance for years to come? Maybe, maybe not. As we discussed earlier, at times all toddlers exert their emerging feelings of independence by offering an emphatic "No!" when asked to do something. This is an absolutely natural and predictable part of life with a two- to three-year-old that children eventually

Some Nos Are Better Than Others

Leon Kuczynski and Grazyna Kochanska's work at the University of Iowa has also revealed important differences in *how* children express their unwillingness to cooperate. Some bode well for the child's future, while others do not. Here are some of the strategies children use presented in order of increasing sophistication, from "unskillful" (without any thought to the impression made on others) to "skillful" (taking others' potential reactions into account).

- **Unskillful.** The child gives no reason for noncompliance. In general, parents are much less tolerant of these strategies than the skillful ones that follow.
  - **Passive noncompliance.** The child simply ignores a parent's request.
  - **Direct defiance.** The child responds with poorly controlled anger. ("No. No! No!!")
  - **Simple refusal.** The child says "no" but without particular passion. ("No, I play more.")

- **Skillful noncompliance.** The child tries to find some "wiggle room" in the parent's instructions through negotiations. In general these strategies are more likely to keep tempers in check.
  - **Bargaining.** The child attempts to win a compromise. ("Just one more?" "Maybe tomorrow?")
  - **Explanations.** The child attempts to justify noncompliance. ("Not done yet." "Need one more.")

Although increasing language skills certainly play a role in how skillfully a child declines to comply, Kuczynski and Kochanska find that, in general, children who depend mostly on unskilled forms as toddlers continue to do so at age five. Similarly, children who depend most on skilled forms as toddlers tend to continue to do so at age five. Research also shows that, just as in every other domain, children tend to model themselves after their parents. Parents who supply explanations, suggest compromises, and consider the child's feelings when asking for cooperation tend to have children who do the same, even if they choose not to comply.

ith the help of wise parenting. Some children, however, never move be-
negative time. We now turn to specific ways you can increase the odds
that your child will fall into the first category rather than the second.

BUILD AN AFFECTIONATE RELATIONSHIP

In a series of research studies also at the University of Iowa, developmental psychologist Grazyna Kochanska has demonstrated very convincingly that something she calls a "mutually responsive orientation" between parent and toddler
vastly increases the likelihood that a child will willingly comply with a parent's
requests. This is a fancy term for two characteristics of a good parent-child relationship:

1. Parent and toddler have lots of good times together, interactions infused with
   love, affection, and playfulness.
2. Parent and child tend to be highly tuned in to each other, each detecting and
   responding sympathetically to the other's distress, bids for attention, and suggestions.

Children lucky enough to enjoy this kind of relationship view the parent-
child relationship as a "partnership" where it is natural and even enjoyable to
follow each other's lead. No "negative baggage" such as distrust or anger is
brought into compliance situations. Instead, the attitude is "If Mommy wants us
to clean up, I'm willing to help." Kochanska calls this attitude "committed compliance."

The "Words of Wisdom and Tricks of the Trade" included in Chapter 2
(page 45) are all aimed at creating a secure bond between the two of you, thereby
helping you create a mutually responsive orientation. But just as a reminder, here
is some specific advice.

◆ **Go the extra mile.** Post a sign in your baby's room that reminds you, "What
I Do Today Makes a Difference for Tomorrow." Remembering that your genuine
attempts to comfort your child will pay off eventually can help you go that extra
mile with a difficult baby. Even when your efforts to hold and interact don't seem

to be working, at some level you are communicating your care and concern in ways that babies apparently can detect and appreciate.

◆ **Grease the nonsticky wheel too.** If your baby is an easy-to-soothe, happy baby, remember it's still important to give him lots of positive attention to help him maintain his sunny disposition. During the hectic demands of everyday life it's all too easy to forget to grease the wheel that doesn't squeak.

◆ **Find the time to play with your child at *every* age.** Remember, children who genuinely enjoy their parents are much more inclined to cooperate with them.

USE POSITIVE RATHER THAN NEGATIVE DISCIPLINE

Please take this to heart! The most reliable finding in the whole research literature on what predicts persistent anger and defiance is that coercive, overcontrolling, negative disciplinary techniques *backfire*. It may feel good in the moment to lose your temper and scream, but consistently doing so is guaranteed to make your child's behavior worse rather than better. Now, when your child is very young, is the time to develop effective parenting habits. Here are some specific tips to help you through the inevitable conflicts that arise during the terrible twos and secure a more peaceful future for both you and your child.

◆ **Take good care of yourself.** Tempers get short when we are exhausted, under a lot of stress, in a rush, depressed, or ill. Put two or more of these together, and the fuse will be shorter still. Slowing down your life and looking after your mental and physical health is a gift you will be giving your children as well as yourself. We are under no illusions that this is easy advice to follow—but that doesn't mean it isn't important.

◆ **Don't expect perfection.** Expecting a toddler always to comply is unrealistic and all too often leads to an unforgiving and punitive attitude that only makes matters worse. Parents who interpret every "no" from their children as a threat to their authority and thwart their toddler's fledgling expressions of autonomy instill feelings of anger in their children. Always remember that a child who feels angry is *more* likely, rather than less likely, to defy your authority.

◆ **Be polite.** Saying "please" and "thank you" to your children both models good behavior and sends the message that you respect them. You can be polite and still be firm. ("Please go get your shoes and socks.") This strategy, like the others in the last news flash, really does help.

◆ **Be clear about what needs to be done.** Avoid vague descriptions like "You need to do something about all this!" Toddlers need precise directions. Saying "Please put all the toys in the toy box" is more likely to get the job done. Think of it this way: How easily would you have learned to read if all you had heard was "That's *not* what it says."

◆ **Acknowledge your child's feelings.** Toddlers, just like adults, feel better about complying when their feelings about the matter are understood and sympathized with. ("I can tell you're really having fun and would like to stay, but it's important that we go now.")

◆ **Decide if you're going to help.** Don't say "We need to . . ." or "Let's . . ." unless you intend to help. Toddlers are literal! And remember, having your help will reinforce the notion of teamwork and make the chore more fun.

◆ **Provide reasons for your requests.** We all feel better about doing things when we know why they are important to do. ("We need to leave now so we can pick up Jason on time.") And "Because I said so!" doesn't qualify.

Baby Hearts in Action:
Out of the Mouths of Babes

It was an idea that sounded good on paper. When your child is angry, Linda had read in a parenting book, put her in her room with a black crayon and a piece of paper and tell her to "express" her anger. Doing so, the promise was, would help the child get the anger out of her system. Well, one day Linda put it into practice—with unanticipated results.

Kate, Linda's six-year-old daughter, was extremely upset with her eighteen-month-old brother, Kai, who had scribbled all over her latest painting. Following the book's instructions, Linda sent Kate to her room and suggested she draw something to make her feel better. After a few minutes, Kate came out and handed over the drawing. Having expected a violent drawing of some kind, Linda thought she was prepared. But what she saw took her breath away. On the paper was a stick figure with a balloon coming out of its mouth and in the balloon were words Linda had

◆ **When possible, give choices.** By letting a child choose between alternatives, you automatically lower the likelihood of hearing "No!" But make sure you're truly comfortable with both outcomes. "Are you coming or not?" is bound to backfire.

◆ **Use "do" words rather than "don't" words.** "Don't" messages—like "Don't run!"—are actually harder for toddlers to understand than "Do" messages, like "Walk!" Because they don't process language efficiently and are impulsive, toddlers tend to miss the word "Don't" and hear only the rest of the message, "...run" thereby automatically leading to disobedience.

◆ **Remember to *show* rather than just tell toddlers what to do.** As we just mentioned, toddlers aren't yet experts at understanding language, especially when they are distracted, tired, or upset. Actions are worth a *million* words to a toddler.

◆ **Praise good behavior whenever possible.** Make a conscious effort to praise your child for *good* behavior. Even little instances count. ("I liked the way you put your toothbrush away.") Write down instances you notice during the day and talk about them again at bedtime. Too many parents spend the vast majority of their time finding fault with their child's behavior. Yes, it's important to know what one has done wrong. But equally important is being told what one has done *right*.

---

never dreamed her innocent little daughter had ever heard: "Kai is a #!@!$#! and I hate him!" What followed was a serious talk about appropriate and inappropriate ways to express one's anger. "Those words are unacceptable. Do you understand, Kate?" asked Linda sternly. Kate said she did.

But the story isn't over. Two weeks later Kate again got angry at her little brother and was sent to her room with a black crayon, paper, and the warning, "Now, Kate, remember what we talked about." This time when she came out of her room she was smiling broadly. There on the paper was the same stick figure and the same balloon, but this time the balloon was filled with numbers. Relieved not to see the awful words, Linda asked "What do these numbers mean?" to which Kate cagily replied, "The *code* is on the back." You guessed it. Once translated using the code (A=1, B=2, etc.), the message was exactly the same! And before Linda could say anything, Kate added proudly, "See, I didn't use the words!" Needless to say, Linda never tried the black crayon technique again.

WHAT IF YOUR CHILD IGNORES YOU?

First, don't automatically assume she is purposefully doing so. She may simply be absorbed in doing something else. Such total concentration is actually a wonderful gift.

Here's what you *do* do. Make sure she's paying attention and can hear you, get down to her level and make eye contact, make sure to include only one instruction at a time, speak clearly using her name ("Sally, it's time to . . ."), and use nouns instead of pronouns ("Pick up the doll" rather than "Pick it up"). If she's busy doing something constructive (other than watching TV), compliment her on being able to pay such close attention to a task and briefly explain why you need her to do something else for the moment.

DEALING WITH TANTRUMS

There will inevitably be times when even your most persuasive, polite, and reasonable requests will be met not only with noncompliance but with the out-and-out tantrum. Here are some tips to help you cope.

◆ **Recognize the danger signs.** The first line of defense is to try to *avoid* having things escalate to tantrum level. It can help to remember that children, like all of us, are more likely to lose control when they are tired, sick, hungry, overexcited, or afraid. The time-honored advice to choose your battles is especially helpful in such situations. If you can postpone requests until the child is back on an even keel, it is wise to do so.

◆ **Use humor and distraction to lower tension.** Your toddler doesn't want her shoes on? Try getting a giggle by putting them on your head or on your own feet. She doesn't want to go upstairs to take a bath? Try making a race out of it. He doesn't want to pick up his toys? Play "beat the clock!" Make up stories, use funny voices, sing nonsense songs, walk funny, and, if all else fails, try a playful tickle.

◆ **Keep your own cool.** Count to ten, recite the alphabet, breathe in and out ten times . . . do whatever you need to do to stay calm. Your own anger will only add to the intensity of the situation and increase the possibility that you will do something you'll be sorry for. But if you do lose control, an apology later will at least let your child know that *you* know what you did wasn't smart and that you still love him enough to admit it.

◆ **Use time-outs instead of physical punishment.** The word "discipline" actually comes from a word meaning "instruction," *not* punishment. *Hitting, shaking, and spanking don't teach anything other than that violence is an acceptable way to deal with things that don't go your way.* They also frighten the child, thereby decreasing even more the possibility that anything constructive will be learned. Instead, remove the tantruming child to a quiet place where he can calm down. This is called time-out and, if done correctly, it does work. See the box on page 232 to find out how we define "correctly."

Just like adults, exhausted toddlers have hair-trigger tempers. Take away an overly tired toddler's plaything—even when it's Grandma's china teapot—and it's quite likely to be tantrum time.

Making Time-Outs Work for You

You've tried time-outs and they don't work, you say? Chances are you haven't given the *right* kind of time-out sufficient opportunity to prove itself. The philosophy behind the strategy of separating a tantruming child from the ongoing action has a solid basis in two research findings: (1) Very young children value your love and attention more than almost anything else, and withdrawing that attention (not your *love*) sends a powerful message, and (2) children who are out of control need practice in calming *themselves* down, and that is unlikely to happen if the child stays in the thick of things.

Here are some guidelines for making time-outs work for you.

◆ **Praise positive behavior.** Be sure your child gets plenty of positive attention when he is *not* misbehaving, a strategy that some folks describe as the "time-*in*" principle. For children who don't get the attention they crave in positive ways, the scolding that follows misbehavior can actually be an incentive to misbehave again.

◆ **Be calm, firm, and brief.** Since one of the goals is to deny your child your much-sought-after attention, keep talking to a minimum and speak in firm, low tones. State the rule and the consequence as simply as possible. ("Time-out. The rule is *no* hitting. Hitting hurts.")

◆ **Keep time-outs as short as possible.** The rule "one minute for every year of age" refers to the *maximum* length of time a time-out should last, not the minimum. Sometimes simply looking away from or looking sternly at a child for a few seconds will be enough. The goal is to take away something the child values—your attention—until he can calm himself down.

◆ **Don't require a jaillike atmosphere.** Personally, we don't favor making the time-out location tantamount to a jail cell with nothing for the child to do but think about things. It's much more to the point for the child to have things available that really *can* calm him down, comforting things such as those found in his own room.

◆ **Don't lecture before or after.** A swift movement into the time-out space and a swift movement back out into the social fray when it's over should be your goal. You can talk over the incident at a later time during the day.

◆ **Be consistent.** Very young children have trouble following rules under the *best* of circumstances. So, if you don't apply rules consistently—condoning hitting on some occasions but not others—you'll only make your child's task (and your life) more difficult.

Any kid will run any errand for you if you ask at bedtime.

—Red Skelton, comedian

LIFE WITH A TODDLER ISN'T EASY

To say that life with a toddler is challenging is like saying that the sun is a bit out of reach. You will have good days and bad days, highs and lows. You will have times when your heart bursts with love and times when you wonder why anyone has children. All this is natural. As they spread their wings and begin to struggle out of the nest and into the wider world, toddlers are bound to get frustrated, cranky, and even belligerent. But if you can keep your cool and understand that the right choices now will pay dividends down the line, you'll be in good shape to weather the storm.

10

Sticks and Stones:
Avoiding Hostility and Aggression

N E W S   F L A S H !

Advice to "Use Your Words!" Finally Possible
for Toddlers Thanks to Signing

Fresno, California. Just two months ago, Kelly and Jim were at their wits' end. Aaron, their twenty-two-month-old son, was going to be expelled from his day care classroom unless something could be done to stop him from shoving, hitting, and biting his classmates. Alert and active from Day 1, Aaron had gone from being a cheerful, adventuresome twelve-month-old to being such a terror on the playground that Kelly and Jim often heard other parents warn their children to stay away from him. What on earth was going on?

Like generations of parents before them, Kelly and Jim began their search for answers with Dr. Benjamin Spock. And, sure enough, they found an important clue in these words:

> Children [between one and two] can't express their frustrations or desires in words, so their frustration or desire to dominate comes out in primitive ways, like biting. Biting usually abates and disappears by the age of three. At that time the child has learned to use words to express his desires or vent his frustrations.

Obviously extremely smart in many ways, Aaron was still not talking very much, and the gap between what he wanted to say and what he could say was contributing mightily to his feelings of frustration and, in turn, to his aggressive behavior. "What a relief it was just to understand what was going on," recalls Kelly. "But we still didn't know what to do about it. We certainly didn't want to just sit around and wait until he was three."

Fortunately, their pediatrician, Dr. Nancy Wheatley, had a solution for them. Why not teach Aaron to communicate with simple signs? Perhaps if he could get his messages across using signs, he wouldn't feel the need to lash out by biting and hitting. Having read the research from the University of California at Davis showing that using signs has only positive effects on learning to talk, Dr. Wheatley knew there was no reason *not* to give it a try. Kelly and Jim enthusiastically agreed.

That was two months ago, and in the interim Aaron has taken to using sign language like a duck to water, says Kelly. "He especially likes the signs for 'more,' 'ball,' 'play,' and 'cookie,' but our own favorites are those for 'please' and 'thank you.' He's so excited about finally being able to communicate that he actually looks for opportunities to use them!"

Dr. Wheatley is also pleased at Aaron's progress but hardly surprised. "Once toddlers have signs to help make themselves understood, a good deal of their need to be aggressive disappears. What's more, the fact that the use of signs also increases the number of positive interactions between a child and other people means that children like Aaron also soon learn how rewarding being nice can be." Looks like Dr. Spock, as usual, knew what he was talking about.

Aggression: A High-Profile Problem

It's no wonder Aaron's parents were worried by his early tendencies toward hurtful behavior. Many parents and professionals share this concern about children in general, asking why youngsters today are seemingly more aggressive than in past generations. Headlines about high school shootings, senseless assaults, and gang violence certainly make this concern understandable.

What's more, recent research on aggression during the first three years has intensified feelings of alarm by uncovering startling levels of stability in aggressive behavior from age two onward. For example, psychologist Mark Cummings and colleagues at the National Institutes of Mental Health found that individual differences in the tendency for children to start fights with other kids remains stable from age two to five, while research from Iceland and New Zealand, as well as the United States, has shown that aggression between ages three and ten is a fairly good predictor of adult inclination toward antisocial behavior.

Whether the problem of youth violence is, in fact, growing more serious within society as a whole or not, the bottom line for parents is the same as it has always been: What can I do to help my own child develop in ways that lead toward positive rather than negative behavior? Thanks to the efforts of researchers around the world, the past twenty years have yielded promising answers to this question. Our own research demonstrating the benefits of helping babies and toddlers use signs as a way to reduce frustration is just one example. We now know more than we ever have exactly what psychological, biological, and societal factors are at work in determining whether a child will choose constructive or destructive means to handle life's inevitable frustrations.

> All children wear the sign: "I want to be important NOW." Many of our juvenile delinquency problems arise because nobody reads the signs.
>
> —Dan Pursuit, educator

Of course, the exact formula for rearing a nonaggressive child will differ from family to family and child to child. What we aim for in this chapter of *Baby Hearts* is to acquaint parents with the most important research findings on the development of hostility and aggression. Then, at the end of the chapter, we describe specific ways parents can start their children on a positive path toward becoming the kind of peace-loving teenagers and adults they wish them to be.

What's Anger Got to Do with It?

In Chapter 9 we dealt with anger and defiance. If you're like most parents, you're wondering why we bothered to separate those two clearly negative behaviors from the two upon which we're focused here—hostility and aggression. Aren't they pretty much the same? Take, for example, a child who gets angry at being told no by his preschool teacher and proceeds to throw a tantrum during which he pushes classmates and throws toys. Isn't that clearly aggression? Of course it is. And you can bet that little Johnny's parents will hear about his "unacceptable aggressive behavior" when they show up at the end of the day.

But the larger reality is that not all anger results in aggression and not all aggression is caused by anger. And because of this fact, the two topics need to be addressed separately. Here are examples that illustrate our point.

ANGER WITHOUT AGGRESSION

Five-month-old Josie is happily playing with a music box that plays "Twinkle Twinkle Little Star" whenever she pounds a big red button with her foot. Suddenly it simply stops working. No matter how she hits it...nothing. In response to this unexpected development, she begins to cry and flail around, her arms and hands jerking about in the air. Is she angry? You bet. There's no doubt she's both frustrated *and* angry. But is she being aggressive? The answer according to researchers is no. To qualify as aggression, researchers have found it helpful to require that an action be *intended* to harm or injure another person (including destruction of objects they value). In fact, even if Josie, in her wild flailing, happened to hit her mother, it still wouldn't count as aggression because the injury was accidental rather than intentional.

AGGRESSION WITHOUT ANGER

On the other hand, consider three-year-old Sammy, who really wants to play with the big toy car that kids can sit in and push around with their feet. The problem is that the popular hot rod is currently being "driven" by somebody else—in this case, three-year-old James. Sammy's solution? Give James a really hard push so that he tumbles out of the driver's seat just long enough for Sammy to jump in and hightail it out of town. Does the pushing constitute aggression? Yes, Sammy did the act intentionally, knowing that it was hurtful. The aggression in this case, however, was not sparked by anger. Sammy wasn't mad; he simply wanted the car and had, unfortunately, learned that pushing is an effective way to get what you want.

Aggression: There's More to It Than Meets the (Black) Eye

As these two examples make clear, in order to understand an action that results in someone being hurt, we really have to go beyond the act itself to the underlying motivation. If there was no intention to harm, then we don't call it aggression. The playmate who was accidentally hugged too vigorously may complain loudly, but chances are the hugger is as surprised as the huggee. That doesn't mean, however, that there aren't important lessons to be learned from accidental injuries— lessons about how to behave more gently and how and why to apologize. But unless there was the intention to injure, it isn't an act of aggression.

Over the last few decades, researchers have gained new and important insights into aggressive behavior by delving even deeper into the motivations that underlie it. This work has led them to identify three main forms of aggression in children (and adults). They call these three types instrumental, hostile, and relational aggression. Because each is fueled by different desires, understanding the differences among them is an important step toward helping children avoid them.

INSTRUMENTAL AGGRESSION

Sammy had such a strong yen to drive the toy car that he enthusiastically pushed his rival out of the way. That's a perfect example of instrumental aggression, where an aggressive act is viewed as an instrument, or tool, to get something the person wants. In this case it was a chance to drive the car. In other cases it might be to get access to a swing, the biggest piece of candy, the top rung of the monkey bars, or the spot at the head of the line.

Less Obvious Rewards. But the payoff isn't always so tangible. Sometimes it's simply attention from adults who otherwise ignore the child. As hard as it is to believe, to a child who has no other way to get important people to acknowledge his presence, the words "Stop that right now!" are actually highly rewarding.

In addition, especially as children get older, instrumental aggression can be fueled by feelings of power and dominance over other people, feelings that all too often are an aggressive child's main, if not only, source of self-esteem.

Television and Aggression: Should You Worry?

For over forty years the scientific community has battled the television and movie industry over the issue of media violence and its effects on children. We're here to tell you that the results were in ages ago and only grow stronger with time: Children who are exposed to lots of media violence are, indeed, affected by it. Here's how: Watching lots of violence on television tends to . . .

◆ Motivate children to engage in more violent behavior themselves.
◆ Make violence seem like an appropriate route to status and glory.
◆ Teach children *how* to be violent.
◆ Make children less emotionally upset by violence and more accepting of it in real life.
◆ Lead children to perceive the world as a meaner, more dangerous place than it actually is.

With all the attention paid to this issue over the years, one would think that the levels of violence on television would have declined. On the contrary, American television programming remains extraordinarily violent. Here are some sobering statistics from a 1997 report:

◆ 58 percent of programs aired between 6 A.M. and 11 P.M. contained repeated acts of violence.
◆ 73 percent of these programs included violent acts that resulted in no remorse or punishment.
◆ *40 percent of the televised violence was committed by characters who were intended to be models for children (such as the Power Rangers).*

None of this means that violence on television is the most important contributor to aggression in children. Far from it. In most cases harsh discipline, a coercive family environment, poverty, unemployment, lack of supervision, poor schools, easy availability of weapons, and drugs are even stronger contributors. But the evidence is clear: Media violence has definitely earned a place on the list. Case closed.

Cool as a Cucumber: The Proactive Aggressor. Children who rely on instrumental aggression to get what they want, including power and dominance over others, are on their way to becoming really scary people. Researchers call such individuals proactive aggressors because their aggression, rather than being a reaction to some slight or frustration, is a cold-blooded tool. Clearly absent from these folks' psyches are sufficient levels of sympathy and empathy to counterbalance the tangible and intangible "goodies" they get from simply taking what they want and pushing people around.

In one recent study of twelve-year-old children already identified as troublemakers, psychologist Paul Frick from the University of New Orleans and his colleagues found a significant number who also scored high on a measure of "CU"—an acronym standing for "callous and unemotional." These kids clearly qualify as proactive aggressors. How sad that researchers even need a test to identify callous and unemotional children.

HOSTILE AGGRESSION

When parents and teachers think about aggression, hostile aggression is the kind that comes most readily to mind. According to David Shaffer, an expert in the area of emotional development, an act of hostile aggression is hurting someone or something just for the sheer pleasure of doing so rather than as a tool to obtain a valued reward.

Hostile aggression is the kind of aggression that often follows angry reactions to intense feelings of frustration. Little Aaron in the news flash is a good example. He was continually feeling frustrated at not being able to communicate and was giving vent to his anger by hitting, pushing, and biting his classmates. Doing so made him feel better. This is hostile aggression.

But even within the category of hostile aggression, there are important distinctions to be made. Hostile aggression can be either:

♦ **Impulsive or premeditated.** Impulsive acts usually follow closely on the anger-producing event, while premeditated acts are planned out in advance. In either case, there's a strong flavor of retaliation or revenge. Obviously, premeditation requires future thinking and planning, skills that don't develop until the third or fourth year.

♦ **Consciously or unconsciously motivated.** A child who, when asked "Why

Looks like Alex is having a very, very, very bad day! Helping children deal with their feelings of anger can prevent them from being translated into hostile aggression toward others.

did you hit Sammy?" can reply " 'Cause he pushed me" is consciously aware of his motivation. However, as discussed in Chapter 9, many children harbor angry feelings at such a deep level that they really can't identify the true cause behind their acts of aggression. These children lash out at others without truly understanding why. They may voice a superficial reason (" 'Cause he looked at me funny!"), but the deeper significance remains beyond their ken.

These two distinctions, between impulsive and premeditated aggression and between conscious and unconsciously motivated aggression, help us understand four different kinds of hostile aggression in children. (See "Hostile Aggression: Hurting for Pleasure" chart on the next page.)

1. Impulsive-conscious hostile aggression: The "He hit me first!" Kid. This is the child who reacts impulsively when challenged and is quite conscious of doing so. Bump into him and he's quite likely to bump back, feeling justified by the other person's behavior. "An eye for an eye" is his motto.

2. Premeditated-conscious hostile aggression: The Revenge Seeker. Rather than reacting on the spur of the moment, the revenge seeker plans his attack and does so quite consciously. He, too, favors an eye-for-an-eye philosophy but takes additional pleasure in planning exactly how that eye will be extracted. "Revenge is sweet" rings especially true for children in this category.

3. Impulsive-unconscious hostile aggression: The "I'm in a bad mood" Kid. Children in this category are likely to lash out at others without any obvious provocation and without truly understanding why they are doing so. For example, children who are overtired and cranky may suddenly become aggressive during play—pinching or biting just because it feels good at the moment.

4. Premeditated-unconscious hostile aggression: The Bully. These are the children whose anger is so deeply rooted that they can't begin to understand the dynamics of why they take pleasure in terrorizing others. They don't need an

---

Hostile Aggression: Hurting for Pleasure

Children who take pleasure in hurting others usually do so out of anger or frustration. Sometimes they know why they are angry, but other times they don't. Also, sometimes they act impulsively, but other times they take time to plan their attack. Here's what these varieties of hostile aggression look like on the playground.

	CONSCIOUS HOSTILE AGGRESSION	UNCONSCIOUS HOSTILE AGGRESSION
IMPULSIVE HOSTILE AGGRESSION	The "He hit me first!" Kid: 2-year-old James punches Sammy after Sammy pushes him out of the toy car.	The "I'm in a bad mood" Kid: 22-month-old Aaron, who can't talk yet, bites a classmate who ventures too close to his toy.
PREMEDITATED HOSTILE AGGRESSION	The Revenge Seeker: 4-year-old Jill hides behind a tree ready to stick a foot out to trip Sara in retaliation for Sara having teased her earlier in the day.	The Bully: Abused and neglected at home, 5-year-old Casio takes pleasure in terrorizing his classmates on the playground.

excuse, either. It's not that they are reacting to any specific challenge; rather, their aggression makes them feel better, at least for the moment.

Of these four groups, the two that consciously use aggression to retaliate against others (the "He hit me first!" and Revenge Seeker categories) have received the most attention from researchers. Often called "reactive aggressors," these children lash out in retaliation for real or imagined slights, injuries, or frustrations. Notice that we include imagined offenses in this list. This is a very important point. One of the sad things about reactive aggressors, and one reason they get into deeper and deeper trouble with peers and adults alike, is that they tend to assume evil intentions behind others' behaviors even when those intentions are not really there. In the minds of reactive aggressors, they are justifiably retaliating. In the minds of their victims, however, the aggression can seem to come out of nowhere.

Many years of careful research by Kenneth Dodge from Duke University have demonstrated this to be true. For example, a child on the playground accidentally bumps into a reactive aggressor. Instead of accepting the child's "Oops!" as genuine, the reactive aggressor pushes back, assuming the bump was intentional. Or the reactive aggressor sees a child whispering into another child's ear and assumes it's about her. Immediately she begins to plan her revenge. Sadly, if a child keeps this kind of overreaction going long enough, pretty soon the slights are no longer imagined. Over time, reactive aggressors are more and more likely to be purposefully rejected by their peers, thereby making it increasingly likely that the whispering really *is* about them. Fortunately, Dodge's discovery has enabled researchers to design interventions to help these children by training them to read body language more accurately. Even better, children whose parents foster awareness of emotions (of both self and others) during the earliest years are likely to escape the problem altogether. (We discuss specific ways to achieve this goal in the "Words of Wisdom and Tricks of the Trade" section of Chapter 3.)

I found one day in school a boy of medium size ill-treating a smaller boy. I expostulated, but he replied: "The big ones hit me, so I hit the babies; that's fair." In these words he epitomized the history of the human race.

—Bertrand Russell, philosopher

RELATIONAL AGGRESSION

Remember the old saying, "Sticks and stones may break my bones, but words will never hurt me"? Well, it's not true. Words can be extremely hurtful, sometimes causing pain that lasts years longer than the pain from any punch possibly could. Calling another child "Fatty!" or "Stupid!" when the goal is to cause emotional pain is a form of aggression. So is purposefully snubbing a child or gossiping about her in order to increase the chance that other children will reject her. Researchers call this kind of aggression relational because the actions are intended to wreak havoc on the victim's relationships with others. The label "Fatty" may increase the chance that other children will avoid a child, and, as many of us can testify, purposefully being omitted from a birthday party can be painful beyond belief.

Have you noticed our use of the feminine pronouns "she" and "her" throughout the previous paragraph? That wasn't just our usual attempt at gender balance. We were referring specifically to girls because research by developmental psychologist Nicki Crick at the University of Minnesota has consistently shown relational aggression to be the weapon of choice for elementary school girls. In fact, the usual sex difference that shows boys engaging in significantly more aggressive acts than girls is eliminated completely when you include relational aggression in the count. Boys and girls are equally likely to be mean; they just prefer different weapons.

Because designing any act aimed at injuring relationships (beyond simple name-calling) requires the ability to understand how others think and feel, this category of aggression is rarely seen during the first three years. However, parents definitely need to begin efforts to prevent their child from engaging in such cruelty in that early period, specifically by paying attention to the development of empathy and sympathy.

Steps Along the Way

No child in the world makes it to preschool without exhibiting aggression sometime, someplace. On the other hand, no child under the age of six months can be accused of instrumental, hostile, or relational aggression. So, obviously, something happens in between. Here's what parents can expect from the typical child.

◆ **Birth to 10 months.** As we described in Chapter 9, infants as young as three months get angry when something they've come to expect suddenly doesn't happen. But, because they don't yet understand cause and effect, this anger doesn't translate into intentional aggression for many, many months.

◆ **10 to 18 months.** Things change pretty dramatically once babies begin to have a sense of what they want to do—and who is preventing them from doing it. Tempers begin to flare when toys are taken away, whether it's by Mom or another child. Children's ability to understand cause and effect also means that

From Sworn Enemies to Bosom Buddies

Almost as soon as Charles Darwin came up with the twin ideas of evolution and natural selection, people began to argue that aggression is built into the human species, that it is "instinctual." Unfortunately, frequently this idea is offered as an excuse for bad behavior. If a behavior is instinctual, the logic goes, it would be futile to try to change or control it. A very clever study done way back in 1930 by a scientist named psychologist Z. Y. Kuo provides the perfect retort.

If there's one behavior that most of us would agree is instinctual, it's the tendency for cats to stalk and kill rats. Or is it? Kuo decided to find out. First he took litters of newborn kittens away from their natural mothers. One-third of these he gave to tried-and-true rat-killing moms to raise. Another third he raised by themselves. And the final third he raised with rats! Then, when the kittens were old enough, he tested to see if they would stalk and kill rats in a natural situation. Here's what he found.

◆ The kittens raised with rat-killing moms learned from them, 85 percent becoming enthusiastic rat killers.
◆ The kittens raised alone split about even, with 45 percent easily persuaded to kill rats.
◆ But of the kittens raised with rats, only 17 percent ever killed a rat in all his tests.

What's the point of all this? Here it is, and it's important: Even something as arguably instinctual as rat-killing can be changed, given the right circumstances. Create an environment that nurtures love and trust rather than violence, and the result will be peace and harmony. Our goal with *Baby Hearts* is to help you do just that.

they notice when hitting someone succeeds in getting what they want. In other words, instrumental aggression rears its ugly head.

◆ **18 to 24 months.** Another cognitive milestone, development of a sense of self as separate from others, further ignites the it's-me-against-you perspective. Toddlers at this age are also still in love with doing things for themselves and, when thwarted by parents or peers, may throw temper tantrums that escalate into aggression. Unfortunately, the period known as the terrible twos is in full swing well before the second birthday!

◆ **24 to 36 months.** By age two, toddlers are beginning to value other children as playmates and to understand the advantages of resolving conflicts peacefully. As a consequence, crude attempts to negotiate, especially if modeled by adults, begin to take the place of physical squabbles—with everyone but siblings! As many parents can testify, both hostile and instrumental aggression among siblings is excruciatingly slow to lose its appeal—and sometimes never does.

◆ **3 to 4 years.** Although physical aggression in the form of hitting and kicking is still fairly common in the third year, especially among boys, physical aggression is about to lose out to verbal forms. By the end of this period, language

Baby Hearts in Action:
She Didn't Stand a "Ghost" of a Chance

Whenever Linda lectures to her undergraduate class about the development of aggression, she always emphasizes the strong tendency for children to imitate people they admire, including the *unacceptable* behaviors they see being performed. That's one reason, of course, that child development professionals worry about the influence of television and movies. She then asks the students to think of occasions in their own lives when they had imitated a character on TV with less than positive results. Of all the stories she's heard over the years, her favorite is the girl who, as a young child, became enchanted with the cartoon character "Casper the Ghost." She reported how she loved covering herself with a sheet and "floating" around the house just like Casper. That was fine. What wasn't so fine was her decision to also try imitating Casper's strategy for getting from room to room: walking through walls! It only took one try—which resulted in knocking herself out—to persuade her to switch her allegiance to a more *substantial* character.

Why are some children aggressive and others not? Researchers have uncovered a variety of contributors, many of them evident in the environments of children even in the first three years of life.

skills have developed sufficiently to enable taunting, teasing, and name-calling to take its place. (At least it cuts down on black eyes and bloody noses!)

◆ **5+ years.** The arts of negotiation and self-control become well ingrained in most children by this point, aided by entry into formal school settings and the developing ability to see things from other people's perspectives. For many parents, therefore, the arrival of the fifth birthday means it's time to breathe a sigh of relief and give themselves a pat on the back for a job well done. Unfortunately, not all parents are so lucky. Let's now take a look at why some parents' problems with aggression are far from over.

What Makes Kids Aggressive?

So, now you know what kinds of aggression to watch for and when to expect them to begin. This knowledge alone is important. Unless you have some understanding of *why* your child has punched, pushed, or pummeled another child,

you're not nearly as likely to hit (forgive the choice of word) on the best way to prevent similar episodes in the future.

But all this discussion of types of aggression leaves an obvious question unanswered: What fuels aggression that doesn't diminish by age five but continues, and even escalates, as a child gets older? Why are some children sweet-tempered and kind to old and young alike while others are so prone to fighting that everyone around them fears for their futures? Research over the last twenty years has revealed a number of factors that clearly contribute to the strengthening of aggressive tendencies. What's more, each one of these tendencies has roots in the first three years of a child's life. We begin our search for answers with a news flash.

N E W S   F L A S H !

Harsh Discipline Linked to Later Aggression, Scientists Say

Nashville, Tennessee. The five-year-olds in Ms. Gardner's kindergarten class are no longer surprised to see two people watching them closely as they play on the playground during recess. Lenny and Sandra, two graduate students from Vanderbilt University, have been coming to the playground for weeks now, clipboards in hand, as part of an ambitious research project being conducted by four researchers from three separate universities: Bahr Weiss and Kenneth Dodge from Vanderbilt, John Bates from Indiana University, and Gregory Pettit from Auburn University. Their goal? To document the link between harsh discipline and aggressiveness in children.

Lenny and Sandra's job has been to observe each child individually for twelve five-minute periods, recording every ten seconds whether the child is doing anything that fits the researchers' definitions of hostile or instrumental aggression. Other graduate students had been given other jobs: interviewing parents at length about how they discipline their children and what their children were like over the past five years, interviewing teachers and classmates about the children's aggressiveness, and giving the children themselves tests to see if they tend to go overboard in attributing hostile intentions to what other people do.

The results are now in, and the message to parents is clear. The more positive and akin to "guidance" a parent's discipline is, the less aggressive his or her child is likely to be. And conversely, the harsher a parent's discipline—including physical punishment like spanking and slapping, as well as emotional punishment like yelling and blaming—the more aggression the child is likely to show. "It's important to point out," says Weiss, "that this same pattern was found no matter what the child's original temperament. It's not the case that the parents using harsh discipline are simply reacting in a justifiable way to difficult kids who are naturally intense and inclined toward aggression. Even children who were originally easygoing are likely to become aggressive in reaction to harsh discipline by their parents."

The researchers also found a link between aggressiveness and a tendency to be suspicious of other people's actions, one that begins in response to the parent's use of harsh discipline. "The fact that they can't trust their parents to treat them kindly automatically leaves them untrusting of others," explains Dodge. In addition, they experience their parents being suspicious of them all the time and quite naturally imitate this attitude in their own interactions with other people. Unfortunately, once established, this tendency to see hostility even when it's not there leads to even more aggression. The accidental bump by another child is interpreted as no accident, and the child pushes back. The ball that accidentally hits the child is considered to have been thrown that way on purpose, and the child retaliates. Thus, a cycle that begins with poor parenting becomes even more deeply entrenched as the child moves beyond the home into the unpredictable give-and-take of the playground. Sadly, the longer it continues unchecked, the harder this cycle is to break and the higher the cost to us all.

"COERCIVE" FAMILIES AND AGGRESSION

The research described in the news flash comes as no surprise to psychologist Gerald Patterson from the University of Oregon. For thirty years Patterson and his colleagues have documented the destructive effects of living in what they call a "coercive" family environment. These are homes in which approval and affection are rare, having been replaced by endless bickering, quarreling, and blaming. Discipline is harsh and arbitrary, fueled by parental anger and frustration, emotions untempered by any memories of sweetness and affection. Marital conflict is frequent and destructive, thereby establishing a level of intense negative emotion in the home that makes cooperation and understanding seem futile. Siblings nee-

> If we force children to submit and attempt to control them, we must accept that as they grow older and stronger we will face the violence we nurtured in them, knowing indeed, we have taught them well.
>
> —Barbara Coloroso,
> educator and author

dle and irritate each other, gradually raising the stakes until open hostility breaks out, whereupon parents intervene with their own hostility. Name-calling and taunting, pinching and slapping, retaliation and grudges are the norm rather than the exception. And *no one* is modeling positive behaviors consistently enough to break the cycle. The product of all this turmoil? Patterson's research is clear: out-of-control, highly aggressive children.

BABY DANDELION AND AGGRESSION

Not every overly aggressive child, however, is the result of a coercive environment at home. Some are put at risk simply by their inborn temperaments. This is particularly true of our little Baby Dandelions. Remember, these are the children who, from birth, seem bent on going everywhere and doing everything as fast as they possibly can. It's as if they are afraid they may miss something if they sit still too long. In addition, they tend to be fearless and impulsive, two qualities that really start getting them in trouble when they begin to crawl and then to walk—although most parents of Baby Dandelions would swear their child skipped walking altogether and went straight to running.

There's nothing intrinsically aggressive about being very active, and with patient, consistent, and *unflagging* parenting, Baby Dandelions can learn to harness their energy and control their impulsiveness. But it's not easy. The problem is that parenting a Baby Dandelion can be truly exhausting and very discouraging. It can also be embarrassing. You may have heard it said that there are no bad dogs, only bad owners. Unfortunately, many people apply this same logic to highly active children and their poor, beleaguered parents. That's not to say that parents of such children bear no responsibility for controlling their child's behavior. Of course they do. It's just that strangers don't seem to ever cut the parents of Baby Dandelions any slack. "If that were *my* child . . ." is easy for strangers to say, but the truth is that, were they to try walking in the parent's shoes, they would quickly appreciate what a daunting task controlling Baby Dandelion can be.

As a result of all this, parents of highly active children all too often become so frustrated that they either lash out with harsh discipline or simply give up. In either case, the result is, eventually, an increase in aggressive behavior. The transition from high energy to aggression is easy to understand. Because Baby Dan-

Sometimes it seems as if "Trouble" is Baby Dandelion's middle name. All too often parents get frustrated trying to keep up with their very active toddler and overreact with physical punishment, thus sending the message that aggression is a legitimate response to frustration.

delions are impulsive, they tend not to reflect on their behavior and simply to barge ahead and do what seems like a good idea in the moment. To the active toddler, this can easily involve taking things from other children, thereby learning very early that aggression is a useful tool to get what you want. Their impulsiveness also causes them to retaliate with aggression in instances where just a little more reflection would lead them toward more positive behavior. In this way the stage is set for the development of both proactive and reactive aggression.

All in all, then, Baby Dandelion and his parents face a tougher challenge than most as they struggle to keep aggressive levels within normal developmental bounds.

LANGUAGE DELAY AND AGGRESSION

Another significant predictor of aggression is poor language skills. In fact, some studies report that 80 percent of preschool and school-age children identified as exhibiting language delays also exhibit disruptive, aggressive behavior. The reason is that the inability to express themselves in words leads to such intense frustration that children tend to lash out, just as little Aaron did in the news flash with which the chapter opened. The good news, as the news flash also illustrated, is that such frustration can be decreased significantly by the use of simple signs. In addition, our study comparing signing toddlers with nonsigning ones showed decisively that using signs actually helps children learn to talk, making it a marvelous way for parents to support language development. (Other tips for how to encourage your child's development of language skills are included in our second book, *Baby Minds*.)

Signing actually continues to be useful even after a child gives up signs in favor of words. We highly recommend adding pertinent signs to your words in high-arousal situations even into the preschool years. The reason is that high-arousal decreases a child's ability to comprehend what you are saying. By adding the physical component of the sign, you are doubling the chance that your message will get through. Preschool teachers, for example, report that when children with a history of signing become frustrated or angry, they are easier to calm down than nonsigners because they still react to the teacher's use of gestures. For a preschooler who is too wound up to listen to words, a firm sign for "Stop!" or "Gentle!" can speak volumes.

How Would You Feel If...?

A significant proportion of the aggression we see in children between the ages of ten months and two years results from frustration at not being able to communicate. Imagine yourself in the following situation and perhaps you'll understand why.

After what seemed like an interminable flight, you finally stumble out of the Frankfurt, Germany, airport and try to find your way to your "nearby" hotel. Unfortunately, your choice of language in high school was Spanish, thereby leaving you totally helpless as you try to decipher the map and street signs. A kindly Fräulein stops to help you, but your failure to understand a word she says leaves you more frustrated and embarrassed than ever. What should have been a ten-minute walk to the hotel turns into a two-hour ordeal as you gradually make your way. Finally standing at the check-in counter, you breathe a sign of relief—only to see the clerk begin shaking his head "no" while talking a mile a minute. That's it. You've had it. Forgetting all your manners, you slam your hand down on the desk and demand to see the manager in the desperate hope that *someone* will speak English and find you a room. The result? Despite your best intentions, another "Ugly American" story is born.

Words of Wisdom and Tricks of the Trade

You may not realize it, but if you have arrived at this chapter after carefully working your way through the rest of *Baby Hearts,* then you already know a good deal about how to help your child reject aggression in favor of constructive behaviors. In fact, many of the specific tips contained in those earlier chapters are applicable here. To avoid repeating them all, we've opted for the shortcut of simply reminding you how the general topics covered in each of the previous chapters relate to the specific problems of hostility and aggression.

◆ **Chapter 1, "The Biology of Emotions."** Childhood aggression often results from frustration untempered by self-control. The child who impulsively throws the bat when he strikes out or kicks the blocks when the castle he's building falls down is demonstrating the inability to regulate his emotions. The biological roots of emotional regulation and the important role parents play in helping children make the transition to managing their emotions themselves is an important theme in Chapter 1. A bit later in this chapter we'll expand on this theme by providing specific tips for helping toddlers develop effortful control, the term researchers use to describe the ability to keep a handle on the kind of impulsive behavior that often leads directly to aggression.

◆ **Chapter 2, "Feeling Loved and Secure."** The lessons of this chapter were designed to help you build a strong and positive emotional bond between you and your baby. Enjoying a secure attachment bond during the earliest years will go a long way toward inoculating your baby against the feelings of anxiety, anger, and distrust that so easily predispose a child toward aggression.

◆ **Chapter 3, "Expressing Emotions Effectively."** In this chapter we highlighted the importance of helping your child *understand* her own feelings as well as the feelings of other people. Being keenly and *correctly* aware of the emotional world around her will help your child prevent situations from escalating into violence unnecessarily.

◆ **Chapter 4, "Evoking Empathy and Caring About Others."** It's hard to imagine a topic more relevant to any discussion of preventing aggression. Children who are helped to not only understand the effects of their behavior on other people, but to care genuinely about others' well-being, are much less likely to inflict either emotional or physical injury intentionally. How to support the development of empathy is what Chapter 4 is all about.

◆ **Chapter 5, "Developing Healthy Friendships."** In this chapter we described the plight of rejected children, children who are so inadequately prepared for social interaction with other children that their peers tend to avoid them. Such avoidance increases the rejected child's feelings of anger and frustration, and often leads to aggression. The ideas at the end of Chapter 5 are designed to help you prevent this from happening.

◆ **Chapter 6, "Having Self-Esteem and Self-Confidence."** The lesson here is quite simple. Children who are overly aggressive have learned to use aggression to bolster their own self-esteem, either by retaliating for perceived slights or by winning dominance over others. In either case, Chapter 6 can help you guide your child toward a sense of self based on positive rather than negative characteristics.

◆ **Chapter 9, "Handling Anger and Defiance."** The fact that anger and defiance so often lead directly to aggression makes this chapter the most relevant of all to the current discussion of hostility and aggression. In fact, all the "Words of Wisdom and Tricks of the Trade" included in Chapter 9 are equally applicable here. Rather than repeating them, we strongly recommend that you review the list beginning on page 226.

UH-OH . . . YOUR CHILD IS ABOUT TO HIT SOMEONE

Even if you've followed our advice to a T and have been rewarded with a basically well-behaved child, there will still be times when the desire to strike out is simply too strong to control. What should you do?

◆ **Head it off at the pass.** Your very first action should be to try to prevent the aggression in some way. As you see tempers escalate, distract the players with another activity, some form of humor, a burst of song, a "Guess what!" announcement (that you make up on the spot), or if worse comes to worst, physical separation.

◆ **It didn't work. Now what?** Either your distractions weren't distracting enough or you were just too late. The end result is the same: Your child has hit, pushed, bit, kicked, pinched, or otherwise assaulted another child. Here's what you do:

1. **Express the rule quickly and aid the victim.** Say something brief like "We do not hit. Hitting hurts!" and immediately move to the victim and begin comforting him. By attending first to the victim instead of your child, you are denying your child the attention he may have been seeking and demonstrating empathy for the other person's feelings. Distract the victim with some other activity so that you can turn your attention to the perpetrator.

2. **Remove your child from the scene of the crime.** It's important for the offending child to realize that something serious has happened. Interrupting the child's activity by physically moving him to a new location sends this message. The move needn't be far as long as the change is obvious.

3. **Explain your disapproval.** After you take your child aside, get down to his level, and start all over again. Using a calm but serious tone, let your child know that you don't like what he did, remembering to criticize the *deed*, not the child. (See Chapter 11 for the reasons why.) It's good to repeat in this statement what specific rule has been broken: "Sammy, do not hit— EVER." Keep in mind that your child is more likely to process these words if he's also heard them under less stressful circumstances, for example, in re-

sponse to TV aggression or while reading books. Also, very briefly explain *why* the action was unacceptable: "Look! You have really hurt Jesse's arm."

4. **Investigate and teach, but don't lecture.** If you don't understand why your child did what he did, ask him to describe what happened as best he can. Listen carefully, acknowledge his feelings, and then suggest what he could have done instead or what he should do next time. Remember, to "discipline" means to "teach."

5. **Decide on consequences.** You may choose to warn of consequences if the action happens again. Just be sure you can follow through with them if your warning goes unheeded.

◆ **What NOT to do.** Whatever you do, don't resort to aggression yourself. Hitting a child who has hit someone else only teaches him that he'd better not hit anyone while you're watching. It obviously doesn't teach that hitting is unacceptable. This general prohibition includes biting or pinching a child who has bitten or pinched someone else "so you can see how it feels." Using physical force only frightens a child, thereby decreasing the chance that he will be able to listen to your words and learn from them. A firm but gentle response is actually much more effective in the long run.

◆ **Be prepared to repeat this list over and over.** Toddlers are not what psychologists call one-trial learners. Parents who think otherwise are being unrealistic. Because toddlers don't think logically or efficiently, they tend to be ruled by their emotions, and it may take many, many individual lessons to tame their tempers. Take our word for it: Being vigilant and consistent will *eventually* pay off.

HELPING YOUR CHILD DEVELOP EFFORTFUL CONTROL

Even better than learning how to handle a situation in which your child has already hauled off and hit somebody is preventing the action in the first place. Because you won't always be there to distract your child when her temper flairs, it's critically important that she develop the ability to regulate her own emotions. In this case what needs to be regulated or managed is the impulse to hit, kick, bite, or push. In other situations other impulses may need to be controlled—such as the impulse to interrupt instead of waiting patiently or the impulse to do something that's off-limits, like playing with a forbidden toy. Researchers call the ability to resist strong impulses like these "effortful control," and some children—particularly

Your Child Is Being Bullied. What Should You Do?

The subject of bullies and their victims deserves much more than just a box. It deserves a whole book and, fortunately, a good one is available: *The Bully, the Bullied, and the Bystander* by educator Barbara Coloroso. As a resident of Littleton, Colorado, the site of a tragic high school shooting triggered by relentless bullying, Coloroso calls on parents, teachers, and *children* to stop tolerating bullying behavior in every way, shape, and form.

Among the wealth of information contained in her book are these tips for parents who suspect or know that their child is being victimized by a bully.

- **Probe gently until you're convinced you know the truth.** Victims are often ashamed of their plight and/or fearful of retaliation if they tell.
- **Help your child understand the difference between tattling and telling.** "Tattling" works only to get someone in trouble ("Teacher, Johnny's reading a comic book!"), while "telling" ends up also getting someone out of trouble (the victim).
- **Don't minimize or rationalize the bully's behavior.** ("Oh, I'm sure he didn't mean it." "Well, boys will be boys.") Bullying in any form is unacceptable.
- **Assure your child you are there to help.** Victims often feel very alone, convinced that no one can or will be able to stop the torture.
- **Report the problem to the proper authorities.** Politely but firmly insist that something be done. Take the problem up the chain of command if necessary.
- **Don't tell your child to fight back.** Chances are good that the effort won't be successful and the bullying will only get worse. You're also sending the message that aggression is the way to solve problems.
- **Use role-play to practice possible responses.** Help your child think of things he might do and/or say and then help him practice through pretend play.
- **Foster a strong sense of self in your child.** Although bullying is always painful, children who are self-confident are less likely to be truly damaged by it.

Finally, it's important to understand that a child who is snickered about, shunned, or openly laughed at is just as much a victim of bullying as one who is beaten up. The scars can run just as deep, if not deeper; they are just not as visible.

very active ones—need more help to develop it than others. Here are some ideas that may help.

◆ **Teach your child specific strategies.** Take advantage of any situation where your child is eager to do something but needs to wait by making concrete suggestions about how she might distract herself. These might include focusing on something else in the room, singing a song, or taking deep breaths to relax. Do them together at first. And be sure to congratulate her when she manages to make any of these strategies work.

◆ **Teach magic words.** In a lovely book called *Playful Parenting*, authors Denise Chapman Weston and Mark Weston suggest giving the slightly older child a verbal "mantra" to recite when she finds herself getting upset, something like "Stop and think!" By helping her practice using the mantra in pretend scenarios, you can prepare her to use it effectively in real situations. "Let's pretend your teddy really wants to grab a toy from my teddy. What can your teddy say to stop himself?" "That's right. 'Stop and think.' "

◆ **Play games that teach impulse control.** Parents and teachers throughout history have struggled to teach children self-control. Once in a while some wise adult would come up with a game to help the effort along. Fortunately, some of these games have been passed down from generation to generation. How many of these did you play as a child? We bet you never knew your teacher had an ulterior motive. Our favorites include "Red Light/Green Light," "Simon Says," "Mother, May I?" and "Statues" (where everyone freezes when the music stops). In addition, any game that requires taking turns (including board games, card games, and hopscotch) will help teach patience. And what better way for very active children to learn to stay still than playing hide-and-seek?

REMIND YOUR CHILD OFTEN THAT YOU ARE A TEAM

Finally, let your child know that learning to refrain from hitting, biting, kicking and pinching is really tough and that if all else fails and you're around, he can count on you for help. After all, the two of you are now, and will always be, a *team*.

11

**Everyone Makes Mistakes:
Steering Clear of Shame**

NEWS FLASH!

Some Toddlers Experience Shame, Others Guilt, Researchers Say

Fort Collins, Colorado. Two-year-old Jayna has suddenly found herself in an unexpected pickle. A nice lady had given her a doll to play with—in fact, the lady's own, absolute favoritest doll named "Pat"—while the lady went away for a few minutes. And everything had been fine, that is, until the doll's leg fell off while Jayna was trying to sit it up straight in a chair to give it a bottle. And now the lady has just opened the door and is coming back in. Oh dear, what to do?

Like the other two-year-olds tested in this same playroom at Colorado State University, little Jayna's reaction to having apparently broken the lady's precious doll is being carefully observed by developmental psychologists Karen Barrett, Carolyn Zahn-Waxler, and Pamela Cole. What they are looking for are the earliest signs of two emotions that everyone from psychologists to preachers to poets has opinions about: shame and guilt. These two morally loaded emotions, although often viewed as one and the same, are actually distinguishable in the behavior of two-year-old children. What's more, as hard as it seems to believe, even at these young ages many children have a bias toward one or the other, some showing what the researchers call shame-proneness and others showing what they call guilt-proneness.

Jayna's reaction when the nice lady comes back into the room provides a good example of the first of these two tendencies. As the experimenter walks in, Jayna turns her whole body away from the door, clearly trying to physically avoid interaction. Even when the experimenter mentions the leg situation, Jayna keeps her eyes turned away, her head bent down, and says nothing, a pattern of behavior that has earned shame-prone toddlers like Jayna the label "avoiders." Like adults who describe shameful feelings as too emotionally painful to confront, these toddlers seem desperate to make the situation go away by withdrawing, as if pretending nothing had happened would make it so. What's more, such behavior, according to their mothers, is also typical of these children at home.

In sharp contrast, other two-year-olds in this study were quick to show the experimenter the damage to the doll and to initiate attempts to fix it. Although clearly upset about the broken doll, these children seemed to get relief from directly confronting the situation instead of avoiding it, seeking solace and assistance from the adult rather than anticipating punishment. "We call them 'amenders,' " explains Barrett, "because their goal from the beginning is to make things right rather than make them go away, a pattern consistent with feeling guilt instead of shame. And the fact that their mothers describe them as also acting this way at home leads us to believe we have tapped an important personality dimension."

What's the Difference and Why Does It Matter?

Researchers Barrett, Zahn-Waxler, and Cole obviously feel it makes a big difference whether a child shows signs of shame-proneness versus guilt-proneness early in life. But is this difference really one parents should be concerned about? The answer is yes. As we'll discuss in more detail later, whether a child tends toward shame or guilt predicts the development of other very important emotions, including negative ones like anger, hostility, and vindictiveness, and positive ones like empathy, sympathy, and altruism.

SHAME AND GUILT: SIBLINGS BUT NOT TWINS

But first, let's get straight exactly why researchers view shame and guilt as distinct emotions. After all, both are reactions to situations where we've done something wrong, where we've clearly violated a presumed standard of conduct. In order to make the difference between shame and guilt clear as it relates to young children, we'll use Jayna's experience with the broken doll. Here are some of the main differences researchers see between these two emotions.

- ◆ **What's the source of the problem?** The most important difference between shame and guilt is where the person feels the error or "deficiency" lies.
  - ◆ **Shame.** The entire "self" is perceived as bad. For example, were we able to look into Jayna's head, we might hear her inner voice saying things like "I'm a bad girl" or "I can't do anything right."
  - ◆ **Guilt.** The specific action, rather than the "self," is perceived as bad. Were Jayna biased in this direction, that same inner voice would be saying things like "Oh dear, I broke it" or "I needed to be more gentle."
- ◆ **What are the physical signs?** One of the reasons researchers feel confident that shame and guilt are different emotions is that they *look* so different.
  - ◆ **Shame.** As is typical, Jayna showed outward signs of shame that included bent head, stooped shoulders, averted eyes—all behaviors that indicate an attempt to withdraw or even "disappear."
  - ◆ **Guilt.** Instead of trying to disappear, the guilty party looks *at* other people, often in a beseeching way with knitted brow and clear anxiety. There's more agitation than normal rather than less.
- ◆ **What's the subjective experience?** To get a sense of what we mean by "subjective experience," think of how the individual might portray himself if asked to paint his own portrait.
  - ◆ **Shame.** Jayna, feeling shame, would be more likely to portray herself as small relative to others and as *exposed*, that is, out in the open in full view of one and all.
  - ◆ **Guilt.** In contrast, a guilty child would portray herself as in the thick of things with long arms trying to make things better. In addition, the degree of discomfort felt with guilt tends to be less than that experienced with shame.
- ◆ **What actions do they take?** Not surprisingly, the two emotions motivate the individual to take very different actions.
  - ◆ **Shame.** The clear inclination is to flee the scene. There is also, unfortunately, a tendency to deal with the intense discomfort by blaming others. Jayna, for example, might think, "It's the lady's fault for letting me play with the doll!"

> The basis of shame is not some personal mistake of ours, but the ignominy, the humiliation we feel that we must be what we are without any choice in the matter, and that this humiliation is seen by everyone.
>
> —Milan Kundera, Czech author

- **Guilt.** Rather than trying to flee, the person feeling guilt is motivated to apologize and make amends, to right whatever wrong was done, and to prove it was a one-time-only lapse of judgment.

WHY THE DIFFERENCE MATTERS

If we had our druthers, we would all prefer that our children never need to feel ashamed *or* guilty. After all, these two emotions both indicate that something has been done that shouldn't have been, and life would be so much easier if we all had perfect children who never did anything wrong. The reality of life, however, is that mistakes—sometimes serious ones—do get made, and children do need to learn when and how their behavior has fallen short of important standards.

Every parent wants to know what to do when his or her child does something wrong. Especially troubling are those cases where the action seems intentional, when there's no doubt that the hit was intended to hurt, the lie was intended to deceive, the damage was intended to make another feel bad. What's a parent to do? The goal, of course, is to react in such a way as to make it less likely the child will choose the wrong path in the future. Research suggests that the best way to do this is to guide the child toward moral behavior *without* fostering feelings of shame. In other words, when necessary, the goal should be to instill guilt but not shame—and here's why.

Shame and Anger. Research by psychologist June Tangney from George Mason University has demonstrated that feelings of shame very often lead to anger and hostility *directed toward the very individuals who suffered from our misdeeds*. Why? What on earth could cause the shamed person to shift responsibility so dramatically? The reason lies, says Tangney, in the intense discomfort that shame arouses, increased in

Uh-oh! Maybe it wasn't a good idea to eat all the frosting off the cake! If this toddler is lucky, her mother will react to her transgression in ways that instill feelings of guilt rather than shame.

the case of children by a worry that their parents won't love them anymore because they are so bad. These painful feelings are so strong that some way out is desperately needed. An easy path to take in such cases is simply to turn the tables by rationalizing one's own behavior and shifting the blame to the other person. Indeed, the term "humiliated fury" is used to describe this illogical reaction. In children (particularly boys), with their less well-developed levels of self-control, such anger often surfaces as out-and-out aggression. In other words, the best defense is a good offense. Clearly, this is not an outcome parents would knowingly instill in their children.

Guilt, by contrast, mobilizes the individual to deal with internal discomfort by taking positive action. Because the pain is peripheral (concern over an action) rather than core (despair over oneself), it is easier both to figure out *how* to fix the problem and to garner the energy necessary to do so. What's more, there is no

effort to shift blame to the victim because the responsibility has already been acknowledged by the individual feeling the guilt. The emphasis on making amends,
according to Tangney, makes guilt a constructive rather than destructive emotion,
one that decreases rather than increases anger, hostility, and aggression.

Shame and Depression. Given what we've already said about shame, it should
come as no surprise to learn that Tangney's research has also revealed a relationship between shame and depression. Painful experiences of many kinds—illness,
loss of a loved one, loneliness—breed depression. Unfortunately, the pain engen-
dered by intense feelings of shame does too. The reason lies in the scope of the
perceived deficiency. It's not just that one did a bad thing; it is that one *is* bad.
And fixing something rotten to the core is a pretty daunting job. Therefore, as
shame builds, so does a sense of hopelessness—and hopelessness is everywhere
and always a prime ingredient of depression.

> The best way to make children good is to make them happy.
>
> —Oscar Wilde, Irish writer

Guilt can also result in depression, but the depression is usually more short-
lived. As soon as the guilty individual becomes mobilized to *do something* to make
amends, the feelings of distress lessen and with them, the feelings of depression.

Shame and Empathy. Unlike the last two categories, the relationship here is a
negative one, that is, the more one feels shamed, the less one feels empathy. Once
again, we have June Tangney and her colleagues to thank for uncovering the relationship. Based on studies of adults whose answers to questionnaires revealed
them to be either shame-prone or guilt-prone, these researchers found that guilt
but not shame was predictive of empathic reactions to the plight of others.

What happens to prevent shame-prone folks from feeling empathic? Two dynamics are at work. First, because they are so used to alleviating internal pain by
blaming other people, they often end up blaming the victims of misfortune. It's a
mind-set that has proven useful so often that blaming others simply becomes a
knee-jerk reaction.

Second, because shame-prone individuals are so used to focusing on themselves and their inadequacies rather than mobilizing to fix things, when confronted with the suffering of others, they tend to dwell on what *they themselves* are feeling rather than what the distressed person is feeling. As we discussed in length in Chapter 4, such a focus on self results in feelings of personal distress that are more likely to lead to withdrawal than to sympathetic action.

Guilt-prone individuals, by contrast, are routinely proactive, a tendency that comes in handy when they encounter someone in distress. Their habit of trying to fix things motivates them to help ease the suffering of the other person in any way they can. Their focus is on the consequences to the other person rather than simply decreasing their own distress, an orientation that leads to the constructive response called sympathetic action.

Guilt Wins Hands-Down! Based on the results of June Tangney's work on the different outcomes for shame-prone and guilt-prone people, it's clear that children will be better off if their parents strive to induce guilt rather than shame when their children miss the mark. Research-based tips for how to do so follow at the end of the chapter.

WHERE DOES "EMBARRASSMENT" FIT IN?

It might have occurred to you, as it did to us, that there is a third "sibling" in this family of self-conscious emotions: embarrassment. Exactly how embarrassment fits into the equation is a question addressed most directly by Michael Lewis of the Robert Wood Johnson School of Medicine.

Purely Public, Never Private. According to Lewis, embarrassment requires the presence of another person, someone who witnesses one's behavior and is assumed to be judging it. Shame and guilt, although they often do involve another person acting as a witness, don't *have* to. Eventually an individual becomes capable of feeling *self-imposed* shame or guilt even when the transgression is private. Standards of behavior have been internalized to such a degree that simply knowing one has violated a rule breeds intense discomfort. This isn't possible with embarrassment. There has to be a witness.

The physical signs of embarrassment are also different from those seen with

Sometimes it's a blessing that babies don't experience feelings of embarrassment before eighteen months! Nine-month-old Jack's expression is one of surprise instead of embarrassment, an emotion that depends on having a sense
of oneself separate from others.

shame and guilt. One particularly vivid telltale sign is blushing—although few
young children and only a minority of adults actually do so. More typical is a particular form of eye movement. Instead of avoiding eye contact, the gaze of embarrassed people goes back and forth. They first glance up and then away, back up
and then away again—a vacillation that is often accompanied by a sheepish grin,
as if to say "I can't believe I just did that." Finally, embarrassment also often leads
to fiddling with the body—touching the face, hair, or clothes or sundry other nervous hand movements.

Self-Conscious Embarrassment. Lewis suggests that there are two kinds of
embarrassment. The one that develops earliest is what he calls embarrassment
from exposure. Starting between eighteen and twenty-four months, children

begin to experience embarrassment when they find they are the center of attention and they don't *want* to be. It's not that they've done anything wrong or shameful. It's just that everyone is looking at them Lewis also calls this self-conscious embarrassment.

Why does embarrassment begin between eighteen and twenty-four months? It's quite simple. This is the age when toddlers become aware of themselves as separate from other people, knowledge that is obviously critical to feeling embarrassed. In fact, Lewis demonstrated a direct connection between self-awareness and embarrassment in the following way. First, he tested a group of toddlers to see

Schyler liked looking at himself in the mirror with his fancy Mohawk hairstyle, but felt very differently about it once Dad got the camera out. At twenty-four months, he's showing unequivocal signs of what researchers call self-conscious embarrassment.

if they could recognize themselves in a mirror—a classic test of self-awareness. As we've described earlier (see page 135), the way to do this is to surreptitiously dab a spot of rouge on a child's nose, set him in front of a mirror, and watch to see if he touches his nose. If he does, then it's clear that he recognizes that the red spot on the nose in the mirror is a red spot on his *own* nose. Some of the toddlers in Lewis's study did touch their noses, while others did not. Lewis then tested whether these same children would show embarrassment. He had their mothers urge them to dance in front of the experimenter to the sound of a tambourine. As you might expect, some children did so without hesitation, while others refused, showing classic signs of embarrassment. Every one of these latter children, and

Baby Hearts in Action:
Dancing with Peter Pan

When Linda's son, Kai, was nearly three years old, he fell in love with *Peter Pan*—or, more precisely, Mary Martin playing Peter Pan. He loved everything about the musical—the flying, the songs, the Indians, the crocodile—and would crow "Rrr-rrr-a-RRR!" at the slightest provocation. One day when Kai was alone in the family room watching the video for about the three hundredth time, Linda happened to peek in. There was Kai trying his darnedest to dance in time to the drums along with the Neverland Indians. The sight was so adorable that she tiptoed out and got her video camera to record the moment for posterity. But no sooner had the camera started rolling than Kai whirled around, saw her, and began howling "No! No camera!" clearly embarrassed to be caught in the act. Taking the hint, Linda retreated—but then snuck back a few minutes later to try again. Kai's second "No! No! No!" was even more convincing, and Linda gave up. What she hadn't noticed was big sister Kate peeking around the corner witnessing the whole thing. That night, having forgotten about the interaction, Linda settled herself in the tub for an early bath. Suddenly the door opened up to reveal a grinning Kai clumsily holding the video camera aimed right at her—with Kate giggling in the background. Big Sister was clearly giving him a valuable lesson in "turnabout is fair play!"

very few of the former, were among those able to recognize themselves in a mirror, a lovely demonstration that the child's developing mind and the child's developing emotions are closely related.

Embarrassment as Mild Shame. Once the child is aware of other individuals as separate from himself, he begins to watch more carefully how they react to his behavior, noting whether their reactions are positive or negative. As he gathers more and more data during the third year, he gradually detects consistencies in what the most important folks (Mom and Dad) like and don't like. The result is a sense of the standards or rules to which he should conform. It's this blossoming knowledge of standards that lays the foundation for shame, guilt, and the second form of embarrassment—embarrassment as a mild form of shame. According to Michael Lewis, when a child realizes she has violated a standard that is very important to either herself or the important people around her, she feels shame or guilt. However, if the standard she violates is only marginally important, then the feeling is one of embarrassment rather than the more emotionally loaded feeling of shame.

So That's Why They Get Upset. There is at least one helpful message for parents hidden in this discussion of embarrassment. Everyone has at one time or another been part of a group of adults sitting around watching the amusing antics of a toddler. Maybe she is busily eating chocolate cake, getting more around her mouth than in it, or maybe she is carefully trying to walk in her mother's high heels. Whatever the behavior, as soon as the child becomes aware that she is the focus of attention, she becomes upset. And no matter how many times she is reassured that no one is laughing *at* her, she remains unconsoled and is too embarrassed to continue. Her new ability to feel self-conscious is generating feelings of embarrassment at being the object of attention. Whether there is a judgment involved is somewhat irrelevant; she simply wants the attention itself to stop... *now*. Understanding this about toddlers can help parents be more sympathetic. After all, would you want everyone watching you stuff chocolate cake into your mouth? We thought not.

N E W S   F L A S H!

What to Do Next Time Is Key Anti-Shame Message, Scientists Advise

Logan, Utah. Thanks to the collaborative efforts of researchers at Utah State University and the University of Utrecht in The Netherlands, parents now have some guidelines to follow in their efforts to avoid strong feelings of shame in their young children. Tamara Ferguson and Hedy Stegge first interviewed five- to twelve-year-old children about how they would react if specific situations were to arise in which their behavior had been less than stellar. For example, what if they came across a young child crying on the sidewalk and they didn't stop to help because they were on their way to a birthday party? How would they feel? The answers the children gave were categorized as either expressing shame, with its emphasis on the whole self as bad ("I would be a mean kid for not helping"), or guilt, with its emphasis on the specific act as bad ("I would feel really sorry for not helping.").

Next, the parents of these children were interviewed about how they would react to their children in these same negative situations, as well as in some positive ones. The results were quite clear. Children who expressed more shame than guilt had parents who tended to react to behavior of which they disapproved with anger rather than with efforts to explain the reasons why the behavior was inappropriate. "All anger does," explains Ferguson, "is scare the child by giving the impression that the parent's love is in jeopardy without offering any way to win back the parent's approval. The result is a sense of failure that leads to despair or hostility rather than to constructive action."

These same parents also showed little interest in rewarding good behavior—as if good behavior were to be expected and therefore not worthy of any special attention. Parents of the ashamed children, in other words, provided very little concrete feedback to their children that might help them decide how to behave in the future.

Parents of the children who tended to express guilt rather than shame did exactly the opposite. They explained why behaviors were inappropriate, they rewarded appropriate behavior, and they expressed calm disapproval of the behavior (not the child) rather than anger. One final difference also deserves note. Parents of children who expressed more shame than guilt were likely to find fault with basic, broad attributes of their child that would be difficult to change (for example, temperament or intelligence), thereby making it even more difficult for the child to figure out how to change to avoid criticism in the future. A much better strategy, the researchers conclude, is to focus on the specific behaviors that need changing. In other words, the more concrete a parent's message, the better.

A lot of growing up takes place between "It fell" and "I dropped it."

—Anonymous

Words of Wisdom and Tricks of the Trade

Ferguson and Stegge's study provides important guidance to parents. To help their children deal constructively with mistakes, parents need to focus on the specifics of the deed rather than shaking the child's confidence in his or her core goodness. Specifically, they need to (1) point out what was done wrong, (2) explain *why* it was wrong, and (3) offer suggestions about how to avoid the problem in the future. Anger isn't the way to do this, nor are words that chastise children for things they can't change.

Here are some other tips for helping you avoid creating a tendency toward shame.

◆ **Know your child.** Following in the footsteps of the scientists whose research was described in the first news flash, observe your child's reactions closely when something unfortunate happens (purposeful or not). Does she frequently seem intent on avoiding you or claim not to have done something when she obviously did? Or is it more typical for her to show signs of wanting to make things better or fix whatever she did wrong? Figuring out whether your child has already developed a bias toward shame or guilt may help you understand other aspects of her behavior—expressions of hostility or defiance, for example.

Also, be sensitive to your child's overall temperament. Some children are simply more vulnerable to feeling shamed than others. For example, children who are extremely vigilant about others' reactions to them may notice the slightest frown and be easily hurt or even haunted by disapproval. Correcting such children requires a particularly soft "kid glove" and lots of loving reassurance. This is also true of children who are perfectionists and view even a minor criticism as a major blow. In contrast, other children are so energetic and risk-taking that it may be difficult to get their attention when corrections are necessary—and they may seem to be necessary all the time. Here's where exasperated parents sometimes go wrong, making general pronouncements like "You drive me crazy!" or "I don't know what I'm going to do with you!" that feel cathartic in the moment but end up causing more harm than good down the line. And remember, your child will be listening and learning from what you say to her brothers and sisters too.

Caught in the act of taking something he shouldn't have, thirty-month-old Shade waits apprehensively for his dad's reaction. Research shows that how parents react determines whether a child will feel shame or the more constructive emotion of guilt.

◆ **Know yourself.** If your observations indicate your child already has a tendency toward feelings of shame rather than guilt, take a close look at your own behavior. What do you say when your child does something wrong? Do you point to the consequences of the behavior and why you disapprove? Or do you emphasize that you are "disappointed in her" or that she's a "bad girl"? Remember, children who are told often enough that they are "bad" gradually find themselves living up to your expectations in what psychologists call a self-fulfilling prophecy.

How Would You Feel If . . . ?

"I'm so disappointed in you. Go to your room and think about what you did." These two sentences are hardly rare. Most parents probably have uttered them at one time or another. However, just because they are typical doesn't mean they are a good idea! In addition to implying that love will be withdrawn, these messages leave out at least two very important pieces of information: (1) why what the child did wasn't a good idea, and (2) what should have been done instead. The words succeed in making the child feel bad, but they don't teach her how to be better in the future.

How would you feel if the same message was addressed to you? Suppose you had just gotten off the phone with a very disagreeable customer whose outrageous accusations caused your own temper to flare. Now suppose your boss, overhearing your end of the conversation, steps into your office and says, "I'm so disappointed in you. Go home and think about what you did." Can you see how unhelpful that is? You probably already know that you didn't handle the situation well; what you don't know is how you *should* have handled it. Have other employees found stock phrases helpful to defuse such situations? Could you have called on your boss to take over? Maybe you should have just put the customer on hold and never come back! Thanks to your boss's choice of words, you still don't know and may well find yourself in the same situation tomorrow. And to make matters worse, you now feel humiliated as well as angry.

Well, guess what? A toddler hearing "I'm so disappointed in you. Go to your room and think about what you did" is even worse off than you are. He has very limited ability to think about what he did even if he *wanted* to! Keep this in mind the next time you are tempted to send this message—to *anyone*.

Self-scrutiny can also reveal whether you are setting realistic or unrealistic standards for your child. Maybe you are a perfectionist who unconsciously expects others to be perfect too. Maybe your knowledge of child development is sketchy, thereby leading you to expect more mature behavior from your child than is remotely possible. Maybe your own self-esteem hinges on your child's behavior reflecting well on you; perhaps that is causing you to react angrily to failure. Acknowledging these tendencies in yourself will help you identify what needs changing in order to prevent shame-proneness in your child.

◆ **Know who else influences your child.** Remember, you aren't the only one giving your child messages about his behavior. Grandparents, babysitters, and older siblings can also contribute to a toddler's notions of being a good or bad person. Be observant when your children are with these individuals, and watch for tendencies to shame your child rather than simply correct his or her behavior. If you find you do need to suggest a different way of interacting, it helps to point out that you are no more pleased with your child's behavior than they are. It's just that you have found it more effective to deal with the problem in a slightly different way.

> We can often better help another by fanning a glimmer of goodness than by censuring his faults.
>
> —Edmund Gibson, 18th-century clergyman

◆ **Highlight positive behavior.** The news flash describing the study by Ferguson and Stegge provides another important tip for parents: Don't overlook positive behaviors. Children who are *only* criticized, who never seem able to do anything right, lose hope and feel both unloved and unlovable. That's why it's so important to watch for opportunities to comment favorably on your child's behavior. Even *baby steps* toward improving her behavior should be praised. For example, a simple comment like "I'm proud of the way you let Emma play with that toy" will go a long way toward strengthening the tendency to share. Not only are you conveying concrete information about *how* to share, you are also increasing your child's desire to do so. Remember, your approval is a powerful reward and should be used liberally, not just on special occasions.

◆ **Remember, to err is human.** Be sure to correctly label mistakes as mistakes and accidents as accidents. The fact that we *all* make mistakes and cause accidents is an extremely important message for children to hear, along with information about how we intend to right the "wrong" ("Oh, dear. I forgot to say thank you. I'll write her a note."). Children aren't perfect, grown-ups aren't perfect, and even Mom and Dad aren't perfect. This fact is important because it conveys the subtle message that making mistakes or causing accidents doesn't make you a "bad" person. The very words "mistake" and "accident" imply that faulty judgment was at the root of things rather than some nefarious impulse, and faulty judgments are easy to change with the addition of more information. In fact, the phrase "I'm sure you didn't mean to..." is a lovely way to let your child know you believe he is basically well intentioned. Remember, self-fulfilling prophecies work in a positive direction as well.

12

The Puzzle Pieces of the Heart:
Putting It All Together

NEWS FLASH!

Search for Perfect Parents Comes Up Short!

Anywhere, USA. The basement of the local community center was the scene of lots of laughter and a few tears last Thursday evening when a group of parents got together to watch a very special video. Entitled *Best Laid Plans,* the film consists of interviews with these very same parents conducted some six years earlier when each couple was expecting its first baby. The prospective parents had been asked to describe their philosophy of child rearing and to predict what life would be like over the next years as they dealt with the challenges posed by their soon-to-arrive bundle of joy. Among the lines generating the most laughter at Thursday night's meeting were:

- "I feel I'm really prepared; I've read all the books and I'm confident that there's nothing the baby can throw at me that I won't be ready for."
- "Whatever happens, I've promised myself I will never lose my temper."
- "What I don't understand is why so many mothers claim they can't get anything done. How hard can it be to take care of one baby?"
- "If there's one thing I won't tolerate it's tantrums."
- "I know it's important to establish routines, so I plan to get the baby up at 7 A.M.,

have him nap from noon to 2 P.M., and put him down for the night at 7 P.M. That will leave my husband and me the evening to spend together relaxing."

◆ "At least I know my husband and I will always be on the same page when it comes to child-rearing decisions."

◆ "I have no patience with parents who can't control their children."

◆ "I'll tell you one thing for sure. I will never let my child out of the house with a runny nose."

As the credits rolled by and the lights came up, one parent was overheard commenting "I can't believe I was that naïve. I think I really assumed that raising a child was like a Paint-by-Number set—just follow the printed instructions, don't color outside of the lines, and everything will turn out perfectly!"

The easier you find it to understand why these parents were moved to laughter and tears by their earlier comments, the better prepared you are to become a parent yourself. These folks clearly thought they had done their homework and knew exactly what to expect, but the reality of parenting turned out to be very different from their romantic daydream. And so it will be for you—no matter how many books you read.

The truth is that no book, not even one as thoughtfully written as we've tried to make this one, has all the answers. No book can join you on the front lines as you try your best to make good moment-to-moment decisions for your unique, one-of-a-kind child. No book can foresee all the challenges you'll face, all the unexpected instances of good and bad fortune, all the special triumphs and tribulations your child will lay at your feet. And no book can guarantee you the unending reserves of patience and insight that you are going to wish you had. In other words, no book will make you a "perfect parent."

What parenting books can do for you is open your eyes to new ideas, new perspectives, and new rationales. Those are the gifts we have tried hard to provide throughout *Baby Hearts*. By helping you understand and appreciate the great strides being made in child development laboratories around the world, we hope to have convinced you to take seriously the general guidelines we've presented. Just to refresh your memory, here are ten common denominators that run throughout all the "Words of Wisdom and Tricks of the Trade" included in the preceding chapters.

1. To parent well you need first and foremost to understand *yourself*.
2. Work as hard as you can to create the bond of love and trust that is the foundation upon which all else rests.
3. Recognize and appreciate your child's uniqueness.
4. Treat your child with respect.
5. Be a good role model for your child.
6. Ask for and accept help from other people.
7. Keep your sense of humor.
8. Educate yourself about development.
9. Remember, there is no perfect child.
10. Remember, there is no perfect parent!

Parenting children is both the most challenging and the most rewarding job an adult will ever face. Fortunately, parents don't have to be perfect. As long as the scale, overall, is clearly weighted in a positive direction, children will return the love you give ten times over. What a deal!

Fortunately, children don't expect or need perfection from us. Children, even during the infant and toddler years, are flexible creatures with a capacity to forgive—just as long as the scale, overall, is very clearly weighted in a positive direction. It's as if Mother Nature has realized that not the richest parent, not the most educated parent, not the most well-meaning parent in the world can be expected to do a perfect job. In other words, we all "color outside the lines" occasionally.

We know from our own experiences that parenting children is both the most rewarding and the most challenging job you will ever face. More than any other life change, the sudden responsibility of having to steer a helpless infant through the murky waters and ever-shifting currents of modern life can seem overwhelming. And with good reason. The world is a vastly different place from the one we ourselves knew as children. As we struggle to raise our children while also dealing with unimaginable technologies, economic and political uncertainty, changing moral attitudes, and growing cultural diversity, it's only natural to make mistakes along the way. However, by reading *Baby Hearts* and taking our advice to "heart," as it were, you can be confident that you will make fewer mistakes than you might otherwise have done.

And, finally, it is our hope that having read *Baby Hearts,* you will now and forever appreciate the profound wisdom contained in these simple words from the noted historian of childhood Lloyd deMause:

> The evolution of culture is ultimately determined by the amount of love, understanding and freedom experienced by its children.... Every abandonment, every betrayal, every hateful act towards children returns tenfold a few decades later upon the historical stage, while every empathic act that helps a child become what he or she wants to become, every expression of love toward children heals society and moves it in unexpected, wondrous new directions.

APPENDIX: Quick Reference Guide

Words of Wisdom and Tricks of the Trade Revisited

Sometimes parents are looking for background information to help them understand their children better, and sometimes they are simply looking for advice on how to handle a situation occurring RIGHT NOW! With this latter need in mind, we have designed the following chart to function as a quick reference guide to the well over one hundred parenting tips included in *Baby Hearts*. Organized by chapter, the chart serves as an index to enable you to scan the tips pertinent to each topic and locate the page in the book where they are discussed in more detail.

You will also notice a column of ages, with one specific age entered for each tip. These ages represent the point in development when, in our judgment, the tip *starts* to be applicable. In each and every case, you can assume that the tip will continue to be applicable from that particular age on. For example, the advice to sing to your baby that we include in Chapter 2 is an activity that's appropriate to start at birth and is therefore followed by the word "Birth" in the age column. In contrast, the advice on arranging playdates to promote social development obviously isn't appropriate until much later. In this case you'll find "12 months" indicated in the age column.

Our real hope is that this index will end up motivating you to read and reread whole sections of *Baby Hearts*. Although the tips are designed to stand alone, we know you will find them easier to remember and to implement if you understand the bigger picture of emotional development they are designed to address.

Part I: The "Big Five" Goals for Healthy Emotional Development

2. "Welcome to the World: Feeling Loved and Secure"

Communicating Love

Play with your baby face to face	*Birth*	*page 46*
Sing to your baby	*Birth*	*page 46*
Whisper sometimes	*12 months*	*page 46*
Cuddle with a good book	*6 months*	*page 46*
Play together	*6 months*	*page 46*
Take advantage of the power of touch	*24 months*	*page 46*

Building Trust

Be sensitive	*Birth*	*page 48*
Learn from your baby what works	*Birth*	*page 48*
Encourage your baby to sign	*6 months*	*page 48*
Keep your promises	*18 months*	*page 48*
Be a secure home base	*Birth*	*page 48*
Establish routines	*Birth*	*page 49*

If You Need to Leave Your Child

Remember, you are still number one	*6 months*	*page 49*
Communicate confidence, not anxiety	*6 months*	*page 50*
Provide reasons	*12 months*	*page 50*
Say when you'll be back	*6 months*	*page 50*
Join the worlds together	*6 months*	*page 51*
Provide reminders from home	*6 months*	*page 51*
Use your voice as a source of comfort	*Birth*	*page 51*

Keeping Yourself Under Control

Post a reminder	*Birth*	*page 52*
Understand your baby	*Birth*	*page 52*

Stay healthy	*Birth*	*page 52*
Develop a support network	*Birth*	*page 52*
If all else fails, seek professional help	*Birth*	*page 52*
Know Thyself		*page 52*

3. "I'm Feeling Sad: Expressing Emotions Effectively"

Preparing the Foundation		
Build a secure attachment bond	*Birth*	*page 75*
Engage in synchronized interactions	*Birth*	*page 76*
Encourage your baby to use signs	*6 months*	*page 76*
Reacting on the Spot		
Help your child identify her feelings	*12 months*	*page 76*
Acknowledge the use of signs	*12 months*	*page 77*
Take advantage of conflicts	*12 months*	*page 77*
Generating Discussion		
Start a "happy/sad" bedtime routine	*12 months*	*page 77*
Branch out from "happy/sad"	*18 months*	*page 77*
Review photo albums or family videos	*6 months*	*page 78*
Use storybooks	*6 months*	*page 78*
Speculate about others' emotions	*24 months*	*page 79*
Start a "gratitude journal"	*18 months*	*page 79*
Practice reflective listening	*18 months*	*page 79*
Providing Practice with Emotions		
Play the "show-me" game	*18 months*	*page 79*
Use emotions in pretend play	*18 months*	*page 79*
Play the "silly song" game	*18 months*	*page 80*
Make a "what are they feeling?" deck of cards	*36 months*	*page 80*
Teaching Self-Control	*12 months*	*page 80*

4. "Kid Kindness: Evoking Empathy and Caring About Others"

Modeling Empathy		
Be a good neighbor	*12 months*	*page 99*
Find "kindness projects"	*18 months*	*page 99*
Expect the unexpected	*18 months*	*page 99*

Practice what you preach	*12 months*	*page 100*
Be reassuring	*Birth*	*page 100*
Acknowledge negative feelings	*Birth*	*page 100*
Help your child cope	*12 months*	*page 100*
Teaching About Empathy		
Use animals to practice being kind	*12 months*	*page 101*
Take advantage of books	*12 months*	*page 102*
Talk about solutions	*12 months*	*page 102*
Help identify feelings	*12 months*	*page 102*
Establish a happy/sad routine	*18 months*	*page 102*
Watch for defense mechanisms	*24 months*	*page 102*
Encourage your child to use signs	*6 months*	*page 103*
Being a Cheerleader		
Acknowledge good deeds	*12 months*	*page 103*
Use positive adjectives	*12 months*	*page 103*

5. "I've Got a Friend: Developing Healthy Friendships"

Know Your Child		
Typical reactions to novelty	*Birth*	*page 124*
Typical reactions to other children	*6 months*	*page 124*
Know Thyself		*page 124*
Provide Opportunities to Play with Other Children		
Choose your neighborhood carefully	*Birth*	*page 124*
Take advantage of classes	*6 months*	*page 125*
Arrange playdates	*12 months*	*page 125*
Make the Most of the Playdates You Arrange		
Choose the playmate carefully	*12 months*	*page 125*
Match your child	*12 months*	*page 125*
Foster ongoing relationships	*12 months*	*page 125*
Keep dates brief	*12 months*	*page 125*
Have the playmate bring toys	*12 months*	*page 125*
Decide on "off-limits toys"	*12 months*	*page 126*
Provide some identical toys	*18 months*	*page 126*

Supervise, but indirectly	*12 months*	*page 126*
Use distraction	*24 months*	*page 126*
Suggest "it-takes-two" games	*24 months*	*page 126*
Teach turn-taking skills	*18 months*	*page 126*
Be a Good Role Model		*page 126*
Use Your Own Playtimes to Advantage		
Play imitation games	*12 months*	*page 127*
Initiate turn-taking games	*18 months*	*page 127*
Encourage pretend play	*18 months*	*page 127*

6. "I Can Do Anything: Having Self-Esteem and Self-Confidence"

Know Thyself		
Don't expect your kids to live out your dreams	*Birth*	*page 143*
Don't compare your child to others	*Birth*	*page 144*
Have realistic expectations	*Birth*	*page 145*
Model self-esteem and self-confidence	*6 months*	*page 145*
Model a try-try-again attitude	*12 months*	*page 145*
Support General Emotional Development		
Forge a secure attachment bond	*Birth*	*page 145*
Help your child interpret his emotions	*12 months*	*page 145*
Use Playtimes Well		
Let your child take the lead	*Birth*	*page 145*
Resist the temptation to take over	*6 months*	*page 145*
Encourage try-try-again activities	*12 months*	*page 146*
Maximize Success Experiences		
Be sure challenges are at the right level	*6 months*	*page 146*
Appreciate the "I do it!" phase	*18 months*	*page 147*
Appreciate tiny triumphs	*6 months*	*page 147*
Let your child make choices	*12 months*	*page 147*
Assign little chores	*12 months*	*page 147*
Review accomplishments at bedtime	*12 months*	*page 147*
Praise your child in others' hearing	*12 months*	*page 147*
Watch Your Reactions to Failure		
Don't attribute failure to lack of ability	*6 months*	*page 148*

Work hard to find a silver lining	*12 months*	*page 148*
Be Careful How You Criticize		
Criticize the behavior, not the child!	*Birth*	*page 148*
Communicate unwavering love	*Birth*	*page 148*
Balance criticism with praise	*6 months*	*page 148*
Avoid "You always" and "You never"	*12 months*	*page 148*
Deliver criticism with love	*6 months*	*page 148*

Part II: The "Big Five" Challenges to Healthy Emotional Development

7. "Monsters and Meanies: Addressing Fear and Anxiety"

Know Thyself		*page 174*
Know the Company Your Baby Keeps	*6 months*	*page 174*
Dealing with Separation Anxiety		
Keep your child's environment constant	*6 months*	*page 175*
Use caregivers your child knows well and trusts	*6 months*	*page 175*
Leave some reminders	*6 months*	*page 175*
Let your child miss you	*6 months*	*page 175*
Avoid being away overnight as long as possible	*6 months*	*page 175*
Prepare your child for longer separations	*12 months*	*page 175*
Plan for reunion	*12 months*	*page 176*
Provide a representation of time going by	*15 months*	*page 176*
Dealing with Stranger Anxiety		
Ask people to approach slowly and soothingly	*6 months*	*page 176*
Provide a prop	*6 months*	*page 176*
Enthusiastically introduce the stranger	*6 months*	*page 176*
Be patient and understanding	*6 months*	*page 176*
Dealing with Other Fears		
Acknowledge	*6 months*	*page 177*
Probe	*12 months*	*page 177*
Promise protection	*6 months*	*page 177*
Provide information	*6 months*	*page 177*
Don't force confrontations!	*6 months*	*page 177*
Use the power of touch	*Birth*	*page 179*
'Fess up	*12 months*	*page 179*

When Your Child Is Afraid of...
   The bathtub   *12 months*   *page 179*
   Monsters   *18 months*   *page 179*
   The dark   *18 months*   *page 181*
Systematic Desensitization   *18 months*   *page 180*
When It's More Than a Few Fears
   Search for the source   *18 months*   *page 182*
   Establish routines   *12 months*   *page 182*
   Seek professional help   *24 months*   *page 182*

8. "No Need to Hide: Dealing with Shyness and Withdrawal"

See Things Through Your Shy Child's Eyes
   Shy children are really and truly scared   *12 months*   *page 200*
   Even asking for help is hard   *18 months*   *page 201*
   The stomachaches can be real   *18 months*   *page 201*
Be Your Child's Secure Home Base   *Birth*   *page 201*
Start Early Making Strangers into Friends   *Birth*   *page 203*
Know Thyself   *page 203*
Make Your Home a Hub of Activity   *Birth*   *page 204*
Arrange One-on-One Playdates   *12 months*   *page 204*
Prepare Your Child in Advance   *12 months*   *page 205*
Remain On Site for as Long as It Takes   *6 months*   *page 206*
Build Social Skills Through Pretend Play   *18 months*   *page 206*
Find the Balance Between Pushing and Protecting
   Outright pushing seldom works   *6 months*   *page 206*
   Be sure you're acting in your child's best interests   *6 months*   *page 207*
   Don't expect too much too soon   *6 months*   *page 207*

9. "Tempers and Tantrums: Handling Anger and Defiance"

Build an Affectionate Relationship
   Go the extra mile   *Birth*   *page 226*
   Grease the nonsticky wheel   *Birth*   *page 227*
   Find the time to play with your child   *6 months*   *page 227*

Use Positive Rather Than Negative Discipline

Take good care of yourself	*Birth*	*page 227*
Don't expect perfection	*Birth*	*page 227*
Be polite	*6 months*	*page 227*
Be clear in your requests	*12 months*	*page 228*
Acknowledge your child's feelings	*Birth*	*page 228*
Decide if you're going to help	*12 months*	*page 228*
Provide reasons for your requests	*12 months*	*page 228*
When possible, give choices	*12 months*	*page 229*
Use "do" words rather than "don't" words	*12 months*	*page 229*
Show rather than just tell toddlers what to do	*12 months*	*page 229*
Praise good behavior whenever possible	*12 months*	*page 229*

What If Your Child Ignores You?

page 230

Dealing with Tantrums

Recognize the danger signs	*12 months*	*page 230*
Use humor and distraction to lower tension	*12 months*	*page 230*
Keep your own cool	*12 months*	*page 230*
Use time-outs instead of physical punishment	*18 months*	*page 231*

10. "Sticks and Stones: Avoiding Hostility and Aggression"

Review Previous Chapters of *Baby Hearts*   *page 254*

When Your Child Is About to Hit Somebody

Head it off at the pass	*12 months*	*page 256*
It didn't work, now what?		
Express the rule and aid the victim	*12 months*	*page 256*
Remove your child	*12 months*	*page 256*
Explain your disapproval	*12 months*	*page 256*
Investigate and teach, but don't lecture	*12 months*	*page 257*
Decide on consequences	*18 months*	*page 257*
What NOT to do	*Birth*	*page 257*
Be prepared to repeat this list over and over	*12 months*	*page 257*

Helping Your Child Develop Effortful Control

Teach specific strategies	*12 months*	*page 259*
Teach magic words	*24 months*	*page 259*
Play games that teach impulse control	*24 months*	*page 259*

Dealing with Bullies   *24 months*   *page 258*
Remind Your Child Often That You Are a Team   *12 months*   *page 259*

11. "Everyone Makes Mistakes: Steering Clear of Shame"

Know Your Child   *6 months*   *page 273*
Know Yourself   *page 275*
Know Who Else Influences Your Child   *Birth*   *page 276*
Highlight Positive Behavior   *Birth*   *page 276*
Remember, to Err Is Human   *6 months*   *page 277*

References

Acredolo, L., and S. Goodwyn. *Baby Signs: How to Talk with Your Baby Before Your Baby Can Talk,* 2nd ed. New York: Contemporary Books, 2002.

Acredolo, L. and S. Goodwyn. *Baby Minds: Brain-Building Games Your Baby Will Love.* New York: Bantam Books, 2000.

Ainsworth, M.D.S., M. C. Blehar, E. Waters, and S. Wall. *Patterns of Attachment: A Psychological Study of the Strange Situation.* Hillsdale, NJ: Erlbaum, 1978.

Asher, S. R., and J. D. Coie. *Peer Rejection in Childhood.* New York: Cambridge University Press, 1990.

Bagwell, C. L., A. Newcomb, and W. M. Bukowski. "Preadolescent Friendship and Peer Rejection as Predictors of Adult Adjustment." *Child Development,* 69, 1998, 140–53.

Bandura, A. *Self-Efficacy: The Exercise of Control.* New York: Freeman, 1994.

Barrett, K. C., C. Zahn-Waxler, and P. Cole. "Avoiders versus Amenders: Implications for the Investigation of Guilt and Shame During Toddlerhood." *Cognitive Emotions,* 7, 1993, 481–505.

Baumrind, D. "Current Patterns of Parental Authority." *Developmental Psychology Monographs,* 4, no. 1, part 2, 1971.

Belsky, J., B. Spritz, and K. Crnic. "Infant Attachment Security and Affective-Cognitive Information Processing at Age 3." *Psychological Science,* 7, 1996, 111–14.

Biringen, Z., R. N. Emde, J. J. Campos, and M. Appelbaum. "Affective Reorganization in the Infant, the Mother, and the Dyad: The Role of Upright Locomotion and Its Timing." *Child Development,* 66, 1995, 499–514.

Bornstein, M. H., M.E. Arterberry, and C. Mash. "Long-Term Memory for an Emotional Interpersonal Interaction Occurring at 5 Months of Age." *Infancy,* 6, 2005, 407–416.

Bowlby, J. *Attachment and Loss: Volume 1. Attachment.* New York: Basic Books, 1982.

Bowlby, J. *Attachment and Loss: Volume 1. Separation: Anxiety and Anger,* 2nd ed. New York: Basic Books, 1982.

Bugental, D., B. J. Blue, and M. Cruzcosa. "Perceived Control over Caregiving Outcomes: Implications for Child Abuse." *Developmental Psychology,* 25, 1989, 532–39.

Burchinal, M. R., A. Follmer, and D. N. Bryant. "The Relations of Maternal Social Support and Family Structure with Maternal Responsiveness and Child Outcomes among African-American Families." *Developmental Psychology,* 32, 1996, 1073–83.

Calkins, S., and M. Johnson. "Toddler Regulation of Distress to Frustrating Events: Temperamental and Maternal Correlates." *Infant Behavior and Development*, 21, no. 3, 1998, 379–95.

Chapman-Weston, D., and M. S. Weston. *Playful Parenting*. New York: Tarcher/Putnam, 1993.

Civitas, 2002, "What Grown-Ups Understand About Child Development: A National Benchmark Survey." Reported in *America's Family Support Magazine*, 21 (Winter 2003): 17–20.

Cloninger, C., D. M. Svrakic, and T. R. Przybeck. "A Psychobiological Model of Temperament and Character." *Archives of General Psychiatry*, 50, 1993, 975–90.

Coloroso, B. *The Bully, the Bullied, and the Bystander*. New York: HarperCollins, 2003.

Conger, R. D., K. J. Conger, G. H. Elder Jr., F. G. Lorenz, R. L. Simons, and L. B. Whitbeck. "A Family Process Model of Economic Hardship and Adjustment of Early Adolescent Boys." *Child Development*, 63, 1993, 527–41.

Cousins, S. D. "Culture and Self-Perception in Japan and the United States." *Journal of Personality and Social Psychology*, 56, 1989, 124–31.

Crick, N. "The Role of Overt Aggression, Relational Aggression, and Prosocial Behavior in the Prediction of Children's Future Social Adjustment." *Child Development*, 67, 1996, 2317–27.

Crockenberg, S. "Infant Irritability, Mother Responsiveness, and Social Support Influences on the Security of Infant-Mother Attachment." *Child Development*, 52, 1981, 857–69.

Cummings, E. M., R. Iannotti, and C. Zahn-Waxler. "Aggression between Peers in Early Childhood: Individual Continuity, and Developmental Change." *Child Development*, 60, 1989, 667–895.

Daniels, D., and R. Plomin. "Origins of Individual Differences in Infant Shyness." *Developmental Psychology*, 21, 1985, 118–21.

DeMause, L. *The History of Childhood*. Lanham, MD: Jason Aronson Publishers, 1995.

Didow, S. M., and C. O. Eckerman. "Toddler Peers: From Nonverbal Coordinated Action to Verbal Discourse." *Social Development*, 10, 2001, 170–188.

Dodge, K. "A Social Information Processing Model of Social Competence in Children." In M. Perlmutter, ed., *Minnesota Symposia on Child Psychology*, vol. 18. Hillsdale, NJ: Erlbaum, 1986, 77–125.

Dondi, M., F. Simion, and G. Caltran. "Can Newborns Discriminate between Their Own Cry and the Cry of Another Newborn Infant?" *Developmental Psychology*, 35, no. 2, 1999, 418–26.

Dunn, J., I. Bretherton, and P. Munn. "Conversations about Feeling States between Mothers and Their Young Children." *Developmental Psychology*, 23, 1987, 132–39.

Dweck, C., and E. Leggett. "A Social-Cognitive Approach to Motivation and Personality." *Psychological Review*, 95, 1988, 256–73.

Eckerman, C. O., and M. Stein. "How Imitation Begets Imitation and Toddlers' Generation of Games." *Developmental Psychology*, 26, 1990, 370–78.

Eisenberg, N., R. Fabes, M. Schaller, G. Carlo, and P. A. Miller. "The Relations of Parental Characteristics and Practices in Children's Vicarious Emotional Responding." *Child Development*, 62, 1991, 1393–1408.

Elicker, J., M. Englund, and A. Sroufe. "Predicting Peer Competence and Peer Relationships in Childhood from Early Parent-Child Relationships." In R. D. Parke and G. W. Ladd, eds., *Family-Peer Relationships: Modes of Linkage*. Hillsdale, NJ: Erlbaum, 1992, 77–106.

Emde, R. N., Z. Biringen, R. B. Clyman, and D. Oppenheim. "The Moral Self of Infancy: Affective Core and Procedural Knowledge." *Developmental Review*, 11, 1991, 251–70.

Evans, M. A. "Communicative Competence as a Dimension of Shyness." In R. H. Rubin and J. B. Asendorpf, eds., *Social Withdrawal, Inhibition, and Shyness in Childhood*. Hillsdale, NJ: Erlbaum, 1993, 189–215.

Feldman, R., C. Greenbaum, and N. Yirmiya. "Mother-Infant Affect Synchrony as an Antecedent of the Emergence of Self-Control." *Developmental Psychology*, 35, 1999, 223–31.

Ferguson, T. J., and H. Stegge. "Emotional States and Traits in Children: The Case of Guilt and Shame." In J. P. Tangney and K. W. Fischer, eds., *Self-Conscious Emotions*. New York: The Guilford Press, 1995, 174–97.

Fernald, A. "Approval and Disapproval: Infant Responsiveness to Vocal Affect in Familiar and Unfamiliar Languages." *Child Development*, 64, 1993, 657–74.

Field, T. *Touch in Early Development*. Mahwah, NJ: Erlbaum, 1995.

Fox, N. A., M. A. Bell, and N. A. Jones. "Individual Differences in Response to Stress and Cerebral Asymmetry." *Developmental Neuropsychology*, 8, 1992, 161–84.

Fox, N. A., and R. J. Davidson. "Taste-Elicited Changes in Facial Signs of Emotion and the Asymmetry of Brain Electrical Activity in Human Newborns." *Neuropsychologia*, 24, 1986, 417–22.

Fox, N. A., K. H. Rubin, S. D. Calkins, T. R. Marshall, R. J. Coplan, S. W. Porges, J. Long, and S. Stewart. "Frontal Activation Asymmetry and Social Competence at Four Years of Age." *Child Development*, 66, 1995, 1770–84.

Frick, P., A. Cornell, S. D. Bodin, H. Dane, C. Garry, and B. Loney. "Callous-Unemotional Traits and Developmental Pathways to Severe Conduct Problems." *Developmental Psychology*, 39, 2003, 246–60.

Fung, H., and E. Chain-Hui Chen. "Across Time and Beyond Skin: Self and Transgression in the Everyday Socialization of Shame among Taiwanese Preschool Children." *Social Development*, 10, 2001, 420–27.

Goleman, D. *Emotional Intelligence*. New York: Bantam, 1997.

Gunnar, M. R. "Changing a Frightening Toy into a Pleasant Toy by Allowing the Infant to Control Its Actions." *Developmental Psychology*, 14, 1978, 157–72.

Harris, P. "Monsters, Ghosts and Witches: Testing the Limits of the Fantasy-Reality Distinction in Young Children." *British Journal of Developmental Psychology. Special Issue: Perspectives on the Child's Theory of Mind*, 1991, 105–12.

Hart, S., T. Field, C. Del Valle, and M. Letourneau. "Infants Protest Their Mothers' Attending to an Infant-Size Doll." *Social Development*, 7, 1998, 54–61.

Hartup, Willard. "The Company They Keep: Friendships and Their Developmental Significance." *Child Development*, 59, 1996, 1–13.

Hesse, E., and M. Main. "Unresolved/Disorganized Responses to Trauma in Non-Maltreating Parents: Previously Unexamined Risk Factor for Offspring." *Psychoanalytic Inquiry*, 19, 1999, 4–20.

Hofer, M. "Hidden Regulators in Attachment, Separation, and Loss." In N. Fox, ed., "The Development of Emotion Regulation: Biological and Behavioral Considerations." *Monographs of the Society for Research in Child Development*, 59, no. 240, 1994, 192–207.

Hoffman, M. "Is Altruism Part of Human Nature?" *Journal of Personality and Social Psychology*, 40, 1981, 121–37.

Howes, C., and C. Matheson. "Sequences in the Development of Competent Play with Peers: Social and Social Pretend Play." *Developmental Psychology*, 28, 1992, 961–74.

Izard, C. E., ed. *Measuring Emotions in Infants and Children*. New York: Cambridge University Press, 1982.

Kagan, J., N. Snidman, and D. Arcus. "Childhood Derivatives of High and Low Reactivity in Infancy." *Child Development*, 69, 1998, 1483–93.

Karen, R. *Becoming Attached*. New York: Warner Books, 1994.

Kingsolver, B. *Prodigal Summer*. New York: Perennial, 2001.

Kochanska, G. "Mutually Responsive Orientation Between Mothers and Their Young Children: A Context for the Early Development of Conscience." *Current Directions in Psychological Science*, 11, 2002, 191–95.

Koren-Karie, N., D. Oppenheim, S. Dolev, E. Sher, and A. Etzion-Carasso. "Mothers' Insightfulness Regarding Their Infants' Internal Experience: Relations with Maternal Sensitivity and Infant Attachment." *Developmental Psychology*, 38, 2002, 534–63.

Kuczynski, L., and G. Kochanska. "Development of Children's Non-compliance Strategies from Toddlerhood to Age 5." *Developmental Psychology*, 26, 1990, 398–408.

Kuo, Z. Y. "The Genesis of the Cat's Response to

the Rat." *Journal of Comparative and Physiological Psychology,* 11, 1930, 1–35.

Ladd, G. W., and B. S. Golter. "Parents' Management of Preschoolers' Peer Relations: Is It Related to Children's Social Competence?" *Developmental Psychology,* 24, 1988, 109–17.

Laible, D., and R. Thompson. "Mother-Child Conflict in the Toddler Years: Lessons in Emotion, Morality, and Relationships. *Child Development, 73,* 2002, 1187–1203.

Lamb, M. "Fathers: Forgotten Contributors to Child Development." *Human Development,* 18, 1975, 245–66.

Lamb, M. *The Role of the Father in Child Development,* rev. ed. New York: Wiley, 1997.

Lewis, M. "Embarrassment: The Emotion of Self-Exposure and Evaluation." In J. P. Tangney and K. W. Fischer, eds., *Self-Conscious Emotions: The Psychology of Shame, Guilt, Embarrassment, and Pride.* New York: Guilford Press, 1995, 198–217.

Lewis, M., and J. Brooks-Gunn. *Social Cognition and the Acquisition of Self.* New York: Plenum Press, 1979.

Lewis, T., F. Amini, and R. Lannon. *A General Theory of Love.* New York: Random House, 2000.

Lieberman, A. F. *The Emotional Life of the Toddler.* New York: Free Press, 1993.

Liu, D., J. Dioria, B. Tannenbaum, C. Caldji, D. Francis, A. Freedman, S. Sharma, D. Pearson, P. Plotsky, and M. J. Meaney. "Maternal Care, Hippocampal Glucocorticoid Receptors, and Hypothalamic-Pituitary-Adrenal Responses to Stress." *Science,* 277, 1997, 1659–62.

Lozoff, B., G. Brittenham, M. Trause, J. Kennell, and N. Klaus. "The Mother-Newborn Relationship. Limits of Adaptability." *Journal of Pediatrics,* 91, no. 1, 1977, 1–12.

Marsh, H. W., and K. T. Hau. "Big Fish–Little Pond Effect on Academic Self-Concept: A Cross-Cultural (26-Country) Test of the Negative Effects of Academically Selective Schools." *American Psychologist,* 58, 2003, 364–76.

Montague, D. P. F., and A. Walker-Andrews. "Peekaboo: A New Look at Infants' Perception of Emotion Expressions." *Developmental Psychology,* 37, 2001, 826–38.

National Institute of Child Health and Human Development Early Child Care Research Network. "Social Functioning in First Grade: Associations with Earlier Home and Child Care Predictors and with Current Classroom Experiences." *Child Development,* 74, 2003, 1639–62.

Parke, R. D. "Fathers and Families." In M. Bornstein, ed., *Handbook of Parenting,* vol. 3. Hillsdale, NJ: Erlbaum, 27–63.

Parker, J., and S. Asher. "Peer Relations and Later Personal Adjustment: Are Low-Accepted Children at Risk?" *Psychological Bulletin,* 102, 1987, 357–89.

Parker, J., K. Rubin, J. Price, and M. DeRosier. "Peer Relationships, Child Development, and Adjustment: A Developmental Psychopathology Perspective." In D. Cicchetti and D. Cohen, eds., *Developmental Psychopathology: Vol. 2. Risk, Disorder, and Adaptation.* New York: Wiley, 1995, 96–161.

Patterson, G., J. Reid, and T. Dishion. *Antisocial Boys.* Eugene, OR: Castalia, 1992.

Perry, B. D., R. A. Pollard, T. L. Blakely, W. L. Baker, and D. Vigilante. "Childhood Trauma, the Neurobiology of Adaptation, and 'Use-Dependent' Development of the Brain: How States Become Traits." *Infant Mental Health Journal,* 16, 1995, 271–91.

Rovee-Collier, C. "The Development of Infant Memory." *Current Directions in Psychological Science,* 8, 1997, 80–85.

Rubin, K., W. M. Bukowski, and J. Parker. "Peer Interactions, Relationships, and Groups." In W. Damon, series ed., and N. Eisenberg, vol. ed., *Handbook of Child Psychology: Volume 3. Social, Emotional, and Personality Development.* 5th ed. New York: Wiley, 1998, 619–700.

Shaffer, D. *Social and Personality Development.* Belmont, CA: Wadsworth, 2000.

Siegel, D. J. *The Developing Mind.* New York: Guilford Press, 1999.

Siegel, D. J., and M. Hartzell. *Parenting from the Inside Out.* New York: Tarcher/Penguin, 2003.

Sorce, J. F., R. N. Emde, J. Campos, and M. Klinnert. "Maternal Emotional Signaling: Its Effect on the Visual Cliff Behavior of 1-year-olds." *Developmental Psychology,* 21, 1985, 195–200.

Spock, B., and S. Parker. *Dr. Spock's Baby and Child Care.* New York: Pocket Books, 1998.

Sroufe, I. A., E. Carlson, and S. Schulman. "Individuals in Relationships: Development from Infancy through Adolescence." In R. D. Funder, R. D. Parke, C. Tomlinson-Keasey, and K. Widaman, eds., *Studying Lives through Time: Personality and Development.* Washington, DC: American Psychological Association, 1993, 315–42.

Sroufe, I. A., E. A. Carlson, A. K. Levy, and B. Egeland. "Implications of Attachment Theory for Developmental Psychopathology." *Development and Psychopathology,* 11, 1999, 1–13.

Steele, H., M. Steele, C. Croft, and P. Fonagy. "Infant-Mother Attachment at One Year Predicts Children's Understanding of Mixed Emotions at Six Years. *Social Development,* 8, 1999, 161–78.

Stern, D. *The Interpersonal World of the Infant.* New York: Basic Books, 1985.

Stipek, D., A. Recchia, and S. McClintic. "Self-Evaluation in Young Children." *Monographs of the Society for Research in Child Development,* 57, no. 1, 1992.

St. James-Roberts, I., S. Conroy, and C. Wilsher. "Stability and Outcome of Persistent Infant Crying." *Infant Behavior and Development,* 21, no. 3, 1998, 411–35.

Swallow, W. K. *The Shy Child.* New York: Warner Books, 2000.

Tangney, J. "Shame and Guilt in Interpersonal Relationships." In J. P. Tangney and K. W. Fischer, eds., *Self-Conscious Emotions: The Psychology of Shame, Guilt, Embarrassment, and Pride.* New York: Guilford Press, 1995, 114–39.

Thomas, A., and S. Chess. *Temperament and Development.* New York: Brunner/Mazel, 1977.

Thompson, R. A. "Emotion Regulation: A Theme in Search of a Definition." In N. A. Fox ed., "The Development of Emotion Regulation: Biological and Behavioral Considerations." *Monographs of the Society for Research in Child Psychology,* 59, no. 2–3, 1994.

Trainor, L. "Infant Preferences for Infant-Directed versus Noninfant-Directed Playsongs and Lullabies." *Infant Behavior and Development,* 19, 1996, 83–92.

Tronick, E. "Emotions and Emotional Communications in Infants." *American Psychologist,* 44, 1989, 112–19.

Urbano Blackford, J., and T. A. Walden. "Individual Differences in Social Referencing." *Infant Behavior and Development,* 21, 1998, 89–102.

Van den Boom, D. "The Influence of Temperament and Mothering on Attachment and Exploration: An Experimental Manipulation of Sensitive Responsiveness among Lower-Class Mothers with Irritable Babies." *Child Development,* 65, 1994, 1449–69.

Waters, E., S. Merrick, L. Albersheim, D. Treboux, and J. Crowell. "Attachment from Infancy to Early Adulthood: A 20-Year Longitudinal Study of Relations between Infant Strange Situation Classifications and Attachment Representations in Adulthood." Paper presented at the biennial meeting of the Society for Research in Child Development, Indianapolis, 1995.

Watson, J. B. *Psychological Care of Infant and Child.* New York: Norton, 1928.

Weiss, B., K. Dodge, J. E. Bates, and G. S. Pettit. "Some Consequences of Early Harsh Discipline: Child Aggression and a Maladaptive Social Information Processing Style." *Child Development,* 63, 1992, 1323–35.

Zahn-Waxler, C., M. Radke-Yarrow, E. Wagner, and M. Chapman. "Development of Concern for Others." *Developmental Psychology,* 28, 1992, 126–36.

Zero to Three. Press release, www.zerotothree.org, September 1997.

Photo Credits

Page 110: Amy Fulmer

Page 113: Janelle Leger

Page 160: Christine Atha

Page 170: Lynn Arner

Page 194: Lynne Field

Page 242: Linda Easton

Index

Abuse, 32, 37–38, 216

Acredolo, Linda, 55

Aggression/hostility
and anger, 237–38, 250, 255–56
as challenge, 154, 235–59, 292–93
and "coercive" families, 240, 250–51
control of, 248, 254–55, 257, 259, 292–93
and discipline, 240, 249–50, 252
and empathy, 85, 86, 95, 241, 245, 255, 256
and expressing emotions, 57, 255
forms/types of, 239–45
and friendships, 115, 118, 122, 255
and gender, 245
as high-profile problem, 236–37
as instinct, 246
and love/security, 246, 255
motivation for, 238, 239–45
news flashes about, 235–36, 249–50
of parents, 257
prevention of, 256, 292
reasons for, 248–53
and self-esteem/confidence, 239, 255, 258
and shame/guilt, 262, 265, 266, 273
and shyness, 187, 196, 198

and steps along the way, 245–58
and teamwork, 259, 293
understanding of, 242, 243–44, 255
and what not to do, 257, 292
words of wisdom/tricks of the trade about, 254–59

Ainsworth, Mary, 26, 27, 28, 72

American Academy of Pediatrics, 5

Amini, Fari, 19

Anger/defiance, 142, 187
and aggression, 237–38, 250, 255–56
as challenge to emotional development, 154, 209–33, 291–92
downside to, 212, 215–16
and expressing emotions, 55, 57, 228–29
and fear, 171–72, 215–16, 217, 220, 221, 222, 231
and maternal depression, 219–20
news flashes about, 209–10, 223–24
of parents, 217, 220–21, 250
as primary emotion, 60, 211
and shame/guilt, 262, 264–66, 272, 273
sources of, 212
and stress, 221–22
and tantrums, 230–33, 292

Anger/defiance (*cont.*)
  and temperament, 217–19
  and "Terrible Twos," 210–23, 227
  underlying advances concerning, 211–15
  upside to, 211–15
  words of wisdom/tricks of the trade
    concerning, 224–33
Animals, 99–100, 101, 288
Anxiety. *See* Fear and anxiety
Arterberry, Martha, 41
Asher, Steve, 117
Attachment, 120, 198, 219–20, 255
  child's role in development of, 42–44
  and contingent responding, 39
  and expressing emotions, 67, 72, 75–76,
    287
  father's role in development of, 31
  and fear, 170–71, 172
  importance of early, 52–53
  parents' role in development of, 34–44
  pioneers of theory of, 26–28
  and self-esteem/confidence, 132, 139,
    145, 289
  steps toward, 32–33
  and Strange Situation, 28–30, 32, 37,
    75–76
  See also Love and security
Avoidance/avoiders, 73, 90–92, 93–94,
  193–94, 195, 230, 255, 262

Bagwell, Catherine, 107
Bandura, Albert, 130, 147
Barrett, Karen, 261, 262
Bates, John, 249
Baumrind, Diana, 218–19
Bedtime, 49, 77, 102, 147, 182, 229, 287,
  289
Belsky, Jay, 23–24, 28
Bevan-Brown, M., 216
Biology
  as destiny, 6, 12, 121
  of emotions, 1–20, 254–55
Biringen, Zeynep, 211
Blackford, Jennifer Urbano, 168

Blame, 91, 93, 102, 172, 188, 263, 265, 266
Bombeck, Erma, 11
Bornstein, Marc, 41
Bowlby, John, 26–28, 72
Brain, 11–12, 14, 16–20, 32, 69, 158, 168,
  186, 188, 190, 192, 198, 201
Bretherton, Inge, 74–75
Brooks-Gunn, Jeanne, 135
Bugental, Daphne, 37–38
Bukowski, William, 107
Bullies, 258, 293
Burchinal, Margaret, 45

Campos, Joe, 157
Chess, Stella, 6, 9
Child care
  and anger, 216, 221
  and fear, 175–76, 290
  friendships from, 108, 123, 125, 288
  and love/security, 49–51
  and shyness, 192–93, 206
Choices, giving children, 138–39, 147, 229,
  289, 292
Cloninger, Robert, 12
Coercive family environment, 240, 250–51
Cole, Pamela, 261, 262
Colic, 10, 14, 43, 46
Coloroso, Barbara, 251, 258
Competition, 134, 137, 138
Confidence. *See* Self-esteem and self-
  confidence
Conflicts, 77, 177, 179, 287
  and aggression, 247, 248, 250
  and anger, 211, 212, 216
  and friendships, 106, 110, 113, 114, 118,
    126
  marital, 220–21, 250
Conger, Rand and Kathy, 45
Contingent responding, 39
Control, emotional
  and aggression, 248, 254–55, 257, 259,
    292–93
  and anger, 212, 218, 227, 230–31, 233
  and biology, 3, 12–16

development of, 12–16
and empathy, 86
and expressing emotions, 57, 68–75, 76, 80, 287
and fear, 173, 176
and friendships, 112, 115, 120–21
and love/security, 51–53, 286–87
and parenting styles, 218–19
by parents, 51–53, 227, 230–31, 233, 286–87
and self-esteem/confidence, 131
and shame/guilt, 265
and shyness, 205
teaching, 80, 287
Cooperation, 118, 126, 127, 224, 225, 227, 250
Cost-benefit analysis, 93
Cousins, S. D., 144
Crick, Nicki, 245
Criticism of children, 49, 77, 148–49, 172, 229, 256, 272–73, 274, 276, 290
Crnic, Keith, 23–24
Crockenberg, Susan, 44–45
Crying, 14, 15, 35–36, 38, 46, 48, 83–84, 171. *See also* Colic
Cuddling, 17, 46, 49, 179, 286
Culture, 144, 189
Cummings, Mark, 236–37

Dandelion ("active") baby, 94, 168, 191
and aggression, 251–53
and anger, 218–19
and biology, 6, 7, 9, 11, 12, 13
characteristics of, 9, 11, 43–44
and friendships, 112, 115, 118, 120
and love/security, 42, 43–44, 52
Daniels, Denise, 121, 204
Defense mechanism, 90–92, 95, 102, 288
Defiance. *See* Anger/defiance
Del Valle, Claudia, 64
deMause, Lloyd, 282
Depression, 131, 187, 219–20, 266
and expressing emotions, 57, 67
and friendships, 106–7, 115, 116

and love/security, 41–42, 45, 53
maternal, 219–20
Didow, Sharon, 106
Discipline, 97–98, 153, 220, 227–30, 231, 240, 249–50, 252, 292
Distractions/diversions, 71–72, 100, 126, 176, 230, 231, 256, 259, 289, 292
Dodge, Kenneth, 244, 249, 250
Dondi, Marco, 83–84
Dreams, 164, 165
Dunn, Judy, 74–75, 76
Dussault, Ed, 19
Dweck, Carol, 140, 142, 148

Eckerman, Carol, 105–6
Eisenberg, Nancy, 89–90, 93–94, 95, 100
Elicker, Jim, 25
Embarrassment, 61, 267–70
Emde, Bob, 62, 157
Emotional development
babies' contributions to, 42–44
"big five" goals for healthy, 21–150, 286–90
challenges to healthy, 151–277, 290–93
contribution of outside world to, 44–45
and expressing emotions, 55–82, 287
parents' contributions to, 34–42
support by parents for child's, 145
See also specific goal or challenge
Emotional regulation. *See* Control, emotional
Emotions
acknowledgment of, 77, 94, 97, 98, 100, 102, 120, 177, 228, 229, 257, 287, 288, 290, 292
appropriate/acceptable, 57, 58, 70, 72–73
awareness of, 58, 86, 244
biology of, 1–20
coping with, 68–75
and evolution, 2, 17, 22
expressing, 55–82, 89, 93–94, 103, 145, 228–29, 255, 287
fading of, 58

Emotions (*cont.*)
   fear and anxiety as mask for troubled, 171–72
   identification/labeling of, 57, 63–65, 74, 76–77, 96, 102, 120–21, 287, 288
   influence of crowd on, 58
   interpreting of, 68, 72, 120–21, 145, 289
   number and variety of, 58
   as "positive" thing in child's life, 75
   practicing with, 79–80, 287
   predicting, 68
   primary, 59–60, 211, 213
   secondary, 59, 61–63
   sharing of positive, 76
   simultaneously experiencing two or more, 58
   social/self-conscious, 61–63
   talking about, 15, 56, 58, 65, 74–75, 76, 77–79, 96–97, 98, 100, 102, 103, 177, 272–73, 275, 287, 288
   understanding of, 68, 112, 120–21, 145, 211, 213–15, 242, 243–44, 255
   and what babies are feeling, 57–59
   what babies know about their, 63–65
   See also Emotional development; Temperament; *specific emotion*
Empathy, 131, 188, 197, 262, 266–67
   and aggression, 85, 86, 95, 241, 245, 255, 256
   "cognitive" components of, 85–86
   definition of, 89
   "emotional" components of, 86–87
   and friendships, 92, 112, 115, 118, 120, 121, 123
   giving voice to toddler, 89–90
   as goal of emotional development, 83–103, 282, 287–88
   and how to help, 92, 96–97, 102
   importance of, 84–85, 282
   modeling, 87, 93–94, 95, 98, 99–100, 287–88
   news flashes about, 83–84, 93–94
   and parents as cheerleaders, 103, 288
   parents' role in developing, 95–103
   practicing, 100, 288
   and predicting success, 94–98
   steps along the way to, 85–88
   and sympathy, 86, 88–92, 97, 98
   talking about, 102, 288
   teaching about, 101–3, 288
   and temperament, 94–95
   words of wisdom/tricks of the trade for, 99–103
Engelbreit, Mary, 52
Environment, 4, 20, 145, 175, 204, 240, 246, 250–51, 290
Evans, Mary Ann, 199–200
Evolution, 17, 22, 246
Expectations, 168, 172, 246
   and anger, 212, 215, 227
   and empathy, 99–100, 287
   and self-esteem/confidence, 136, 142, 143–44, 145, 148, 289
   and shame/guilt, 271, 275, 276
   and shyness, 205, 207–9

Fabes, Richard, 89–90, 93–94, 95, 100
Face-to-face interactions, 38, 39, 41, 46, 62, 67, 76, 77, 220, 286
Facial expressions, 15, 86, 109, 203, 212
   and expressing emotions, 58, 64, 67, 76, 79, 80
   and fear, 158, 168, 176
   and self-esteem/confidence, 137, 144, 145
Failure, experiencing, 133–34, 137–38, 139–42, 145, 148, 272, 289–90
Failure-to-thrive syndrome, 1–2, 14
Fakes, Dennis, 68
Fathers, 31
Fear and anxiety, 139, 263
   acknowledging, 177, 290
   and anger, 171–72, 215–16, 217, 220, 221, 222, 231
   "catching," 157–58, 169–70, 174–75, 176, 203, 221
   as challenge, 154, 157–82, 290–91
   common, 179–82
   Don't! list for, 172

healthy and harmful, 158–59
hierarchy of, 180–81
and love/security, 49, 164, 170–71, 172,
175, 177, 286, 290
as mask for troubled feelings, 171–72
multiple, 182, 291
news flashes about, 157–58, 173
origins and reasons for, 159–66, 182, 291
of parents, 174, 179, 221, 290
as primary emotion, 60, 211
and shyness, 188, 190–91, 194, 195,
197–98, 199, 200–291
systematic desensitization to, 180–81, 291
those at special risk for, 166–72
words of wisdom/tricks of the trade
about, 174–82
See also Separation anxiety; Stranger
anxiety
Feelings. *See* Emotions; *specific feeling*
Feldman, Ruth, 76
Ferguson, Tamara, 272–73, 276
Fernald, Anne, 67
Field, Tiffany, 47, 64, 179
Fight-or-flight responses, 12, 17–18, 158
Flowers
as representative of temperament, 7–9,
11
See also Dandelion ("active") baby; Holly
("difficult") baby; Orchid ("slow-to-
warm") baby; Sunflower ("easy") baby
Fox, Nathan, 192
Freud, Sigmund, 26
Frick, Paul, 241
Friendships
and aggression, 115, 118, 122, 255
and average kids, 116
from child care, 108, 123, 125, 288
and empathy, 92, 112, 115, 118, 120, 121,
123
as goal of emotional development,
105–27, 288–89
importance of, 106–8
and language skills, 106, 110, 112,
121–22, 125, 127

and love/security, 119–20
and neglected kids, 116
neighborhood, 107, 124, 288
news flashes about, 105–6, 117–18
opportunities for making, 122, 124–25,
288
and parents, 123, 124, 126–27
and popular children, 110, 112–13, 118,
121, 122
and predictors of success, 118–23
and rejected kids, 115–16
and self-esteem/confidence, 131, 132
and sharing, 105–6, 108, 114, 125
and shyness, 197, 203, 291
steps along the way to, 109–10
and temperament, 113, 118–20, 124
when things go right and wrong in,
111–17
words of wisdom/tricks of the trade for,
124–27

Galtran, Giovanna, 84
Gelatin mold metaphor, 2–4, 14, 69
Genetics, 4, 11–12, 121, 192. *See also* Nature
and nurture
Gibran, Kahlil, 107
Gibson, Edmund, 276
Ginott, Gaim, 175
Gonzalez-Mena, Janet, 140
Goodwyn, Susan, 55, 89
Gratitude, 63, 79, 287
Grey, Kathleen, 55–56
Guilt. *See* Shame and guilt
Gunnar, Megan, 173, 174
Gwynne, J. Harold, 8

Happiness, 41–42, 60, 211. *See also*
Happy/sad routines
Happy/sad routines, 77, 102, 147, 287, 288
Harris, Paul, 63, 165
Hart, Sybil, 64
Hartup, Bill, 117
Hartzell, Mary, 52, 53
Hau, K. T., 137–38

Help, asking for, 72, 201, 281, 291. *See also* Professional help
Hesse, Erik, 169–70
Hofer, Myron, 1, 2
Hoffman, Martin, 84
Holly ("difficult") baby, 76, 95, 217
  and biology, 6, 7, 8–9, 10, 13
  characteristics of, 8–9, 42–43
  and friendships, 116, 118, 119–20
  and love/security, 35, 42–43, 52
  and shyness, 188, 191
Hostility. *See* Aggression/hostility
Howes, Carolee, 117–18
Humor, 206, 210, 230, 231, 256, 281, 292
Hunter, Edith F., 98

Imagination, 164, 165, 197
Imitation, 105–6, 109, 110, 111, 126, 127, 145, 195, 247, 250, 289. *See also* Modeling
Individual differences, 114, 145, 189, 236–37
  and biology, 4, 6, 7–9, 11
  and empathy, 90, 92
  and love/security, 35, 48
  See also Temperament
"It-takes-two" games, 118, 126, 289
Izard, Carroll, 59

Jealousy, 64
Johnson, Laura, 199–200

Kagan, Jerome, 167–68, 185–86, 188, 191–92, 197, 198
Killebrew, Harmon, 171
"Kindness projects," 99, 287
Klinnert, Mary, 157
Kochanska, Grazyna, 224, 225, 226
Koren-Karie, Nina, 37
Kuczynski, Leon, 224, 225
Kundera, Milan, 264
Kuo, Z. Y., 246

Laible, Deborah, 77
Lamb, Michael, 31

Language skills
  and aggression, 235–36, 247–48, 253, 254
  and anger, 211, 212, 225, 229
  and empathy, 102
  and friendships, 106, 110, 112, 121–22, 125, 127
  and shyness, 199–200, 202
Lannon, Richard, 19
Learned helplessness, 141–42, 148
Leaving children, 49–51, 148, 172, 175–76, 192–93, 206, 221–22, 286, 290. *See also* Separation anxiety
Letourneau, March, 64
Lewis, Michael, 135, 267, 268–70, 271
Lewis, Thomas, 19
Lieberman, Alicia, 6, 35, 38, 50, 172
Liu, D., 15
Love and security, 20, 98, 119–20, 281
  and aggression, 246, 255
  and anger, 210, 215–16, 220, 221, 226–27, 291
  and attachment theory, 26–44
  babies' contributions to development of, 42–44
  communicating, 45–46, 48
  and criticizing children, 49
  and expressing emotions, 56, 70, 72, 75
  father's role in, 31
  and fear, 49, 164, 172, 175, 177, 286, 290
  as goal for healthy emotional development, 23–53, 282, 286–87
  importance of early, 24–26, 282
  and leaving children, 49–51
  and memories, 23–24, 40–41
  news flashes about, 23–24, 33–34
  outside world's contribution to development of, 44–45
  and parental self-control, 51–53, 286–87
  parents' contributions to development of, 32–42
  predictors about, 25
  and self-esteem/confidence, 132, 139, 148–49, 290
  and shame/guilt, 50, 265, 272, 275, 276

and shyness, 196, 197, 201, 291
and Strange Situation, 28–30, 32, 37
and trust, 47–49, 53

Main, Mary, 169–70
Marital conflicts, 220–21, 250
Marsh, H. W., 137–38
Mash, Clay, 41
Massage, 46, 47, 179, 199
Mastery skills, 130, 131–32, 137, 140–41
Matheson, Catherine, 117–18
McCullers, Carson Smith, 39
Memories, 23–24, 40–41, 62, 63, 65, 77, 78, 159, 165–66, 204, 215, 216, 250
Menninger, Karl A., 220
Miller, Bradley, 85
Modeling, 70, 145, 281, 289
    and aggression, 240, 247, 251
    and anger, 221, 224, 225, 229, 230, 292
    and empathy, 87, 93–94, 95, 98, 99–100, 287–88
    and friendships, 114, 126, 289
    See also Imitation
Montague, Diane, 66
Moral values/behavior, 88, 131, 264
Munn, Penny, 74–75
Music/singing, 33–34, 46, 49, 51, 80, 181, 286

Nature and nurture, 1–20, 85, 121, 193–94, 196
Neglected children, 116
Newcomb, Andrew, 107
Nightmares/night terrors, 164, 165
"No," saying, 38, 214–15, 224, 225, 226, 227, 229

Orchid ("slow-to-warm") baby, 9, 42, 94, 95, 167–68
    and biology, 6, 7, 9, 12, 13
    and friendships, 116, 118, 120
    and shyness, 188, 191, 192–93
Others
    caring about, 83–103

development of sense of, 63
and expressing emotions, 57, 61–63, 66–68, 74
and shyness, 193–94, 197
speculating about emotions of, 79, 287
what babies know about feelings of, 66–68

Parents
    authoritarian and authoritative, 218
    "catching" fear from, 157–58, 169–70, 174–75, 176, 203, 221
    as cheerleaders, 98–99, 103, 288
    as disciplinarians, 97–98
    and friendships, 124, 126–27
    "gelatin molds" metaphor about, 2–4, 14, 69
    ignoring of, 225, 230, 292
    "mutually responsive orientation" between toddler and, 226
    and parenting styles, 123, 216, 218–19
    perfect, 279–80, 281
    permissive, 218–19
    as role models, 93–94, 95, 99–100, 126–27
    taking care of, 227, 292
    as teachers, 67–68, 95–97, 101–3, 288
    teamwork between child and, 259, 293
    See also Modeling; specific topic
Parke, Ross, 31
Parker, Jeff, 117
Patterson, Gerald, 250–51
Peers, 68, 92, 106–8, 134, 137, 187, 244, 255. See also Friendships
Perfection, 228, 274, 276, 277, 279–80, 281, 282, 292, 293
Perry, B. D., 15
Peterson, Wilfred, 169
Pettit, Gregory, 249
Photo albums/family videos, 51, 78, 287
Physical development, 14, 20, 131
Play, 179, 182, 191, 196, 227, 291
    and aggression, 243, 259, 293
    and expressing emotions, 79, 287

Play (*cont.*)
    and friendships, 106, 109, 117–18,
        124–26, 127, 288, 289
    and love/security, 31, 46, 286
    and self-esteem/confidence, 137, 138–39,
        145–46, 289
    See also Playdates; Pretending
Playdates, 120, 125–26, 204, 288–89, 291
Plomin, Robert, 121, 204
Politeness, 224, 227–28, 292
Pool, Rodger A., 26
Popular children, 85, 110, 112–13, 118, 121,
    122
Praise, 103, 200, 207, 288
    and anger, 229, 230, 232, 292
    and self-esteem/confidence, 141, 147–48,
        289, 290
    and shame/guilt, 272–73, 276, 277, 293
Pretending, 164, 165, 206, 258, 259, 262, 291
    and expressing emotions, 58, 63, 75,
        79–80, 287
    and friendships, 110, 127, 289
Price, Alvice, 203
Pride, 61, 63, 130, 133, 134, 136–39, 141,
    145, 147–48
Professional help, 52, 165, 174, 182, 220,
    287, 291
Promises, 48, 286
Punishment, 172, 218, 231, 233, 250, 292
Pursuit, Dan, 237

Reflective listening, 79, 287
Regulation. *See* Control, emotional
Rejected children, 85, 115–16, 255
Revolving sweater, case of, 141
"Rouge Test," 135, 270
Routines, 49, 77–79, 102, 147, 182, 199,
    232, 286, 287, 288, 291
Rovee-Collier, Carolyn, 129–30
Rubin, Kenneth, 191, 196
Russell, Bertrand, 244

Sadness, 60, 211. *See also* Happy/sad
    routines

Satir, Virginia, 145
Security. *See* Attachment; Love and security
Self
    categorical, 135–36
    See also Sense of self
Self-concept/image, 88, 98, 138
Self-efficacy, 130, 147
Self-esteem and self-confidence, 55, 106,
    116, 188, 207, 218, 219, 276
    and aggression, 239, 255, 258
    components of, 131–33
    and expectations, 142
    as goals of emotional development,
        129–49, 289–90
    importance of, 130–31
    and love/security, 49, 132, 139, 148–49,
        286, 290
    news flashes about, 129–30, 138–39
    and predicting success, 139–42
    and shame/guilt, 134, 137, 273
    steps along the way to, 133–38
    words of wisdom/tricks of the trade for,
        143–49
Self-evaluation, 133, 136
Self-knowledge, of parents, 13, 124, 143–45,
    174, 203–4, 227, 230–31, 233, 275–76,
    281, 288, 289, 290, 291, 293
Self-talk, 195, 196
Sense of self
    and aggression, 247, 255, 258
    and anger, 211, 212, 213–15
    development of, 62–63
    and empathy, 86
    and friendships, 106, 110
    and self-esteem/confidence, 130, 134,
        135
    and shame/guilt, 263, 269–71
Sensitivity, 35–37, 38, 41, 48
Separation anxiety, 33, 159–60, 172,
    175–76, 290
Shaffer, David, 241
Shame and guilt
    and aggression, 262, 265, 266, 273
    and anger, 262, 264–66, 272, 273

as challenge to emotional development, 154, 261–77, 293
child's reactions to, 261–62, 263–64
differences between, 262–64
and embarrassment, 267–70
and empathy, 262, 266–67
and fear, 263
importance of showing, 262–71
and influences on children, 276, 293
and love/security, 50, 265, 272, 275, 276
news flashes about, 261–62, 272–73
as secondary emotion, 62
and self-esteem/confidence, 134, 137, 273
and sense of others, 63
source of, 263
subjective experience of, 263
words of wisdom and tricks of the trade for, 273–77
Sharing, 105–6, 108, 114, 125, 196
Shyness and withdrawal
and aggression, 187, 196, 198
and anger, 187
benefits of, 197
and biologically solitary child, 195–97
and biologically wary child, 191–95
categories of, 189–99
as challenge to emotional development, 154, 185–207, 291
and developmental pathways, 189–99
and empathy, 188, 197
and fear, 188, 190–91, 194, 195, 197–98, 199, 200–291
and friendships, 197, 203, 291
as good or bad, 189
and love/security, 196, 197, 201, 291
news flashes about, 185–86, 199–200
parent's perspective about, 187–88
as problem, 186–87
and pushing and protection of children, 206–7, 291
reasons for, 189
and self-esteem/confidence, 188, 207
and "shy-through-hard-knocks" child, 197–99
and sometimes shy child, 190–91
words of wisdom/tricks of the trade for, 200–207
Siblings, 122, 127, 144, 159, 204, 221, 222, 247, 250–51, 274
Siegel, Daniel, 39, 52, 53
Signing, 122, 200, 213
acknowledging use of, 77, 287
and aggression, 235–36, 237, 253
and empathy, 89, 102, 103, 288
and expressing emotions, 55–56, 64, 65, 70, 73, 76, 77, 287
and love/security, 48, 286
"Silly song" game, 80, 287
Simion, Francesca, 84
Skelton, Red, 233
Social impact, 112–17
Social preference, 111–17
Social referencing, 67–68, 157–58, 159, 168, 169–70, 174, 221
Social skills, 68, 195, 198. See also Friendships
Sorce, Jim, 157–58
Spock, Benjamin, 69, 235–36
Spritz, Becky, 23–24
St. James-Roberts, Ian, 209–10
Steele, Howard, 75
Stegge, Hedy, 272–73, 276
Stern, Daniel, 62
"Still Face" procedure, 39–40, 41, 220
Stipek, Deborah, 138–39, 145–46
Storybooks, 46, 78, 102, 181, 200, 286, 287, 288
Strange Situation, 28–30, 32, 37, 75–76
Stranger anxiety, 33, 159–60, 176, 190–91, 194, 290
Strangers, 67–68, 158, 186, 190–91, 203, 291.
    See also Stranger anxiety
Stroufe, Alan, 25
Success, experiencing, 134, 137–38, 139–42, 146–48, 194–95, 196, 198, 289
Sudden Infant Death Syndrome (SIDS), 5
Sunflower ("easy") baby, 6, 7, 8, 13, 35, 42, 94, 112, 118, 191

Support networks, 43, 44–45, 52, 72, 287
Swallow, Ward, 195, 200, 206
Sympathy, 86, 88–92, 97, 98, 226, 228, 241, 245, 262, 267
Synchronization, 3, 38–40, 41, 46, 67, 76, 287

Tangney, June, 264–65, 266, 267
Tantrums, 213, 230–33, 247, 292
Television, 240, 247
Temperament, 94–95, 167–68, 188, 274
    and aggression, 250, 251–53
    and anger, 209–10, 217–19
    and biology, 4–5, 6, 7–9, 11–12
    cataloging infant, 6
    flowers as representative of, 7–9, 11
    and friendships, 113, 118–20, 124
    inborn, 4–5, 6, 7–9, 11
    and love/security, 35, 42
    mismatch between parent and child, 13
    origins of, 11–12
    of parents, 13, 218–19
    See also Dandelion ("active") baby; Holly ("difficult") baby; Orchid ("slow-to-warm") baby; Shyness and withdrawal; Sunflower ("easy") baby
"Terrible Twos," 210–23, 227, 247
Thomas, Alexander, 6, 9
Thompson, Ross, 69, 72, 77
Time-outs, 231, 232–33, 292
Touch, 3, 46, 47, 179, 286, 290
Toys, 15, 51, 125–26, 175, 176, 179, 288
Trainor, Laurel, 33–34, 46
Traumatic losses, 198–99
Travers, P. L., 62
Tronick, Edward, 39, 41, 46, 220
Trust, 86, 139, 281
    and aggression, 246, 250, 255

    and anger, 215, 216, 226
    building, 47–49, 53
    and expressing emotions, 56, 72, 75
    and fear, 171, 174, 175, 290
    and friendships, 119–20, 125
    and love/security, 47–49, 53, 286
    and shyness, 196, 197, 198, 199, 201
Turn-taking, 106, 110, 126, 127, 259, 289
Twins, 11–12, 192

Van den Boom, Dymphna, 42–43
Voice, tone of, 34, 46, 51, 67, 158, 168, 176, 232, 256, 286
Vulnerability
    and empathy, 100
    expressing feelings of, 93
    and fear, 166–72, 176, 182

Walden, Tedra, 168
Walker, Alice, 100
Walker-Andrews, Arlene, 66
Waters, Everett, 25
Weiss, Bahr, 249, 250
Weston, Denise Chapman, 180, 259
Weston, Mark, 180, 259
"What are they feeling?" deck of cards, 80, 287
Wheatley, Nancy, 236
Whispering, 46, 286
Wilde, Oscar, 266
Withdrawal
    and friendships, 115–16, 118
    of love, 98
    and shame/guilt, 263, 267
    See also Shyness and withdrawal

Zahn-Waxler, Carolyn, 86–88, 261, 262

About the Authors

Linda Acredolo, Ph.D., is professor emeritus of psychology at the University of California, Davis. Susan Goodwyn, Ph.D., is professor of psychology and child development at California State University, Stanislaus. Their pioneering research and discovery that babies could learn to use simple sign language to communicate before they can talk resulted in the renowned *Baby Signs* book and program, followed by the popular *Baby Minds*.

A Trilogy of Research-Based Advice for Parents

BABY HEARTS

Giving Your Baby ...nal Head Start

...N SUSAN GOODW...

Baby Minds

Brain-Building Games Your Baby Will Love

Birth to Age Three

Linda Acredolo, Ph.D., and Susan Goodwyn, Ph.D.
Authors of *Baby Signs*

BABY SIGNS

NEW EDITION!

How to Talk with Your Baby Before Your Baby Can Talk

LINDA ACREDOLO, PH.D., AND SUSAN GOODWYN, PH.D.
WITH DOUG ABRAMS

by

Linda Acredolo, Ph.D., and Susan Goodwyn, Ph.D.

Baby signs®

nurturing little hearts & minds